Exotic Groves

A PORTRAIT OF

Lady Dorothy Nevill

✳

GUY NEVILL

WITH AN INTRODUCTION BY
ELIZABETH LONGFORD

MICHAEL RUSSELL

To the memory of
PHILIPPA CHELSEA

Text © Guy Nevill 1984
Introduction © Elizabeth Longford 1984

First published in Great Britain 1984
by Michael Russell (Publishing) Ltd
The Chantry, Wilton, Salisbury, Wiltshire

Typeset in Linotron Sabon
at The Spartan Press Limited, Lymington, Hampshire
Printed and bound in Great Britain
by Biddles Ltd, Guildford and King's Lynn

Designed by Humphrey Stone
Indexed by Sibylla Jane Flower

ISBN 0 85955 114 8

Contents

Acknowledgements

I would like to thank Mrs Philippa Pullar who drew me to my subject and without whose enthusiasm this book would never even have begun; the Countess of Longford; the late Mrs Jeanne Nevill, Lady Dorothy's granddaughter-in-law; Mr and Mrs John Nevill, her great-grandson and his wife (the present owner of 'the Gate'), and Mrs Ian Hastie, her great-granddaughter, on whose material I feasted for years; to the many people whose lives I interfered with for my research: particularly Lord and Lady Walpole; the Hon. Robin Walpole; the late Mrs Colin Davy, granddaughter of Lord Walpole and the Countess of Lincoln; the Duke of Wellington and the Marquess of Douro; the late Major Hankey; the Marquess of Abergavenny; Mrs Virginia Surtees; Miss Sibylla Jane Flower; Mrs Phyllis Cumberland Brown; Mrs E. M. Hawley from the Primrose League; Mr Bevis Hillier; Mr David Rose; Mr John Henderson; the late Mr Wilmarth S. Lewis from Connecticut, authority on Walpoliana and acquisitor of Lady Dorothy's childhood diaries; Edward Cazalet's sister, Mrs Thelma Cazalet Keir, and his nephew Mr Edward Cazalet QC; the late Earl of Mexborough; Mr Angus Macnaghten; the Hon. Guy Strutt; Mr Kenneth Rose; my mother; Mrs Mildred Field; the whole family of the Hon. Nicholas Assheton in whose house I often stayed; Miss Joan Quennell, who now rules Dangstein without the twenty-seven gardeners a-scything; the Marquess of Dufferin and Ava in whose library I discovered the character of George Smythe; the Dowager Countess of Airlie; Mr Harold A. Alpert and Miss Rachel Crutch; Mrs Patricia Ducas and Mr Michael Wells, who never stopped feeding me; Kew Gardens; Churchill College, Cambridge; the Universities of Birmingham and Keele; the National Trust; the Hon. David Lytton Cobbold; Lady Soames; Mr Christopher Gibbs; Lady Lucinda Lambton; Mr Charles

Denton, who gave me a year's sabbatical from television to start this; Miss Diana Fitzgeorge Balfour and Miss Sabrina Horne, who had the horrible task of deciphering and typing out my longhand; and Sir Mark and Lady Palmer.

Introduction

It is high time we had a biography of Lady Dorothy Nevill. Like her contemporary, Lady Jeune, she was a Victorian 'character' as well as being an exceptional 'lady' who went everywhere and knew everyone. One might even call the pair of them the Lady Cunard and Lady Colefax of the nineteenth century. And as Lady Dorothy was compulsively articulate, not to say literary, she became the source of invaluable Victorian and Georgian stories, information and gossip. When she died on 24 March 1913, her family were able to make up a huge leather-bound volume of 200 obituary notices. The headlines were universally flattering: 'Reminiscences of a Notable Victorian'; 'The Woman Who Was Discreet'; 'Death of Aged and Genial Anecdotist'; 'Brilliant Society Leader'; 'A One-time Confidante of Kings, Statesmen and Diplomats'. She herself wrote several memoirs, the most popular being *Under Five Reigns*; for she was born in 1826 under George IV and died under George V. Yet today she is in danger of being forgotten.

Perhaps her own lively memoirs seemed sufficient while she was alive, but now that two world wars have swept over our heads since her death, the memories are becoming blurred. Nevertheless the double picture – a picture of Lady Dorothy the personality and Dorothy's own picture of a vanished world – are still sure of a welcome both from the general reader and among historians and biographers. As one who was personally grateful to Dorothy Nevill for her sprightly reminiscences, when I was writing a life of Queen Victoria and of the Duke of Wellington, I do not hesitate to put forward her claims to fuller recognition; and I feel sure that what may have been undertaken as a duty to history and scholarship, as well as family, will also give immense pleasure.

Fortunately it is a young member of the family, Guy Nevill,

9

who has had the interest and industry to collect all the material about Lady Dorothy and to tell her fascinating story before it is too late. He has naturally had the benefit of her letters, diaries, albums and many original family photographs. Though this is his first book, he handles his large canvas with unusual skill and lucidity, keeping a sensitive balance between his subject and her background.

Her 'background', however, is the 'foreground' to many other Victorian biographies. No life of Disraeli, for instance, is complete without the light thrown upon it by his friendship with Dorothy Nevill. She it was who helped to found the Tory Primrose League in his memory, while admitting with a characteristic smile that the great man did not much care for primroses. She made this confession at dinner to another great man, Mr Gladstone, no less, Dizzy's hated rival. Guy Nevill tells the story of Gladstone asking Dorothy whether she really ever heard Dizzy express any fondness for the primrose. When she had to say no, Gladstone commented, 'The glorious lily I think was more to his taste.'

Dorothy was not one of Dizzy's 'glorious lilies' like, say, the voluptuous Lady Sykes, but she was a very intimate friend. Their friendship was founded on Dorothy's sparkling ambience and Disraeli's need for feminine reassurance, preferably when expressed in a smart London salon. She treated London as 'one long whispering gallery', it was said, and relayed what she had picked up to those worthy of her confidence. One of the best 'whispers' had come from the learned Bishop Blomfield who found himself at a party with a lady wearing an extreme décolletage. 'Did you ever see anything like it?' whispered a shocked fellow guest to the Bishop. 'Never,' he replied; 'at least not since I was weaned.' Dickens once told Dorothy that he thought of writing a cookery book. Dorothy might have done the illustrations for Pickwick Pudding, with Oliver Twist asking for more, for she was a talented decorator of her own albums. She designed her own bookplate which consisted of the simple inscription, 'Stolen from Dangstein', the name of her country home in Sussex.

Though her salon in Charles Street, Berkeley Square, was mainly a Tory stronghold, it was continually invaded by friendly Liberals and Radicals. Dorothy was glad to stay with the great free trader, Richard Cobden, and included in her album a photograph of his country house, with its splendid Victorian croquet hoops on the front lawn, each one wide enough, surely, to let through any possible political ball.

Not that Dorothy's Tory friends approved of her Liberal associates. Disraeli's beloved old Lady Chesterfield, recounts Guy Nevill, was in the habit of sending Dorothy a turkey every three months, but when she heard that Dorothy had taken up 'Radical Joe' Chamberlain, she sent her friend a tart note instead: 'I hear you have had Mr Chamberlain to lunch. I therefore cannot send you a turkey to feed such a democrat . . . ' Dorothy replied blandly, 'I promise if you send me the turkey that nothing but a Conservative tooth shall touch it.'

The photograph album of Dorothy's that I myself have seen is brilliant with mosaics and filigree paper frames. It is a joy to see the plain Victorian face of the Duke of Marlborough wreathed in delicate gilding, or the Abergavennys (her husband's family) enshrined in medallions found by her in illuminated manuscripts at the British Museum. Lady Dorothy was careful to suit the frame to the person – banners or a portcullis for her soldier friends. Among these, Field Marshal Lord Wolseley was quite the most rewarding, for she got a flirtatious letter as well as a photograph from him after a country-house visit. He hoped to visit her again in three days' time, he wrote, wearing his best clothes – and she in her 'airiest of summer costumes copied from the classic coins of ancient Greece'. In other words, flimsy and transparent.

There are photographs of dogs, too, in their little paper frames, Trip and Pixie and, more romantically, Camellia. This last may have been named after one of the botanical specimens at Dangstein, Dorothy's 'exotic groves'.

It was her own and her husband's aristocratic families, however, for whom Dorothy produced her most elaborate work, particularly 'rolled-paper work', a mosaic craft practised in England from the late seventeenth to the earth nineteenth centuries but now forgotten. A daughter of the third Earl of Orford, she counted in her pedigree the inimitable Horace Walpole; while her husband Reginald Nevill was a grandson of the first Earl of Abergavenny, who built that impressive neo-Gothic façade to ancient Eridge Castle.

Guy Nevill has benefited from Lady Dorothy's family papers. As a reward for his patient delving into his predecessors' past he has discovered an intriguing and very human skeleton in one of Lady Dorothy's cupboards. I must not spoil his story by giving away the secret of that Victorian paragon, that 'discreet' woman. I will allow myself merely to wonder how many of the prettiest, cleverest, most blameless Victorian ladies did not also have something to hide – if one only knew.

ELIZABETH LONGFORD

One

Lady Dorothy Walpole was born in London on April Fools' Day 1826, at 11 Berkeley Square. She was the fifth and youngest child of Horatio, third Earl of Orford, and his wife Mary, and she was christened after her kinswoman Dorothy Walpole, wife of 'Turnip' Townshend, the agricultural reformer. The Walpoles were a family endowed with intelligence and style, enjoying a social position which tended to blur their more preposterous idiosyncrasies, though without concealing the fact that Horatio was extremely small. As his young nephew once pointed out, seeing him enter the room, 'Here is Uncle Orford and he hasn't growed a bit.' He was at pains, as a result, to emphasise his physical prowess and once knocked out his dentist with a single blow from the chair. But he and Dorothy's mother must have presented a bizarre spectacle throughout their forty-six years of marriage — he diminutive, nervous, sharp-featured, always restless, in nankeen shorts, white stockings, exquisitely embroidered waistcoat and brass-buttoned coat, she tall, gentle and beautiful. There was, too, a touch of the exotic in her background. Born Mary Fawkener, she was the great-granddaughter of Nance Oldfield, Pope's Narcissa. Her father, William Fawkener, as well as being Minister Plenipotentiary at Lisbon and Florence, was Envoy Extraordinary at St Petersburg, where he was on such close terms with the Empress Catherine that — besides her rather exacting favours — she gave him quantities of her dresses.

Horatio seems to have had an allergy to foreigners. It extended even to the aliens within the Royal Family. When William IV died he scandalised everyone by driving out in a particularly light pair of checked trousers, and he strongly disapproved when Queen Victoria married Prince Albert. Yet, oddly, he loved to travel, and for years employed a Russian valet — a giant from St Petersburg, where Horatio had been attaché during Napoleon's invasion – whom he repeatedly threatened to throw out of the window.

Both alcohol and gout contributed to his bad temper. When he was Colonel of the West Norfolk Militia he was so incapacitated by gout that he was obliged to drill the regiment from a fly. The drinking cannot have helped. He would consume prodigious quantities of wine, chased by a mixture of port and sherry, and was once found by the morning watch hung over the lamp-post outside White's Club. Once on the Continent the postboy found him so alarming that he unfastened the traces of the chaise and made off at a gallop yelling 'Je ne veux pas conduire le diable'; and 'le diable' was obliged to pass the night alone in a wood.

He was a man of strong prejudices. He violently disliked change, especially that which interfered with his territory in Norfolk and Dorset. He fiercely resisted the approach of the railways, though in this he was not alone. Opposition to the railways was strong in the country and not confined to any particular class, although agriculturists felt themselves more threatened than the rest. There were numerous cases of cattle straying on to the line, causing indignant denunciations from the local press – one paper became so agitated it reported that 'owing to the new-fangled invention, an innocent cow had been cut into calves'.

Horatio feared public education and so detested the new police force, introduced in 1836, that he presented a petition against the County Constabulary in Norfolk, on the grounds that it produced nothing but expense and caused people to be prosecuted for offences of a very trivial nature. Nor could he stand the hypocrisy of social reformers, public officials, and what he called 'meddlers in society': 'I am surprised and annoyed by the contents of your letter,' he had replied in 1824, when invited to become President of the Norwich Bible Society:

. . . surprised, because my well-known character should have exempted me from such an application, and annoyed because it compels me to have even this communication with you. I have long been addicted to the gaming table. I have lately taken to the Turf. I fear I frequently blaspheme, but I have never distributed religious tracts. All this was known to you and your Society. Notwithstanding which, you think me a fit person to be your President. God forgive your hypocrisy. I would rather live in the land of sinners than with such saints.

His passion was racing – the Turf. Known in Newmarket circles as the Little Lord, he was subject to bouts of extreme moodiness brought on by frequent trips to the racecourse, where he anticipated one day he would certainly make his fortune. His younger daughter's first memories were of her father optimistically setting out in his carriage accompanied by such bigwigs of the Turf as Admiral Rous, George Payne and Lord George Bentinck – Lord George with a delicately moulded hand trailing from the carriage window. He backed his horses for large sums, but was not helped by their usually unfit condition. Even so, he did manage to win the Two Thousand Guineas with Clearwell in 1833 and his colt Ascot only lost the 1835 Derby to Mundig by a head.

To counter his turf disasters Horatio economised by keeping his family in the country, alternating between Ilsington in Dorset and Wolterton in Norfolk. Both places were more or less self-sufficient communities complete with fine houses – 'magnificently equipped bird cages' Virginia Woolf called them. At Wolterton a room was set aside especially for two old retainers to pick at the feathers of chickens and game birds, which were then used to stuff rather uncomfortable couches and beds. The house itself had been created at the beginning of the 1740s by Horatio's ancestor, Lord Walpole, who had been ambassador at the court of Louis XV and an intimate friend of Cardinal Fleury. In a sense Fleury is the inspiration behind Wolterton; it was in memory of their strolls together at Versailles and Fontainebleu that Walpole planted the parterres and terraces, while his friend's magnificent present of the Gobelins tapestries were the centrepiece around which the Houghton architect, Thomas Ripley, designed the State Rooms.

By the 1830s the bricks at Wolterton had weathered to a beautiful pale red, contrasting subtly with the Portland stone which dressed the lower storey. Even Horace Walpole, who had fallen out with his uncle the ambassador, was grudgingly forced to admit that 'Wolterton is one of the best houses of its size in England', and on another occasion: 'I really was charmed with Wolterton. It is all wood and trees.'

Horatio however found little there to amuse him, apart from his favourite project which was enlarging the lake. He would indulge his capacity for fidgeting about by pulling down walls, removing and replacing windows, relegating eighteenth-century furniture to the attics or bonfires and replacing it with fashionable Victorian maple and satinwood furniture or the famous 'Dowbiggin' leather sofas. He even cut out figures from the family portraits and Dorothy remembered his hacking into pieces Amigoni's painting of the ambassador and his family. There is no knowing how many works of art he may have destroyed. But whether by luck or good management treasures survived that are now museum pieces – besides the Gobelins the tapestries included the Mortlake Sea Battles now in the Victoria and Albert Museum, while the dining room housed the Rainbow Rubens, now in the Wallace Collection. Also in the dining room was a group of George II's family given by Queen Caroline to her friend Lord Walpole. For Dorothy and her sister Rachel the whole of Wolterton was a never-ending source of delight: the ground floor of six huge rooms leading one into another through exquisite carved doors of American walnut; the finely moulded ceilings and marble fireplaces; to say nothing of all the works of art inherited from Strawberry Hill and the Nelson family, and the beautifully worked suite of French chairs and sofas, depicting Aesop's Fables, on which the children skipped about learning the stories.

From the upper windows of the schoolroom the girls could see the dubious sight of their father – dressed in his nankeen shorts – training the gasping racehorses with the inadequate stud groom, who had already failed as farm bailiff. Otherwise, when not engaged in study, they spent most of their time out-of-doors. They would walk or ride to Blickling, jumping the stream that separated the place from Wolterton. Once out of the park gates, a web of tracks lined by briared banks offered different expeditions round the neighbourhood – to the pre-Saxon church of Wick-mere, burial place of the Walpoles, or through the woods to the thirteenth-century manor, Mannington, with its sacred groves, landscaped walks, sunken avenue of oaks, strange sepulchres and ivy-clad ruins. The sisters also had the freedom of the neigh-bouring Norfolk estates, riding across to Felbrigg or to Melton Constable, tasting the fresh salt breezes which swept across the fens. They would listen to tales of folklore, how men died at the fall of the tide, and bees sang and cattle knelt in their stalls at midnight on Christmas Eve. They would return at nightfall searching the lanes for Shuck, the phantom dog that haunted these parts, terrified all the while that they might encounter the White Lady, whose appearance flitting around Wolterton, they had heard whispered, ordained a death within the family.

The highlight of the year was the ball in the Assembly Rooms at Aylsham when their neighbour, Lady Suffield of Blickling (nicknamed 'The Double Dow'), would ceremoniously cut the cake. Her father, the Earl of Buckinghamshire, wanting a male heir, was so gloomy at her birth that he told the butler to 'go and drag the baby through the horse-pond'. Whatever this baptism may have implanted, it was not social humility. Dorothy once overheard her complaining, horrified that two local tradesmen had gained admittance, 'It is most unpleasant here. I can hardly see across the room for the flour dust.'

The trip from Norfolk to Dorset was made generally by way of London. The family coach was preceded by two fourgons of luggage and its occupants sustained by a box of the celebrated Threadneedle Street biscuits that had made a fortune for the Lemanns family. The careless cooking and tough meat at country inns could thus be avoided. Naturally any form of public transport was out of the question; ladies did not go in post chaises.

To recover from the two-day journey the family would stay in London, sometimes for several weeks. The Orfords rented an apartment in Berkeley Square since their own house, once Horace Walpole's, had been sold the year of Dorothy's birth following one particularly disastrous afternoon on the Turf. From there Lord Orford and his daughters would sally forth to museums and galleries, though Dorothy was bored by these progresses through what she remembered as galleries filled with musty, badly stuffed animals. The girls preferred to walk with their governess down St James's Street where they were told to avert their eyes from the bay windows of White's Club bulging with languishing bucks; or, worse, from the sight of the scandalous Lady Blessington with her young Count d'Orsay, driving out in her barouche, her face enveloped in scarves, which Dorothy thought gave the impression less of beauty than of toothache.

Apart from drives in the West End, the family would go to neighbouring market gardens. At that time the fields of Paddington and Battersea were not submerged by undistinguished building but grew vegetables and other produce; and during the strawberry season it was fashionable to make parties to eat the fruit there. Battersea was renowned for its asparagus – the best in London – while Hammersmith and Fulham were noted for the profusion and flavour of their fruit, particularly strawberries and raspberries.

Occasionally the Orfords would drive out as far as Twickenham to call upon Horace Walpole's fiancées, the two Misses Berry – to both of whom he was supposed to have proposed marriage. Dorothy was appalled by these two old things, dressed in their mob-caps. Years later, in *Life and Letters*, she wrote:

I myself own that I felt as any young girl would, very shy, when I found myself in the presence of these two celebrities. And all I could notice was that they were so old, and dressed up like two mummies or ghosts. Shades of my kinsman, Horace Walpole, how they would have horrified him!

They would also visit their aunt, Horatio's blind sister, Lady Charlotte Walpole, at Richmond, and their cousins, Miss Charlotte and Miss Fanny Walpole, granddaughters of Clive of India, who were now well over ninety and lived in apartments at Hampton Court. One day, while waiting for dinner, there was a great to-do: Miss Charlotte remarked, 'Fanny, I am going to be ill, too. I feel so hot about the head it must be apoplexy.' 'Nothing of the sort,' exclaimed Miss Fanny, dashing at her sister's head, 'your cap is on fire and I'm going to put it out.'

After such excitements it was soothing to arrive at Ilsington in Puddletown. This was a long grey stone manor reputedly built by Inigo Jones, and surrounded by topiary. Johnny Garth, the famous huntsman, had been brought up there. He was the son of Princess Sophia, daughter of George III, by her brother, the Duke of Cumberland, and was adopted by some of Dorothy's relations. Marie Belloc Lowndes (*Diary*, 22 August 1912) records that Queen Charlotte made the Princess ride down Windsor High Street the day after the birth 'to show the people – who of course knew all about it – that it was not true'.

Horatio, as at Wolterton, busied himself with his 'improvements', once removing all the Georgian casements while his family was in residence. He seemed indifferent to any discomfort this might cause. The wind howled, draughts whistled through the house and in this rude climate he received Colonel Chatterton of the Dragoons from Dorchester, much to the latter's astonishment.

During these country visits, Horatio attended to the education of his daughters – his 'babies' as he liked to refer to them. He procured for them a delightful governess, Eliza Redgrave, sister of Richard Redgrave the painter and Royal Academician and a watercolourist herself of some note. (Another brother, Samuel, produced a *Dictionary of Artists*.) She cultivated her charges much as Roger Ascham had educated Lady Jane Grey, or at least Dorothy was pleased to think so. They were taught to read and write in Italian, Greek, French and Latin, and at a time when most young ladies were instructed in little but sewing and piano-playing, they were enjoying '*Les Oraisons Funèbres* de Bossuet', the works of Fénélon, Barenti's *L'Histoire des Ducs de Bourgoyne* and Sismondi's *L'Histoire des Français*. At the time, however, she much preferred going for long rides across the countryside – to Tolpuddle, for instance, or to Athelhampton Hall, a derelict medieval house which in those days, Dorothy remembered, had cattle wandering to its door and fowl invading the fifteenth-century dovecote. Sometimes they would visit the cottager tenants pursuing their ancient craft of buttony, manu-facturing buttons for hunting waistcoats and ladies' corsets by spinning them on small wheels.

His lordship sometimes employed himself by supervising his daughters' lessons. He would sit dozing peacefully but at the first mistake his eyes would shoot open and he would leap up and rage around. Though French literature was encouraged English novels were not, and the girls' elementary reading consisted of Mrs Warner's *Cautionary Tales*, which were supposed to instil a suitable sense of morality and discipline into a child's life, with such couplets as:

> Why mayn't I when I dine,
> Eat ham and goose and drink port wine?
> And why mayn't I as well as you
> Eat pudding, soup and mutton too?
>
> Because, my dear, it is not right
> To spoil the youthful appetite.

At meal times the children were not allowed to speak unless their mother signalled to them by special codes. Crossed forks signified that their father was about to erupt into a terrible tantrum. Sitting at the head of the table he would take so long to carve the joint that the girls were too nervous to suggest second helpings. This was tantalising, as the food was delicious: 'well roasted lamb, ducklings with green peas, small turbots, followed by beautifully cooked apple or apricot tart'.

Visitors were few, but when they did come they stayed a long time. Horatio's relations were sometimes guests, and these included one very curious pair – his sister Lady Georgiana and her husband Dr Wolff, a missionary who had escaped being murdered in Bokhara because he entered the town reading aloud the English Church service in surplice and college cap. The populace thought he was mad, and therefore sacred. Back home he met the very plain, nearly middle-aged Lady Georgiana Walpole. Rumour had it that at a luncheon she dropped her fork and Wolff, bending to pick it up, by mistake pinched her foot. This quasi-caress unleashed such passion that she fell in love. Horatio at first would not approve the match because of Wolff's Jewish blood; he said the fellow had phylacteries sewn into his very trouser legs. 'Our children, Lord Orford,' pleaded Wolff, who was also very snobbish, 'will be of glorious lineage, for in them will be united the holy blood of David with the illustrious blood of Walpole.' Horatio was so amused by this reply that he agreed, saying that if Wombwell (the famous menagerie keeper of the day) could get hold of these two, his fortune would be made.

Certainly Dr Wolff's behaviour was a little strange. He would wander round and round the house making a tremendous noise. Lady Georgiana would allay all fears: 'Oh, it's only Dr Wolff', she would explain, 'trying to find his way.' (It was a wonder, as Dorothy pointed out in *Under Five Reigns*, how such a man had ever found Bokhara.) And another idiosyncrasy was his aversion to changing his clothes. Once Lady Georgiana sent him off for a short stay with a clean shirt for every day he was to be away. He did on this occasion use them all – but by placing one over the other.

Another visitor was Mr Jermy, who with his child was savagely murdered by Rush, the keeper of the sweet shop at Wolterton, who used to serve the girls with peppermints on their ponies. 'From then on', wrote Dorothy, 'murder and peppermints were inseparably associated in my mind.' But only slightly less dire were the associations engendered by Colonel Netherthorpe, an ugly old comrade of her father, who was a semi-resident. He had a room and a stable at his disposal both at Wolterton and in London. Dorothy thought he was the most hideous specimen she had ever seen. On his death he cut up well but much to Lady Orford's dismay bequeathed a large fortune to his servant 'Wulliam'. Although usually unworldly, she entertained hopes that he would will it to her daughters.

Saturday nights were bath nights. The mutton and deer fat candles spluttered and smelt, while the girls were rubbed vigorously with a soaped flannel. Bathing in fact was considered dangerous and likely to induce colds – and with good reason, since the cans of hot water conveyed from the kitchens were generally lukewarm by the time they had travelled down the long passages to the school room. It was no wonder that the children dreaded the weekly torment.

Occasionally there was a party. Then the girls' hair, which they always wore parted down the middle, was braided on either side of their faces and covered with gold nets to give a classical effect, and they wore white figured silk bodices with lace stomacher fronts, muslin skirts and white satin shoes – quite elaborate costumes for days when it was unusual to spend money on children's dresses.

On Sundays the whole family, including Horatio if he could not think of an excuse, went to the Norman church in Puddle-town where, seated in the carved oak gallery, they endured a doleful service and inspected the congregation. The girls would peer round at the tombs of knights and crusaders, at the preposterous crests with their posturing monkeys, and at brasses with strange inscriptions – as, for example, 'Nicholas ye first Nicholas ye last Goodnight Nicholas'. The vicar, often late after his Sunday morning gallop, would clatter up the aisle, his vestments barely screening boots and spurs. Then the village orchestra of two clarinets, two bass viols, a flute and a bassoon would shriek and wail in the nave, accompanied by children who sang hymns in a discordant Dorset dialect.

Sometimes the family would drive to Dorchester for the Dragoons' parade. They would cross the little stone bridge and approach the wide boulevard along the magnificent avenue leading up from the water meadows, while the girls dreamed of being snatched from the Orford fly by a handsome Dragoon officer, resplendent in huge gold epaulettes, red coat and crested Roman helmet.

At other times they went on to Weymouth – made fashionable by George III – for fresh Channel air; and these excursions usually ended in tears, either through weariness or torn and dirty clothes. They lodged there with an old lady who had gathered from a fortune-teller that she would end her days in a palace, and had accordingly hurried out and purchased the villa where the King had stayed.

So life continued until the elections of 1835. Politics were the appanage of the upper classes. The Old Parliament, changed by the Reform Bill, was represented by property; candidates for membership and government office had to possess a certain amount of land. Therefore the houses possessed by large landowners such as the Orfords at Wolterton and the Rutlands at Belvoir – 'comfortably padded lunatic asylums' Virginia Woolf called them in her *Portrait of Lady Dorothy Nevill* (1917) – had an influential place in English politics, where men of different opinions could discuss affairs of the day. The aristocracy was still a politically effective class, the system working by graft and patronage. The Walpole family themselves were ennobled in the eighteenth century for service to the state. Horatio, as a peer and a powerful landowner, wielded enormous political influence. He was a fierce and uncompromising Tory. When deprived of the office of Lord High Steward of Yarmouth by the Liberal Government, he wrote:

Gentlemen, my appointment of Lord High Steward of Yarmouth in the late Government was received with pride and pleasure. My dismissal by the present Government confers almost equal pleasure upon

Your obedient servant

ORFORD

The Tory party opposed radical movements and political reform and clung to hierarchical and aristocratic notions of society. Horatio had already spent a large fortune during several elections in order to prevent radical returns for Norfolk. Born in 1783, he believed – as did most landowners who had lived through the French Revolutionary Reign of Terror – that any radical sentiments were treason. He believed also that the seat of Norwich was, unofficially at least, the property of the Walpoles. He decided in 1835 that his son Horace should stand as a candidate in the General Election. The young Horace, charming, intelligent and indolent, was totally uninterested and escaped to Dresden, refusing to return and be part of the saturnalia which inevitably took place at election times. His younger sisters, however, went canvassing on their ponies, decked out with Tory ribbons; and their absent brother was selected by proxy of his cousin, Spencer Walpole (later to become Home Secretary). He, known for his unnatural dress, stoop and height as the 'High-Stepping Hearse Horse', was triumphantly chaired around Norwich while one of the old feather ladies, Phoebe Barwick, grabbed the gong and rushed on to the lawn in front of Wolterton to celebrate the victory. Horace returned only once to take his seat, and then only to please his friend Disraeli. Otherwise his only recorded action as a Member of Parliament was to send his constituents a load of dead hares.

The next year, when Dorothy and Rachel were ten and eleven years respectively, the routine of their life was even more interrupted by their father's decision that they should all travel across Europe to Munich. Bad sight was the family malady. Not only had Horatio's sister lost her vision but his son Henry, eight years Dorothy's senior, was blind from birth. So they decided to take him to Dr Walter, the famous German oculist. A party of ten set out including Eliza Redgrave, two maids, a French cook, and a courier of limited intelligence dressed in gold braid, with two fourgons for the *batterie de cuisine*, six beds which had to be unpacked and made every night, the family coach and barouche, as well as two attendant grooms and six saddle horses, one of which, Testina, seventeen hands and bred for racing, was ridden by ten-year-old Dorothy all the way from Antwerp to Munich. The mare, becoming increasingly temperamental, returned some years later to the racecourse and killed a jockey.

England had been at peace for twenty years yet the journey through Europe upon which the Orfords embarked was fraught with inconvenience. Horatio's spleen did little to alleviate it. In spite of his previous diplomatic career he had great difficulty curbing his contempt towards foreigners generally, and almost no control over his annoyance with postilions, innkeepers and all officials. But then the English of this period tended to regard foreigners with hostility. During the old wars it was considered policy to indoctrinate the population with a spirit of contempt which lingered after all reason for it had departed. 'Skip the long words,' said a patriotic tutor to his charges, 'they're only the names of foreign countries in which you'll never want to be.'

The existence of so many separate states in Germany caused particularly exasperating delays. Dorothy remembered her father roaring with rage as customs officers effected their boring regulations, while she roasted in the hot sun expecting to faint, pressed by a grumbling crowd. In Italy, Horatio outraged the customs officers by screaming in Italian, 'Your King is a swindler.' He was apparently not the only one. Hotels or inns were few and far between and fixed tariffs non-existent; mendacious innkeepers believed the English milord was there to be fleeced. They had reckoned without Horatio, however, who was so incensed at the enormous charges levied on candles that he took around an ever-increasing load of partly consumed stumps, until the bag became so heavy it had to be abandoned. The best accommodation they could hope to find was a dusty, uncarpeted room with a brick floor, containing a couple of beds, each big enough to sleep three or four persons, a few wooden, rush-bottomed chairs, a wine-stained deal table, a basin and a jug. The routine became automatic. They would mount the staircase, which apparently had never been washed since the stones were laid, and peruse the bedrooms. Dorothy remembered the horror of beds consisting of boards laid on iron trestles, with a great sack of maize leaves mounted on top, a wool mattress and flat hair cushions as bolster. Admittedly they were generally clean, unlike the staircase, and at least the Orfords and their family never had to survive an ordeal like that of the Duke of Devonshire and his brother who, arriving exhausted at an inn, awoke to discover they were sleeping with a corpse between them.

Dinner was usually a standard *table d'hôte*. The soup was warm water thickened by vermicelli, the wine was sweet and sour at the same time, the bread made of beans. Usually there were chickens, skinny and freshly killed, with coarse cotton diaper for table linen, pepper as coarse as gruel and, to crown everything, dirty salt. This the Orfords supplemented by a travelling larder, which contained mutton chops and portable soup, replenished as supplies grew thin.

Ablutions were usually limited to a little warm water brought in a milk jug. Heating was not understood, and the whole family would fall early onto their beds to escape the incessant draughts. Even then, sleep was difficult. Travellers were tormented by fleas and the noise from the streets was often made even more offensive by bad music intended as a serenade.

The railway, which Horatio so resented in England, was still a rarity on the Continent, although the Ferte–Nuremberg line had just been constructed. Whenever there was a train, however, Horatio, at great inconvenience to all concerned, would have his carriage hoisted on to the tracks. Years later, in 1879, Dorothy was astonished to see two old ladies hoisted in this fashion on to the line at Bournemouth.

The Grand Tour specified what sights the traveller should see – Lake Geneva for example, the Castle of Chillon and Chambercy – but the inaccurate road maps caused the party continually to trespass. The local inhabitants were outraged by the sight of the English cavalcade tramping about their properties. Dorothy remembered that the shouts of 'Zum Richter! Zum Richter' – 'To the judge, to the judge!' – seemed to pursue them everywhere. Nevertheless she detected the 'spirit of William Tell' in Switzerland and of Andreas Hofer in Bavaria, even if by the time she rode into Bavaria the discomforts of the journey were making her eye a little critical. She seemed to notice only the 'faded worn condition' of the female peasants' attire. They compared most unfavourably with the country girls at home who wore 'pretty red cloaks and black silk bonnets'.

Upon reaching Munich they moved into a magnificent apartment below Lord Erskine, the English minister. This at least succeeded in raising Dorothy's spirits. Now she saw women in gay tinsel, with swallowtail gold and silver head-dresses, and glamorous Bavarian men with long tail coats, cocked hats and hessian boots. As for the postilions, 'they were decked in bright Bavarian blue trimmed with silver lace, and sporting shiny hats with a tall blue and white feather – all so merry and clean'.

Life in Munich was old-fashioned and simple. Open fireplaces were seldom seen, carpets were practically unknown. The Orfords' apartment was elegantly furnished, yet there was not even a rug on the floor. Some of the habits of the people, too, were strange and uncomfortable. Bavarian officers in full regi-mentals walked about covered with enormous military cloaks whatever the weather, preceded by their footmen who always carried umbrellas. As the great families disliked having living-in servants, when ladies returned at night they must ignite their lamps from the flames carried by the liveried footmen who attended their carriages. The footmen would then clatter off in their plumed hats to their quarters, leaving the ladies to fend for themselves.

For a while the family endured long boring evenings at the mercy of old Count Mongelas, Prime Minister of Bavaria in the time of Napoleon. Horatio and he droned on about the Napoleonic wars. Dressed in snuff-coloured clothes Mongelas seemed, for some reason, like an old vulture to the children. But then Horatio rushed away on some diversions – drinking and racing – leaving his wife and children with various introductions and instructing them to enjoy the festivities.

The children were presented to the three daughters of King Ludwig I: Hildegard, Adelgund and Frederica. The King would come to play with them in the nursery. To their delight, his favourite game was to hide a ring in a mountain of flour which he would then proceed to hunt with his nose, emerging from it with his face and shaggy hair coated with dust. Dorothy very much enjoyed that joke. On their royal circuit they went also to Possenhofen, the country palace of Prince Charles of Bavaria. There an English governess, Miss Newbolt, had charge over the three young Wittelsbach Princesses, the future Queen of Naples, Princess of Thurn and Taxis and Empress of Austria, to whom Rachel and Dorothy seemed heroines having ridden all the way from Antwerp at a time when no German lady ever mounted a horse.

They spent days roaming the sculpture and picture galleries, the Glyptothek and the Pinacothek, stupefied by the liveried giant who guarded the door of the former. Wherever they were, Miss Redgrave paid attention to their artistic education, and Lord and Lady Orford would introduce their daughters into artistic company, visiting artists' and sculptors' studios. Ludwig himself had turned Munich into an architectural dream of neo-classicism, so the city was in itself an education for the young girls.

It was not all learning. Quite inseparable from this first visit to Munich was Dorothy's memory of the marriage of an English lady to a Bavarian, celebrated in the English church, in which the bridegroom, having no idea of to what he was replying, kept on murmuring 'All dis I say' – the only words of English he knew.

Whenever Horatio was in Munich they went to the market. He would choose and buy vegetables, fruit and game, stuffing some of it into his own pocket while the main portion was placed in an enormous basket which the girls would carry back to the palace. If the King had been hunting the spoils were put up for public auction and on these occasions Horatio would always bid for a roebuck, taking a manservant to help him carry it home.

When the time came to leave Munich, the whole family was sad and they 'were in their turn regretted by those who,' as Eliza Redgrave put it, 'privileged by acquaintance and friendship, followed us with kind adieux to the carriage which bore us away.' Flowers and fruit, according to Continental custom, were put in the carriage on departure and the cavalcade set off for Verona.

They were back again to the dismal routine of lodgings. At Radstadt in Bavaria, the landlord of the inn appeared semi-naked on the staircase. He offered them two rooms, at the sight of which they could scarcely hide their disgust. In the first room the sheets appeared to have been used by a succession of malodorous guests and the room stank of mice-droppings, while in the other room the beds were bare. The landlord refused them dinner, so they lay on the bare beds and shared a piece of bread. At dawn they escaped and reached the next stage, where they consumed enough bread, butter and eggs to sustain them until their arrival in Salzburg in the evening. Here they had rooms in the fashionable Goldener Schiff where it seemed there was never a dull moment. The other apartments were taken by two bridal couples, a

Hungarian couple on their honeymoon and the Potockis from Poland who had just been married by the Neapolitan minister. Their party was coming in from the Archbishop's Palace all ready for the wedding feast when the Hungarian countess was carried out, having expired after a short illness. The incident shook Dorothy considerably.

This seemed to herald an epidemic of doom. Arriving at the next stop, she saw from her window the plain coffin of a poor man's child carried into the church, attended by dirty little boys. Moments later, the sound of a bassoon announced another coffin – this time a rich man's child. White-robed priests and torch bearers attended the body, the coffin strewn with artificial flowers and supported by four boys with plumed helmets and great wings flapping from their backs. Undaunted, Dorothy and her governess entered the church for Mass, but were horrified to see yet a third coffin dropped beside the other two, giving them the feeling that they were in the midst of a city consumed by plague. The final straw was the hotel brochure that they read just before lunch. It indicated the charges for boarding the dead before disposal of the corpse. The information did nothing for their appetites.

Before crossing the Brenner they encountered a terrible storm but managed to struggle to lodgings in St Anton. As usual there were fleas in the butter, fleas in the milk; they were told in the town that gentlefolk never stayed in that particular house. Unrefreshed, they began the climb and were hardly able to enjoy the breathtaking view before the postilion had reached the summit and set off down the mountain at a brisk trot, urged on recklessly by Horatio. More terrifying still was crossing the Splügen in a slushy snowstorm. They had been warned that the carriages would have to be fixed on sledges and so were accompanied by eleven men as well as the postilions, three being appointed to clear the road. Some members of the party chose the britzka, but Dorothy joined her mother in the coach. The sledges were narrow and the snow, obscuring the route, soon reached higher than the road markers. They climbed in zigzags. All went well until the pacemaker slipped and fell, spilling out the boxes and two servants. Dorothy and Lady Orford, feeling their carriage about to capsize, baled out, preferring to travel unprotected on the sledges pulled by horses. The melting snow made matters worse and the men, jumping from side to side to hold the zigzagging carriages, were up to their waists in slush. The dangers were not over at the summit. On the descent to Isola, they could hear the roar of avalanches threatening them on every side and could see snow gushing through rocky galleries and ledges.

At last they arrived at Verona. Horatio, complaining that one could not even get a decently cooked mutton chop, immediately left the family to their own devices. They spent two weeks exploring and enjoying the sights until a quarrel broke out in the kitchens between the Italian and English servants, which ended with the Italians victorious. Mary Orford, fearing a massacre, felt it wise to repair to Vicenza, there to await her husband's directions. It proved to be a very dull eight weeks; they had soon exhausted every object of interest – Palladio's Rotonda (the inspiration for Chiswick House and Mereworth) and the rival castles of Montecchi and Cappelletti. However, one of Horatio's friends attempted to relieve the monotony. He produced novels, the letters of Madame de Sévigné and a pigeon pie. He took them to a picture gallery which, Dorothy thought, 'was in sober truth a collection of daubs', but would not invite them to his house as he thought his house party was too Bohemian to meet an English countess. The only pleasant interludes were when some Austrian officers allowed them to use their riding school and as a compliment asked them to a ball. Meanwhile Eliza Redgrave painted views from their inn which Horatio later had transferred onto plates to illustrate their journey. Dorothy treasured these all her life.

Horatio finally contacted them: it was too late to go to Rome so they should proceed straight to Florence. Here Dorothy went to her first public entertainment, a diorama – an exhibition of illuminated pictures viewed through the opening of a darkened chamber – at the Church of Santa Croce. The effect, she remembered, was enhanced by the extremely fine music 'which simulated the swelling strains of an organ'.

Shortly before they left Florence they witnessed the taking of the 'black veil' by a young and beautiful novice at the Church of St Apollonia. During the service the bishop was given a salver covered with rose leaves, on which was placed the black veil and a silver crown set with a semblance of precious stones. These were placed upon the head of the nun, prepared, it seemed, for sacrifice. Afterwards at the celebration breakfast she presented them with delicious sweets, nosegays and framed prints of her patron saint.

Retracing their steps over the Brenner they returned at leisurely pace via Wiesbaden, Mayence and Toplitz. Here they bought such quantities of glass and garnets that the Jewish shop owners rewarded them with an invitation to a wedding ceremony to hear the 'true word of one god'. Throughout the celebration they were devoured by fleas, which Horatio pronounced to be of the 'true Jerusalem breed'.

Just before they left they were all shocked to read the following description in a German newspaper of Princess Victoria, soon to become Queen, purporting to be translated from an English court journal:

She gobbled her food and was so greedy, eating and drinking all day. Many helpings of turtle soup sufficed to send one suitor back to France, and at breakfast she consumed prodigious amounts of 'slices of bread roasted on the coals and buttered hot'.

Nevertheless they pulled themselves together and, stopping at Frankfurt, arrived home in the spring of 1837.

Two

Hostesses were an important factor in English politics. Lady Jersey was known to her friends as 'Silence'. Her house in Berkeley Square was the hub of the Tory party. It was to Lady Jersey's support that Disraeli owed his position; while Lady Holland, who was divorced, exercised absolute sway over the Whigs, from Holland House. Lady Holland's gatherings could be so overcrowded and uncomfortable that there was hardly room for the guests. She once asked the assembly to make more room for some unexpected arrivals: 'Yes, we must make it,' they replied, 'for it doesn't exist.' She was totally demanding. Staying with Lord Melbourne at Brocket she ordered a magnolia tree in full bloom to be felled forthwith as it was spoiling the view from her window. On another occasion, while residing near Eridge, a house little visited because of the eccentricity of its owner, Lord Abergavenny, she stormed it with a huge party, even including her maid; and when Count d'Orsay first entered Society and was placed beside her at dinner, she kept dropping her handkerchief to see how many times he would pick it up.

She had first married Sir Godfrey Webster of Battle Abbey, by whom she had a daughter, Harriet. When she eloped from Sir Godfrey she hid the child away, pretending it was dead – actually performing a funeral service over the body of a kid. Harriet then returned to her mother's house as an adopted daughter, and in due course became the mother-in-law of Dorothy's brother Horace. It was as a result of this somewhat tenuous connection that Dorothy was taken to see Lady Holland. 'Oh yes,' she told Edward Cazalet seventy-five years later, 'I remember the great Lady Holland and she terrified me out of my wits – she used to wear a huge old-fashioned cap.'

Lady Jersey on the other hand was vivacious, versatile, volatile and very beautiful even when old. 'No white paint, no agues, no messes and mixtures . . . but like her conversation still the child of nature,' Disraeli described her. She was Zenobia in *Endymion*. 'Society was her passion and she had every quality to make it agreeable. Inexhaustible animation, unrivalled tact and no wish to show off.'

The winter sessions would assemble in February, bringing to London the men who ran the country, and their wives. Entire households would travel to London with their coachmen and carriages, housemaids, grooms, butlers, housekeepers and minions. Regularly on 1 May the season burst into full bloom. Lord and Lady Orford now involved themselves and in May 1840 the girls, who were sixteen and fourteen years old respectively and had for the past three years resumed their quiet country routine, were sent for by their parents. Horatio allowed Rachel £50 and Dorothy £45 annually, while Lady Orford received £300, a sum that was considered adequate for someone in her situation. Life was delightful, if exhausting; Dorothy filled her diary with a round of visits and entertainments. Lady Orford, as the wife of a great landowning peer, held a regular salon for Tories of different opinions to meet one another. She left cards all round Mayfair and kept open house at 24 Portland Place which they had rented for the summer. She received so much it made her ill.

Dorothy began noting down details of the guests and their conversations. Though still too young to attend Society dinners and balls, the girls always dined with their parents on Sunday nights and on other occasions were allowed down after the dessert to be shown off to the guests. Dorothy lived in that world that lies somewhere between an adult's and a child's, never knowing quite where she was. It was provoking when Rachel, although her senior, was allowed downstairs to dine when she was not. However, her disappointment was soothed a little when her mother began taking them both out to breakfasts – light and leisurely repasts in those days, beginning around midday. These included the celebrated ones at St James's Place with the old banker-poet Samuel Rogers, whose famous collection of paintings was constantly being shifted round the walls to its best advantage by a singular mechanism. It was here, Dorothy tells us, that she first encountered the London literati and heard the Irish poet Tom Moore sing 'When I first saw thee' 'most expressively'. She remembered Rogers as a dried-up little figure, hunched in his chair, dressed in a blue coat and nankeen waistcoat he was maliciously nicknamed the 'Dug-Up Dandy', apparently feeding his taste for aesthetics by gazing out at the changing hues in the sky. Outside the window an artificial nightingale sitting in a cage would serenade him with music. She also went to Mr Eliot Warburton's[1] where she met A. W. Kinglake.[2] She told Warburton she was related to Amy Robsart, wife of Elizabeth I's favourite, Leicester. 'Oh what pretty blood!' her host replied.

Once she was taken to the villa of the profligate Lord Hertford, whose name was a byword for debauchery (he was even to die with a prostitute in the house). Known as the Caliph of Regent's Park, he erected Hertford Villa with a spectacular portico of eight huge free-standing Corinthian columns and a roof, tent-shaped with gilt pinnacles, under which he staged extravaganzas. In the gardens he set up Roman antiquities and columns, and cows drank from sarcophagi. Rumour had it that while one was breakfasting respectably downstairs the entire *corps de ballet* were above in the bedroom sleeping off last night's orgy behind locked doors. But the only hint of intemperance that Dorothy saw was a cow being milked into a pan for a syllabub – a dish of wine and milk, curdled, whipped into a froth and boiled.

Mornings generally were of a more sober nature with Miss Redgrave supervising their lessons. English reading included the *Life* of Sir Robert Walpole. Here was the man they were taught had instituted the office of Prime Minister together with collective responsibility of ministers to the Crown. Dorothy learnt to intone 'Sir Robert' as if in an act of worship. It planted in her an exaggerated sense of reverence for her family which stayed with her all her life. Yet innuendo reached her that Sir Robert and his family were guilty of malpractices: how he had misappropriated funds from the Exchequer to build Houghton and set up their good fortune. Years later Dorothy joked to Augustus Hare about her family. There had been a burglary at Wolterton. A man had

[1] Author of *The Crescent and the Cross*. Drowned or burnt to death when the mail ship *Omoza* caught fire while he was trying to reach a friendly agreement with the Indian tribes on the Isthmus of Darien in 1852.
[2] Alexander William Kinglake (1809–91) was the historian of the Crimean War and author of *Eothen*.

come supposedly to measure the dining room. He asked the old housekeeper to go up to the top of the house and fetch him a tape, and while she was doing so he stole two of the best pictures and disappeared. 'I could swear to them anywhere,' said the old woman, 'for they were members of the Orford family.' 'They were the Virgin and St Sebastian,' added Dorothy, 'and I leave you to imagine how far they were ever likely to have been members of the Orford family.'

Rachel was gifted musically. Monsieur Benedick came to instruct her every day. Three times a week Scipione Petrucci, an Italian, exercised them in drawing, and Dorothy was drilled in German by Fräulein Zocher, a governess from Dresden. French history embraced the fall of the Bourbon dynasty. Dorothy was fascinated by the tragic figure of Marie Antoinette, who became her heroine.

After lessons the girls lunched with their parents, then drove out in the open carriage or their mother's barouche, visiting the stalls in the Pantheon for purchases: wrist bands for Agnes (a German maid just leaving their service for Hamburg), eggs for the canaries to hatch or a pot of tamarinds. On 9 May Dorothy recorded materialistically in her social diary:

Mama gave me some money to buy her a smelling bottle, 6d. I went also to a work-shop and bought two Berlin patterns to work from for Jane West. They cost 1/8d. the two. I bought three skeins of shades of green worsted for the cushion I am working on for papa, 3½d. the skein.

Miss Redgrave would escort them to exhibitions. She talked about the fashionable artists and introduced some of those she knew – Wilkie, Webster and Maclise – to her charges. This certainly influenced Dorothy's developing tastes. They visited the Royal Academy on 11 May:

At half past eleven went to see the Royal Academy. Admired very much one of them, Mr Redgrave's, called the Poor Gentleman's daughters in search of a situation, and the banquet scene in Macbeth, where the ghost of Banquo is seen by Macbeth alone by Sir David Wilkie, and the four children of the Lord Chancellor, Lord Cottenham, are very like. Lady Seymour as Queen of Beauty in the Eglinton Tournament is very well done, we thought the Bust of Lady Sarah Villiers as like but not flattering. It is by Macdonald and also one of Lady Canning. We came home at nearly two.

Occasionally they trotted about at Mr Davis's Riding Academy and frequently cavorted at the school for dancing run by Madame Michau, a plain, lumpy little lady who danced to perfection. There they met other young ladies whom they invited for tea – what a bevy they were: their cousins, the Longs and the Wests, the Pepys girls (daughters of the Lord Chancellor). Sarah Mary Cavendish, Horatia Rushworth, Adeline Horsey de Horsey (Admiral Rous's niece who later married Lord Cardigan) and the lovely Villiers girls, daughters of Lord Jersey. One evening when Dorothy and Rachel were sitting reading, the Jerseys' French governess burst in, crying 'Est-ce que Lady Adèle est ici?' She had not been seen, however, and the governess rushed out again, shrieking 'Alors, tout est fini!' The next day London reverberated with the news that Lady Adèle had bolted with an officer of the Hussars.

Sometimes there were children's balls, at one of which Dorothy noted she had met twenty-four young ladies her own age, but the high spot of the season was Madame Michau's ball at the Dancing Academy (at the Willis Rooms where Almack's was held). 'Madame Michau intends giving a Great Ball next Thursday for her pupils,' wrote Dorothy excitedly, 'therefore from today many fancy dances were practised such as the Minuet de la Cour, the Bolero, the Cachoucha, Cracovienne, the Mazurka and the Karot Shawl dance.' Madame Michau herself would sometimes wait on Portland Place since Rachel, a promising dancer, was learning the minuet de la cour. Once even Monsieur Michau tried to come and watch Rachel dance, but he was so late, Dorothy reported in her diary, that they were eating their lunch, and she, always a stickler for punctuality and etiquette, especially where employees were concerned, refused to admit him. Even as a child Dorothy was not going to tolerate bad manners and familiarity from a dancing teacher, arrogantly believing – then as always – that servants were a world apart. The incident did not however in any way affect their enjoyment of the ball:

Went at 4 o'clock to Trewfitt to have our hair cut for curling, then came home and dressed for Madame Michau's Ball. It was not at all full which was very good for the dancing.

Lady Orford, too, loved dancing and was used to going out without her unreliable husband, who would dash off nervously to the country at a moment's notice. She would go off to balls – to Lady Jersey's, Lady Palmerston's and Lady Charleville's – often accompanied, Dorothy noticed, by the two young Mr Rushworths. At other times daughters, visitors and servants would admire as, dressed in black for the death of the King of Prussia, she climbed into her carriage and drove off to the young Queen's drawing rooms. The vague and charming Mary never knew the number of guests that filled her corridors. Thursday 1 July, for example, saw a stream of callers – the Cottenhams, Lord Strangford and his daughter, Miss Smythe; Mr Gawler and the Sayerses, the 'Double Dow' with her niece and the ubiquitous Colonel Netherthorpe. 'A great many more came in the evening,' scribbled Dorothy, 'Aunt and Uncle West, Jane, William Hoste, Kate and Sophy Walpole, and Reginald Nevill dined. We passed the evening very agreeably without dancing.' On another day her diary recalls: 'The Cannings came. Rachel and I had tea. I had extra. The rest went down to dinner – . . . and we all when Mr and Mrs Canning were gone romped and played in the corner.'

Meanwhile her father would be at Newmarket with Lord George Bentinck or at Epsom supervising the running of his hopeless horses. 'Papa's horse again came third. This is indeed sad news,' moaned Dorothy in her diary, dreading the gloom, economies and hangovers that would ensue. But when he was at home Horatio delighted more and more in the company of his daughters and life became a hive of activity. He flew off with them to buy American Turkies, clothes, carpets and presents: 'Set down at the Egyptian Hall, Piccadilly, saw some magnificent carpets just imported from Aubusson, then we walked down Pell Mell, and there saw some very fine pictures,' Dorothy wrote on 13 June. He whirled them off to buy white veils at Hodge and Longmans, to Ackermanns to buy a sketch book, to the Burlington Exchange to buy pairs of short kid gloves; he ordered china buttons for them, and the next day, never still, set out with Dorothy to buy a hearth rug for one of the drawing rooms at Ilsington, and to Rogers the Carver to collect some magnificent carvings he had commissioned for Wolterton. Meanwhile Rachel and Miss Redgrave visited friends, 'to copy with watercolours the colour of their rooms'.

Dorothy recalls a typical day in her diary:

We went to Tessier and Griffins jewellers, 32 South Audley Street, to know if our things were done. After we went to Gunter Confectioners where we each had (not Mama) a fresh strawberry cream ice and sponge biscuits and each a glass of iced water. We then went home and walked to the Pantheon with Aunt Maria, Fanny, Georgy West and us two. I went and fetched at Goodals, 52 Pantheon, a workstall, a pocket handkerchief which I had left there to be embroidered with my name, Dorothy. I paid 1/ 9d. for it. We went home and Georgy, Algy, Fanny and me went to tea. R and Mama, Aunt Maria, Jane and Kate and Sophy Walpole went to dinner. After we came down to dessert and we talked and played music the whole of the evening.

Every Friday, a basket of provisions came up from Wolterton and included such items as mulberry leaves for the silk worms that her cousin Georgy West had given her. On Sundays they attended the church nearby in Portland Place which Dorothy, for reasons of her own, always referred to as the Extinguisher, and afterwards perambulated in the fashionable Circus Gardens. Sometimes they went to the singular Polytechnic to see the Stalactite Cavern.

We saw some very curious things – the diving bell which goes down in the water at 3 o'clock, some things from the wreck of the Royal George, quantities of models and machines. We saw the microscope which magnifies thousands of times . . . we all went down the diving bell which hurt our ears exceedingly.

The girls saw little of their brothers at this time. Frederick, at eighteen years old, was a midshipman, while Horace, aged twenty-seven, now lodged at the St James's Hotel. He would come to meals and bring bracelets to spoil his little sisters. He was something of an aesthete and a rake, the lover of Mrs Norton (one of the three beautiful Sheridan sisters) and much in demand for his elegant dinner-party conversation. 'I never met anyone like him,' wrote Disraeli, 'such a stream of humour, fancy, philosophy, and quotation in every language.' He was describing a dinner party at the Misses Berry's:

. . . the party consisting of Miss Montague, Guizot and Pollington – very recherché and Strawberry Hillish. The old ladies a little in love with the Horace Walpole of the nineteenth century, who, by the by, is more elegant fantastical and interesting than ever, and talks of changing his name and retiring to Parma or Cremona or some city equally decayed and unvisited. Venice too vulgar with Monckton Milnes[1] writing sonnets in every gondola, and making every bridge 'a bridge of sighs'. I breakfasted with him today and he really was divine.

On another occasion that year he was not so heavenly. His ex-valet, Courvoisier, had distinguished himself by murdering his employer, Lord William Russell, and Horace booked a window from which to witness the execution. Unfortunately he had drunk so much that he fell asleep before the hanging and could remember nothing. His family, whose dinner it was and who were longing to enjoy all the horrors exquisitely presented, were thoroughly put out. For this lapse he was the model for 'Lord Tom Noddy' in the *Ingoldsby Legends*.

On 10 July the festivities came to an end and a huge waggon arrived to collect all their belongings. Stopping with friends along the route, they travelled slowly back to Dorset to resume their country life – lessons, riding, pottering in the garden, gathering mushrooms on the heath and walking through the woods. They attended archery meetings, shot a little and once visited Dorchester gaol. Horace came to stay, bringing friends to while away the summer months, one of whom was Lord Pollington, heir to the Earldom of Mexborough, who had been an M.P. before the passing of the Great Reform Bill. Pollington paid attentions to Rachel, who was dancing even more delightfully and becoming prettier and gayer all the time. Indeed it was difficult not to notice her high spirits, for she scattered convention to the winds, and was considered to behave quite unlike other young girls.

There were fewer visitors in the autumn. Horace and Lord Pollington left, the colours on the heath and in the woods turned to gold. A snowy winter set in and the pace of Dorothy's diary slackened: 'Did nothing particular today.' They practised worsted work and fashioned paper into spills, drove to Dorchester to see the judge ride in, visited the Sapient Pig in the village, or watched the foxhounds nosing for scent on Puddletown Heath. Her chickens hatched four chicks, but her favourite cock was pecked to death. The steward's wife at Wolterton died, and so did Dorothy's friend, Bob Ponsonby: 'We heard on Thursday of

[1] Richard Monckton Milnes, later Lord Houghton (1809–85), poet, writer and administrator.

poor Bob Ponsonby's death,' she wrote. 'How awful, one so young.'

Dorothy wrote no more diary for three years. In January 1842 Rachel became officially engaged to Lord Pollington. Encouraged by the Orfords they decided to marry. Unfortunately the alliance did not find favour with the Mexboroughs. The Orfords had gambled away their fortune and were thought to be dissipated, what with Lord Orford's rackets on the racecourse, Lady Orford's goings on in artists' studios, seeking out Bohemian society, Lord Walpole's gambling and various emotional entanglements. The Orford life style could not endear them to the puritanical Mexboroughs. In the eyes of good society the Orfords had declassed themselves. It was not surprising that Rachel, so young that she had not yet been presented at court, was considered flighty and unconventional. She already had a host of admirers. Lady Holland considered her

very wild and gay, but most people believe it is merely from excess of animal spirits, and that her Boys as she calls her troops of suitors, are merely playfellows. But as [Pollington] is perfectly satisfied the dragons of virtue must be silent.

Lord Pollington was terrified of his parents, and his grandmother, old Lady Hardwicke, and refused at first to admit he was even engaged. His first cousins, Louisa Stuart, a gifted painter who later married the Marquess of Waterford, and her sister, Charlotte, Viscountess Canning, lady-in-waiting to Queen Victoria, kept their father, Lord Stuart de Rothesay, who was away in St Petersburg, abreast of family events. Louisa wrote:

Grandmama is perfectly well and happy at the moment having Pollington's marriage to Lady Rachel Walpole to talk over. He kept on denying it long after the other side had publicly announced it.

Her sister added:

At last [he] allows this to be talked about and letters of congratulation fly about *de part et de l'autre*. The Orford family talk of Pollington's qualities and how his wife is to deserve such great happiness – while the answers from his side look rather hypocritical though they do not attempt to reach Lady Orford's raptures.

Mary Orford was indeed fortunate to marry off such a

wayward daughter so early and so well. The Walpole idiosyncrasies were already ominously apparent, with Rachel writing to her fiancé in December, before the actual announcement, as her 'dear, dear husband' and signing herself 'Your truly affectionate and attached wife'. No wonder Lord Pollington was said to be scared. The Mexboroughs stayed the nuptials for a three-month engagement and Rachel wrote in the same letter:

I have not the slightest wish for you to deny our engagement as Lord Mexborough has now given his consent. Pray write and tell me all what he said as I am dying to know all about it. I am afraid, dearest, he made a great many objections.

In spite of these Rachel married Lord Pollington in March and the marriage was a happy one, even if the Mexboroughs, so different from her own family, could never quite stomach her behaviour. At first Rachel tried to please them, daring to hope they would like her. Lady Stuart de Rothesay wrote to her husband on 25 April 'Pollington and his bride were at the Queen's Ball where she looked very pretty and danced with great delight. It was her first Ball.' On the 26th Grandma Hardwicke added a stiff postscript: 'Pollington's little wife is a gay, wild, pretty creature, and I suspect very clever – they were NOT of our party.' The same day Lady Stuart described the visit to Tyttenhanger:

It went vastly well. The young pair of Pollingtons who went away that morning, having been in great fashion, were quite forgotten in the interest of the new acquaintance, and there were also Charlotte and Canning.

The Mexborough connection were much more satisfied with the betrothal of Louisa to Lord Waterford. Poor Rachel never could make herself popular. They were all scared by her unconventional behaviour, which was not improved by long sojourns in Dover Street, followed by weeks in the country: in Methley, Downham, Tyttenhanger – always Mexborough houses. Charlotte Canning wrote:

Aunt Mex has got the Pollingtons in Dover Street for the moment; she [Lady Pollington] is tolerably good but she does not do well with them and I am afraid is not very amiable. She ran riot abroad and there are no end of stories of her odd pranks.

Rachel was in high spirits and refused to be crushed. She was headstrong, capricious, a true Walpole. Lady Canning wrote from her mother's house in February 1843:

Rachel was as much in want of being kept in order as ever, all the pleasant things about her diminish. Pollington is dreadfully afraid of her, and Aunt Mex too – so no-one will do her the slightest good.

Such were Rachel's cavortings that she stayed in London longer than the official summer. In late August, when the city became a desert, only 'Aunt Mex' remained, Charlotte wrote, 'determined to outstay the Pollingtons'. Yet Rachel's tactics paid off to the extent that they were allowed their own home. Lady Canning wrote unsympathetically a year later:

Pollington and his wife, that little, wild Rachel, had emancipated themselves and established themselves in Bolton Street, which was in a higgledy piggledy state, but she seems to like a house of her own of all things.

It is not surprising that Rachel's leaving left a void at Wolterton. Dorothy, without the company of her vivacious, riotous sister and her Band of Boys, grew bored and listless. It affected her parents as well. So in 1843 the Orfords decided to spend the year in Italy. This idea titillated Dorothy's enthusiasm and she resumed her diary and her travels. The journey out was no more comfortable than the one seven years before, added to which the translation of the menus was sometimes as bad as the meals themselves. Here is Dorothy's souvenir of Modena station:

Travellers will find in the Refreshment Room
(Buffet of the station), which is in direct
communication with the Customs Office,
luncheon and dinner at the price of 3 francs,
wine included.

Porridge

–

Slender at the Saint Germain

–

Pike forced meat ball sauce of the
financial Beef to bake vegetables
Poultry Snow-drop of the Bresse at the Jelly

–

41

Salad of the time

Side dish: Chees and dessert

(½ bottle of wine)

The prolonged stoppage of this train to Modena
is long enough to allow travellers to lunch
and look over their baggage with a custom officer.

In Florence they settled in the Palazzo San Clemente, the former residence of the Countess of Albany, who had lived there with the poet Alfieri after she separated from her husband, Charles Edward, the Young Pretender, whose initials and portraits in medallions were the interior motif. Their current landlord was the parsimonious Marquis Torregiani. Over eighty years old, he could be seen, gaunt, thin and melancholy, crippled with arthritis, struggling beneath a green silk sunshade round the groves he had planted, sometimes laboriously mounting a tower to scan the horizon for the grave of the peasant girl whom he had loved but whom pride had prevented him from marrying.

His palace was situated in the filthiest of streets, thronged by dirty, semi-clad urchins. To reach its entrance the Orfords had to stumble over rotten cabbage stalks, and horrible lumps of hair, which emanated from a barber's shop and got attached to the ladies' petticoats. But, once within the walls, there was a paradise of a park, grand trees, wonderful foliage, banks of roses. Luscious bunches of grapes dripped from a hundred pergolas and there were tuberoses in profusion. Through her medallioned window Dorothy would sniff the delicious scents and gaze at the prospect: hills crowned with olives and speckled with white villas reaching up to the purple snow-capped Apennines.

The Orfords were sucked into the social whirl of Florence – reputedly known at this period as 'le paradis des femmes galantes' – and immediately Dorothy and her mother dazzled Florentine society. One ecstatic observer wrote:

The Hollands are much preoccupied with Lady Orford and her daughter Lady Dorothy Walpole, the prettiest, most captivating little creature that I ever beheld. Sun in her eye and mischief in all her thoughts. The only day I was out she rode up to me with General Ellice, hung over with flowers, a large straw hat and a red ribbon round it, and a bunch of peacock feathers on the side of it, her habit quite open, and little gauntlets, to be, as she said, 'like the Lifeguards'. We were all enchanted with her.

Indeed Dorothy was enchanted with herself and her success. Guests flocked to pay her court and it was at this juncture that she met the glamorous young painter G. F. Watts, who was to become so famous and for a short disastrous time to marry Ellen Terry. Here in Florence he painted in the colours of Titian a romantic and ravishing portrait of Dorothy, signing his name in the ribbons streaming from her hair.

Society at this time was led by Prince Demidoff and his beautiful wife Mathilde (Napoleon's niece, daughter of Jerome, King of Westphalia). Dorothy encountered the Prince at a fancy dress ball. A mysterious gentleman concealed by a domino approached her and hissed 'Dieu! Tu es blanche comme tes fleurs!' He then revealed himself and begged to be introduced to Lady Orford. Dorothy spent many days at the Villa Donato with the Demidoffs and was their guest at the chariot races held in the Piazza Santa Maria Novella. Every house was hung with brilliant damasks of crimson and gold. Plumed chargers, drawing gilded and painted chariots, dashed round the arena and later there were spangled explosions of fireworks and fire balloons with flaming parachutes. The outrageous Lord Ward amused their balcony by tossing red hot money to the boys and precipitating jugs of cold water over the crowd – behaviour which caused him to be interviewed by the police.

In Florence Dorothy met several exiled members of the French Royal Family as well as the prominent sculptress Mademoiselle Felice de Fauveau. Fine-looking but crop-headed, and in a close-fitting, tailor-made dress, she had resolved not to let her hair grow until the Comte de Chambord sat on the French throne as Henry V. She had been incarcerated for plotting against the Republic and she stimulated Dorothy's obsession for Marie Antoinette. Then, at the end of June, the Orfords departed to spend the summer around Padua – but not before the old Marquis Torregiani had creaked down onto his knees to count the grease spots that his tenants and their admirers had deposited on his furnishings.

The summer heat was unendurable, the conveyance unbearably stuffy and the inns as usual infested with fleas. The staggering temperatures made Horatio's humour even more peppery, but his tantrums with officials at least secured them an unhampered if undignified progress. They spent twelve thundery horrible days at Padua, which they all found an exhausting place. Miss Redgrave and Dorothy sheltered in the church of San Antonio, drawing their favourite frescoes, dodging out between storms to make perspiring expeditions round the dreary town, where the only form of life seemed to be the students who flitted about the ramparts and perched like crows against the skyline. In the cool of the evening the party would ride towards the Euganean Hills which seemed to glow in the twilight, all purple and blue, and throw strange, subtle reflections onto the plain below.

It was a relief to reach Venice, where they were entertained by an English patriarch, Mr Cheney, collector of antiquities – his speciality being the large bronze knockers peculiar to the city – and Mr Rawdon Browne, who was supposed to be the greatest living authority on Venice.[1] His rooms at the Palazzo Ferro were a delight, overlooking the Grand Canal and Santa Maria della Salute, and arranged with 'old carved chairs, antique writing tables, and ancient tapestries'. Browne conducted Dorothy round the sights, which included the last surviving Foscaris, two venerable sisters, descendants of the poor Doge who fell dead upon hearing the Campanile's bell ringing to celebrate the election of his successor. One sister was decrepit the other lively and gay. They inhabited a crumbling apartment in their palace, the only remnants of magnificence being the worm-eaten figures which formerly supported the bed canopy. Otherwise the room contained only a large, scrupulously clean but poor bed, a few miserable chairs, a table, and a bare old settle from which the two ruined sisters ceremoniously received their guests. It was Lord Alvanley, man of fashion and wit, who heard of their plight and settled on them for life the annuity they said would enable them to live happily (about three shillings a day).

The itinerary of the Italian journey is somewhat vague.

[1] He discovered and removed the gravestone of Thomas Mowbray, Duke of Norfolk, banished by Richard II for quarrelling with Bolingbroke and who 'toil'd with works of war retired himself to Italy, and there at Venice gave his body to that pleasant country's earth'. Shakespeare, *Richard II*.

Presumably at some stage the family returned home to England. But next year again, Dorothy tells us in her memoirs, they made a winter excursion to Naples, arriving by boat from Genoa and settling in yet another bad inn, the Croselle. Naples was ruled by King Bomba who seems to smack of the decadent Roman Emperors in general, and Caligula in particular. He loved to pepper his subjects with bullets and screw over their heads the 'cap of silence', a barbarous appliance last used in an English prison in 1818, when one Thomas Haggerty was prevented from singing 'rollicking songs'. Bomba spent a lot of his time concocting dishes with his cook, Beppo, a well-known Neapolitan character. Together they conjured up the most wasteful consommé ever invented. An anchovy was encased in an ox, in the following sequence. A round of veal was introduced into a round of beef and served as an envelope for a turkey; inside this lay a fowl, a pheasant, a partridge, a woodcock, an ortolan, and last of all, filling up the unbelievably small space, the anchovy. From this conglobate Beppo would produce the phenomenal cup of essence for the dissipated Bomba.

Perhaps His Majesty's corruption was too much for Horatio, who conversely decided to make his table one of his areas for economy. If he considered that they had eaten enough at midday he would tell the evening waiter: 'Pour dire le vrai, nous avons dîné', a phrase which blighted their existence and was only mitigated by Mary Orford's clandestine provisions. This is not to say that the Orfords had lost their taste for the disreputable. Now abroad, Dorothy at eighteen wallowed in Bohemian society, feeling quite at home in it and thoroughly enjoying the Casino Ball. While in Naples they hurried down through flower-studded paths and pergolas to see the scandalous Lady Strachan, mistress of Lord Hertford, who had purchased the title of Marchesa de Salsa and acquired a husband with the extraordinary name of Pisollili. She served them claret and Threadneedle biscuits before showing them around. She had arranged the Villa Rocca Matilda – which she persisted in calling her cottage – with a view to coolness, the floors paved with tiles and the rooms furnished with light chintzes. From her bed she could see the sun rising beyond Vesuvius. Dorothy settled down on the balcony overlooking the sea to sketch the caves from where Lucullus fed the Muranae with the flesh of slaves.

The Orfords left for Rome in a deluge on 4 January. 'Never was so unhappy on leaving dear Naples,' confided Dorothy to her diary. Swarms of blind beggars dressed in blue and crimson petticoats besieged them on arrival at Capua. Horatio, remembering that robbery was rampant in this part of Italy, had made plans with Pareti, the Neapolitan postmaster, to ensure their comfortable and easy progress. Everything had been paid for in advance, down to the last postilion's tip, in order, so he thought, to save trouble and danger, but the drivers grumbled, and in fact his plan increased every annoyance that it was intended to prevent. On leaving Capua the rain pelted down and the horses champed. In the middle of the stage from St Agata, a postilion ran up to the family barouche to let them know that the coach with the fourgon containing the menservants had overturned. Happily this was not true but nothing could persuade Pareti's poor postilion to investigate in pitch darkness. After crossing the Carrigiano they reached the post house and lit their lamps, but Pareti had again failed them – here were only a jaded pair of horses; the coach in front with the maids had taken the fresh ones. The old nags carried them for about a mile when suddenly they jibbed, kicked, plunged and pulled the light carriage into the roadside ditch. The two fourgons with the menservants were still waiting at the post house for horses, so the party was left unattended in the pouring rain. Suppose, said Miss Redgrave, brigands, attracted by their lights, should fall upon them in their defenceless situation. They were close to the marshes of Minturnae. Even Marius, she added, never at a loss for a scholarly reference, could scarcely have spent a more dreadful night here than that with which they were threatened. Her forebodings, however, came to nothing. Eventually a new postilion arrived with fresh horses, which tore up the street of Mola di Gaeta at a great pace, striking sparks from the cobbles; and soon they were all seated at supper in front of the blazing logs in the villa of Cicero.

Next day they resumed their journey along a route thinly scattered with small crofts resembling haystacks. They laid out on cloths a midday meal of wine, bread and oranges. The country was filled with people, sandalled labourers in the fields, women bathing in pools or drying their clothes on the sunny banks. The party continued pleasantly along until reaching the Pass of Lantalae.

At the entrance to the Pontine Marshes, with no sign of human habitation except the crude wigwams and occasional square buildings for the Guardia, a 'flippertigibbet', as Dorothy called him, mounted their barouche and whipped on the horses as if there were a race to the next post house. The result was that fresh horses were soon required, but the only ones available were not only very small but running about loose in the fields. Everyone had to rush about catching them, and this took a good while. Nevertheless, once harnessed, they went a fair speed, charging past peasants on horseback (armed whether for 'sport or defence' Dorothy was never sure) and shepherds clothed in coats of sheep's wool and breeches made of long shaggy goat-hair. After Cisterna they traversed wonderful country bordered by daphne, phyllera and other evergreens, and eventually caught their first glimpse of the Campagna, at first believing the long, level line was the sea. A few stages later Dorothy saw in the misty distance the dome of St Peter's towering massively above Rome.

The sun was setting as they entered the city by the Porta San Giovanni. A double rank of carriages lined the whole length of the Corso to the Spanish Steps, where their residence, the Hotel Melloni, lay. Here they stayed three months, and the Continental festivities began all over again. As in Florence Dolly managed to dazzle the galants and in doing so achieved a certain notoriety. Cardinal Zacchia, the last papal governor, was quite bewitched and presented her with a locket containing a relic of her patron saint, St Dorothy. She even captivated General Ramsay, who was usually interested only in his poodle, which was even represented on his visiting cards; the General and his dog were spoken of always in one breath, and the two exercised absolute rule over English visitors. One of Dorothy's admirers, George Cadogan, penned a letter depicting in the margin all his rivals – Cardinal Zacchia, General Ramsay and his poodle, Dwarkanath Tagore, the distinguished Bengali, and other lords-in-waiting at 'ye court of Queen Mab' – climbing the stalk of a flower on whose buds sat demurely the winged seductress, Dorothy.

47

Horatio was in his spending vein. He ordered a cast of the *Dancing Faun* by Roerich, commissioned a portrait of his wife by Blaise, a Tyrolean artist, and another of 'Queen Mab' herself from the popular young Buckner, who painted her whimsically *'en fête champêtre'* busy feeding poultry. A keepsake volume of 1851 was illustrated with Dorothy's portrait by Buckner, together with an abysmal verse:

> O Lady! were the biped folk unfeathered
> Who flock around you for your notice here,
> What eager hopes would straightway be untethered,
> What brawls stirred up for all the town to hear!
> Then, since your chance is made no more to waver,
> Look but on birds with favour!

For diversion the Orfords ventured to see a play in a theatre so asphyxiating it was enough to put them off for ever. Roman Society at this period only went to the opera, and no wonder. The Orfords were overpowered by the pungent audience; most of the men took off their coats and sat in sweaty shirt sleeves which, wrote Dorothy, 'for colour could have shamed an Irish labourer . . . might have been Old Westminster and St Giles put in the pit and boxes.' The length of the performance was the same as an English play of those days – lasting from seven to half-past eleven – consisting of a melodrama, a pantomime and then a farce. The latter on this occasion satirised the English and their riding – 'more laughable than fair', thought Dorothy. The hero, an immensely corpulent John Bull, with a pert booby of a son, who answered 'Yes, Papa' to everything and walked about with his thumb in the armholes of his waistcoat, was seen mounting a horse for the first time. This he accomplished by means of a crane, which lifted him up with his legs spread out, a good height into the air, and then let him drop on to the horse's back.

Whenever the north wind blew, or the hot sun exhausted them, they found a sanctuary in the changeless temperature of St Peter's. Unpopular parties of English tourists shuffled round, armed with guidebooks and astounded by the wonderful music. Dorothy wrote that her fellow countrymen caused great offence by desecrating monuments, chipping off portions, and inscribing their names at inappropriate places. One tourist stopped a religious procession in order to light his cigar from one of the holy candles, disappearing back into the crowd before he could be lynched.

The Orfords attended the elaborate ceremonies at Easter, witnessing the illuminations when all St Peter's Square blazed with paper lanterns and a thousand torches. It seemed to Dorothy that the lanterns were burnished silver enveloping the golden light of the torches. The ceremonies ended with a carnival. Processions passed through the streets showered by storms of confetti and flowers, lit by wax tapers. The carnival ended in a battle, with each participant trying to extinguish his neighbour's flame while retaining his own. The Romans enjoyed it all enormously. 'If Paradise can be half as delightful as the carnival, what can be so happy?' one Roman lady simpered to Dorothy. Dorothy however was not so sure. 'It seemed more like purgatory than Paradise.'

They left for England on Friday 4 April, travelling slowly and stopping often, immersing themselves in classical ruins and works of art until they reached Bologna exhausted. Much to their fury Horatio, as usual consumed with energy and drink, suddenly abandoned them and dashed off to Florence. An exasperated Dorothy wrote in her diary: 'When he chooses to come back remains to be proven, knowing our great wish to get back. Of course he will hinder us as much as possible from doing that.'

Three

The age of twenty was late for a young lady to be presented in London. It was certainly the only thing that was retarded about Dorothy: Lord Hertford's breakfasts, Lady Strachan, the Casino Ball, Mary Orford's Bohemian circle, her education and long sojourns abroad had combined to give her a much broader experience of life than the other girls. Indeed, as the youngest member in the family, Dorothy had virtually lived the life of an adult for several years. Now she launched herself into the 'Curly days', as she liked to refer to her début, a jamboree of fifty balls, sixty parties, about thirty drums[1] and thirty-five breakfasts –one of the last being given at Syon House in honour of Ibrahim Pasha, a wonderful creature who made salaams to himself and to all the guests. Later he was entertained to a cricket match. Having viewed the inactive players for some time he ordered the game to begin, not realising it was half way through.

Dorothy's presence caused eyebrows to be raised and heads to turn as soon as she entered a room. At one of her first balls a resplendent dandy, with black ringlets, rings and a cane, the epitome of a Curly character, spied her across the floor. 'Pray who is that young lady who looks as if she had come out of a picture of George II's time?' she overheard him inquire. It was Disraeli. Then he at once approached her, saying: 'You are dear Walpole's sister and I must know you.' That night a friendship began that was to last a lifetime. He was forty-two years old. Dorothy believed his foppery was merely an instrument for him to draw attention to himself and that when he had achieved the premiership he no longer cared for dress and ornament.

London's prime hostess at this time was Lady Palmerston. Hers

[1] Large and tumultuous evening parties – said to be so called because rival hostesses vied with each other in 'drumming up' crowds of guests.

was the salon *par excellence* in Europe, where you heard all the *bons mots*, anecdotes and gossip. The food, too, was delicious; one of Lord Palmerston's most violent political opponents had to admit: 'Lord Palmerston is redeemed from the last extremity of public degradation by his cook.' Smoking was forbidden. Lord Palmerston had such an aversion to it that he once sent a sharp rebuke to the attachés of Constantinople because their dispatches smelt of tobacco.

At the Palmerstons' house Dorothy met such Curly characters as Talleyrand, Pozzo de Borgo and the Princess Lieven. She told Edward Cazalet sixty-five years later how much she had enjoyed the salon. 'You sat and talked to your friend and were happy.' Nowadays, she added, you went to a drawing room or tea party and the crowds were so great you couldn't get in at the door. But London in the 1840s was so small that Lady Palmerston wrote out her own invitations by hand, and her neighbour Lord Anglesey (of Waterloo fame) actually kept a slate in his hall on which people who wished to be asked to dinner could write their names.

Two other well-known hostesses were Lady Desart and Lady Cowper, who was witty and experienced and had a secret formula: 'To make a ball successful, three men should always be asked to every lady. One to dance, one to eat and one to stare.' Nothing was duller than a ball which lacked cavaliers, and as Lady Desart pointed out, 'For a ball to go well you must have the dancing dogs.' Other hostesses had their own peculiarities. One, clever but loquacious, Dorothy likened to Johnson's dictionary – 'full of information but a little disconnected'. Another was so grand that people were asked if they were going to her house to be insulted. Mrs Lawrence's gatherings were foppish – certainly in the 'Curly' category. Her specialities were Lady Blessington, Count d'Orsay, in his brown coat and tight pantaloons, and Lord Harrington, unsuitably married to Miss Foote, an actress no less. He was always dressed in a long coffee-coloured cloth coat braided all over down to his heels and a beaver hat trimmed with brown. A cousin once remarked to Dorothy she always felt the richer for seeing him; as if she had seen a sight without paying for it.

Dorothy once more kept a diary:

Went to the drawing room, Rachel presented me. I wore a ribbed silk train, tarlatan double petticoat trimmed with blush roses, body to correspond, headdress feathers, Valenciennes lace lappets and a wreath of blush roses. In the evening went to an evening party at Madame Dietrichstein's (wife of the Austrian Minister) and afterwards to a small dance at Lady Londonderry's. Danced three times with Lord Seaham, once Lord Goderich, once Lord Adolphus Vane, once Lord Keane. Came home early . . . Drove with Papa and Mama to a nursery garden in Chelsea. Went down with Rachel and the Duke of Beaufort to Woolwich then went onto his yacht, the Intrepid, down to Gravesend, were becalmed, obliged to wait for a steamer to tug us up to Woolwich when we drove back to London. In the evening went to the Adelphi to see Jenny Lind. Dined at the Disraelis. Met Count d'Orsay, Lord Harry Vane, Mrs Maberly, Lord and Lady Ponsonby, Lord Brooke, Lord Ossulston and Lady Duncannon.

Next they were off to a sale which took place on the death of the old Duchess of Somerset. The catalogue, adorned with ducal arms, contained pages and pages of items. She had hoarded everything. There was a large room full of silk stockings in bundles of a dozen, tied up with pink ribbon, 'never undone since they had been purchased'. Another room was filled with petticoats, but most curious of all was the 'immense collection of bonnets of all ages', some of them poke, some with immense plumage, starting from the crown, others turban-like. There was also her court train and about thirty boxes of 'toothbrushes and hair'. Dorothy resisted these temptations, restricting herself, rather quirkily, to one of the Duke's court suits – bought for £5 on account of the 'exquisite workmanship of the stalk buttons'.

Fashionable fêtes were held in Vauxhall Gardens – for a while. There was an old gypsy woman in the grotto to tell fortunes and the ham sandwiches were celebrated, with a carver reputedly able to cut from one ham enough slices to cover the whole park. Unfortunately the whores from Cremorne Gardens were so angry at Society's penetration into their territory that they squirted ink all over their fine clothes. The result was no more fêtes were held and the gardens were abandoned to the prostitutes.

Dorothy excelled at dancing. At Gunnersbury, another diverting haunt, she remembered making up a quadrille with a company of elegant ladies and their partners, to the amazement and amusement of the more humble frequenters of the pleasure gardens. Her ear for music, however, was not developed. Occasionally she would attend the fashionable opera, but she longed only for the intervals and the informal party in the crush room where the élite withdrew to await their carriages, lingering sometimes at least an hour. She found the ballet more interesting. She met the dancers Cerrito and Taglioni: 'Taglioni was, of course, not generally received, but I nevertheless once met her at a party, though I cannot remember when, or how she got there.' The truth was that Dorothy only liked street music. Nearly seventy years later a professional violinist came to dinner, bringing her Stradivarius with her. Dorothy as usual laid out her game of patience while the woman began to play. 'I 'ate that scratchin' sound,' Dorothy hissed to her neighbour under cover of some vigorous bowing.

Dancers, like actors and actresses were not admitted to Society. Dorothy explained in *Under Five Reigns*:

Although several men of high rank had married actresses, society still rigidly closed its portals to the profession . . . Whenever they saw any theatrical celebrity in the street [they] would watch their movements closely, and would apparently be much disappointed at not perceiving any eccentricity in their walk or manner, hoping that after a few steps the actor would invert himself and proceed on his hands, or that calling for a cab would spring in head foremost through the window, and disappear like a harlequin.

The prejudice against the acting profession reached such a pitch that the son of Dorothy's friend Alfred Wigan actually had to be withdrawn from his school in Brighton because the other parents disapproved of their boys associating with the son of an actor.

The season progressed like a series of thoroughbred auctions. Most parents hoped to put their fillies under the hammer and marry their daughters to a rich elder son before having to face the expense of a second season. Likewise the beaux were on the lookout for fortunes to squander. Property, riches and good looks were passports to an early bid. But that year good matches were sadly lacking. 'Alice enjoyed her Ball very much yesterday and looked very nice in a black tulle gown. I think people will approve of her quiet and unpresuming manners,' Mrs Stanley told her mother-in-law, Lady Stanley of Alderley. Lord Pomfret and Lord Goderich were introduced to her:

Certainly they are two of the most insignificant little mortals I ever saw. Eldest sons do not shine this year. I am getting to know many of the infants who frequent Balls.

Mrs Stanley was getting to know a great many things. Nothing escaped her, and certainly not the behaviour of 'Dotty' Walpole, so unlike the unpresuming Alice. During the summer it was rumoured that Dorothy was to be engaged to Lord Feversham's son, Mr Duncombe – though there is certainly no mention of him in her diary. She describes Lady Ailesbury's ball at Uxbridge House:

Had luncheon with the Cadogans, a drum at Mrs Wyndham's, afterwards a Ball at Uxbridge House. Danced first quadrille Lord Goderich, second Lord Henley. I was engaged to Lord Goderich, but there were none. First waltz Prince Lieven, second Lord Dupplin, third Lord Henry Lennox, cotillon Lord G. Paget. Polka, G. Cadogan.

'Lord Goderich, who is nineteen, is on the high-road of being entangled with Dolly Walpole,' Mrs Stanley dashed off indignantly to her mother-in-law. 'It is well to keep these boys out of London as long as one can.' Dorothy, however, was leading the boys on for all she was worth. Certainly she was not interested in infants. Her eyes strayed on to more experienced prey. On the whole Lady Orford trusted her daughter's friendships, but sometimes they went too far. Louis Napoleon Bonaparte, for example, the future Napoleon III, who had recently escaped from a French fortress, was thought to be a bad match and a rascally adventurer. He was a friend of Lady Blessington and a member of the daring Gore House Set. Dorothy found him attractive and was told not to see so much of him. She turned her attentions instead to George Smythe.

A Tory politician, Disraeli's closest aide, George Smythe was the son of the Irish peer and diplomat Viscount Strangford. At Cambridge he was considered outstandingly talented and charming. His heroes were Byron and Disraeli, his looks Byronic. He was both romantic and cynical, contemptuous of middle-class morality and a rebel. He had been crippled by an over-affectionate and dominating father (Lady Strangford had died in

Constantinople), who alternately spoilt, coerced, petted and abused his son, encouraged him in mischievous pranks and doubtful follies and then censured him. George was the favourite on whom Lord Strangford pinned all his hopes and he was aware of the undue favouritism he showed to his first-born: 'His hold over my affection becomes so painfully strong,' he wrote to his mother, 'that I feel and fear the sinfulness of my adoration for that child and dread the awful punishment that may one day attend it.'

Lord Strangford's letters to his family are filled with descriptions of what George was saying and doing. At one moment 'George is now a perfect Methodist and thinks nothing but of his devotions'; and then, while his sister Ellen[1] 'continued to attend Mass . . . the other day George danced before her on a picture of the Pope.' And extracts from different letters at the time George left Eton show the mixture, according to his varying mood, of Lord Strangford's adulation and censure.

George has grown two inches taller than I am, looks as strong as Hercules and as handsome as Adonis. No one is more certain to achieve a brilliant future. . . . George is utterly devoid of every quality that could lead to success in public life. . . . No one has a finer spirit or a better heart than George. . . . He wants application, ambition and all those natural affections through which youth is capable of being influenced. . . . I am sure that George will do well now that he has exhausted the budget of these follies. . . . I fear that George is hopelessly lost to every good feeling. . . .

G.S.S. was very popular at Cambridge, but incurred debts beyond his means and took a disappointing degree. He summed up his college career in a letter to his father in 1846, when he was already embittered by life.

Born a pauper and the son of a poor nobleman who had acquired a great name and position, and a few of his hereditary acres, my life at best can be seen as always a venture for any person to back me in.

With talent, high spirit, courage, a spice of that genius that borders on madness, I was given as became my rank, and not my fortune a noble education, and made, by the monstrous caste system of the English Universities, the associate of men who could spend a pound

---

[1] George's elder sister, Ellen, married the Marquess of Sligo in 1847.

with less inconvenience than I could spend a shilling. What followed? What generally follows with the impetuous and the sensitive. I was not to be outdone. I gave dinners to those from whom I received them and got involved in debt way beyond my means. I took my degree, one which if utterly unworthy of my talents and university reputation, was yet no proof that I did not read and hard too, but with the example of abler and better men, I may say that here again the false system of fee exacting mathematics was much to blame.

I came up to London with my boyhood over, with extravagant habits and owing £1200 . . . Now what I ought to have done was to have told you this; paid my debts out of income, lived economically, and I humbly think have travelled. For many good reasons, and for one very bad one you objected to this . . . after your refusal I stayed in England, owing a great deal of money . . . ready to jump at the first expression of sympathy.

Although it was as often on himself that he turned the knife, this letter demonstrates Smythe's tendency to moral vivisection. He was utterly regardless of the agony he might inflict on his victims.

Women adored him and were only too ready to provide sympathy, but he was too dissolute and poor to settle down. By 1846 he was also extremely debauched; forbidden by his father to marry a girl he had really loved, he had taken to drink as an anaesthetic and an opiate. Elected as M.P. for Canterbury in 1841, an exercise which cost £7,000 and almost ruined his family and his sisters, his father urged him to make a lucrative marriage but he was averse to it, not wanting to be seen as a fortune hunter. He was also bored by conventional society. He wrote to his father:

The moneyed young ladies of England require being waltzed with, and I don't waltz. They require being followed from party to party, being dangled after, and that does not suit my habits and health either. Nor have I a temper that can endure the comments of chaperons and dowagers. 'Will it be a match?' 'He hasn't got a penny!' 'There it is on again, or off!' The only way of marrying in England, and that suits me better as a sort of a clever fellow, is country house life. Propinquity makes marriages, but who in a million ever met an heiress in a country house?

And he confided to Disraeli:

Family I don't care in the least for: would rather like to marry into a rich vulgar family. Madness no objection. As for Scrofula why should I care for it more than a king? All this ought to be a great pull in my favour.

Dorothy was certainly neither rich nor vulgar. Daughters and younger sons rarely shared in the patrimony, and anyway the gambling had seen to that. Although Lord Strangford and his daughter had been part of Lady Orford's social whirl in 1840 it was probably at breakfast with Disraeli that she had met the irresistible G.S.S., who by then had had a string of unsuccessful love affairs behind him. He was thirty-one years old, experienced and the very devil. It promised disaster for both of them, but Dorothy was bowled over by his attentions from the very start. There was also another side to Smythe's fascination: he was the embodiment of the Young England Movement. Dorothy had grown up in the spirit of Young England, its leaders all being friends of her elder brother, and when she fell for George Smythe she fell in love with the spirit of Young England – even though by this time it was a myth and Smythe had accepted a post in Peel's Government as an antidote to his financial and parental problems. 'I don't pretend to have any principles, but I have a heart and I am a gentleman,' he told Disraeli.

Young England, launched by Smythe and Lord John Manners, sought to arrive at a new Toryism. It was both symbolic and an example to the otherwise dull course of party politics, and it was a culmination of the whole contemporary revival which reached its peak in the mock medieval tournament organised by Lord Eglinton in 1838 at a personal cost of £85,000. Besides, the resuscitation of a benevolent feudal system was an understandable reaction of a class defeated by the Reform Bill and the railways. Soon Disraeli was its leader; in a sense it was to remain the inspiration of his life and to fashion his reforms. But great landowners resented the hold that Disraeli held over their sons. 'It is grievous', wrote the Duke of Rutland to Lord Strangford, 'that the young men such as John [Lord John Manners] and Mr Smythe should be led by one of whose integrity of purpose I have an opinion similar to your own though I can judge only by his public career. The admirable character of our sons only makes them the more assailable by the arts of a designing person. I will write to John and I shall enquire of him whether there is any truth in the report of his having engaged himself to a great dinner at Manchester under the Presidency of Mr Disraeli.'

There was in the Young England creed just that spice of the poetical and picturesque to attract George Smythe – to say nothing of Dolly Walpole. The nobles of England were once more to occupy their legitimate place around the throne and in the order of chivalry; the Church was to become the revered guardian and benevolent educator of the masses; commerce and industry and art were to be fostered by generous patronage;

and a grateful and contented peasantry, clustering for shelter under the shadow of lordly mansions, were to vary the monotony of their toilful lives by merry dances on the village green, and perennial feasts of roast oxen and barrels of ale provided by their munificent Lords and masters, the hereditary owners of the soil.

It was a Utopian dream which Disraeli recorded for posterity in his Young England trilogy, *Coningsby, Sybil* and *Tancred*. Smythe hero-worshipped Disraeli, who according to his penchant for young aristocrats adored his handsome young disciple. Smythe's last surviving letter to Disraeli sums it up:

You were of old the Cid and Captain of my boyish fanaticism and after that I was seduced to desert you (out of domestic reasons). I could never help feeling you were the Cid and Captain of my every sympathy. . . . I once heard that you had said of me that I was the one man who had never bored you.

In *Coningsby* Smythe is Coningsby, in *Endymion* Waldershare – 'whose versatile nature becomes palled even with the society of Duchesses . . . '

Waldershare was profligate but sentimental; unprincipled but romantic; the child of whim, and the slave of an imagination so freakish and deceptive that it was impossible to foretell his course. He was alike capable of sacrificing all his feelings to worldly considerations or of forfeiting the worlds for a visionary caprice. [*Endymion*, chapter 2.]

From the start Society tongues wagged delightedly. The Stanleys flew back to their writing desks: 'I heard of Lady Dolly from Mrs Hibbert, pretty doings again of aristocratic young ladies,' scribbled Lady Stanley. Rumours were rife and pursued Dorothy into the country at the end of the season. She had gone in August with her parents to stay with Mr Gawler near Andover.

George Smythe followed her thither and, horror of horrors, she was discovered with him in a summerhouse folly. Before they could return to Norfolk she fell ill and a defamatory article appeared in a scurrilous newspaper. Every mother's nightmare come true. Quite regardless of what may or may not have happened within the summerhouse, her reputation had been deflowered and her marriage prospects ruined. What was more, Queen Victoria was to banish Dorothy from her court for ever. It was the convention – all males were in search of prey and all females must be saved from deflowering. The whole system was geared to protecting the loss of a young girl's reputation just as much as her virginity. If a girl disappeared for half an hour it could mean that something might have happened and potential suitors might evaporate. Almost immediately the Stanleys were at it again. Rumour had it that Dorothy was pregnant. Lady Stanley had to 'say another word':

Aunt K [wife of the Bishop of Norwich] says the report of Lady Dolly cannot be true as she is going to balls in the neighbourhood and going riding every day. That does not prove she has not miscarried.

Dorothy was apparently quite unaware of her publicity and fluttered around Norfolk wondering what everyone was whispering about. Her parents were also ignorant of any scandal until the New Year when the horrified Miss Redgrave happened belatedly upon the newspaper article, and a visiting nephew confirmed the stories to Horatio. There was pandemonium now in the 'Bird Cage'. Dorothy's parents were desperately worried about what was to become of their hitherto promising daughter. Needing a confidante, Lady Orford poured out the dreadful saga to Disraeli's effervescent, pretty wife, Mary Anne – a 'rattle', as the term went in those days, older than Disraeli and of decidedly middle-class origins. Mary Anne wrote bright, gossipy letters which Dorothy said in her memoirs were so ill written it was like deciphering a cuneiform inscription. Lady Orford's were hardly easier to decipher as she scrawled her narrative diagonally across the writing paper.

Feb. 2nd.

Dear Madame Disraeli,
    I have been intending to write to you for some time but we have had so many people in the house that it has left me so little time unoccupied – in

a letter I cannot enter into every particular that has led to the disgraceful stories that have been in circulation respecting Dorothy, which doubtless you must have been made acquainted with for I understand that the most dreadful calumnies have been put about concerning her. We only heard of these *stories* a short time ago otherwise they would have been contradicted long since. When we left London the middle of August we went into Hampshire to visit an old friend of Lord Orford's and were accompanied by Dorothy. Lord O remained with us two days then returned to London having business there. The day after Lord Orford left us Mr Smythe made his appearance and came to Mr Gawler's uninvited by him and unknown either to Lord Orford or myself – it was in the evening that Mr S came. I did not see her or him for not being well I had returned to my room but Mr Gawler told Mr Smythe that he must beg him to quit the neighbourhood as his visit to Dorothy was *unsanctioned by* either Lord O or myself – Mr S had taken up his abode at a small hotel about a mile or rather more from Mr Gawler's residence. The day after this visit Mr G finding that Mr S was still at the hotel asked me to write to him to beg him to quit the hotel and retire from the neighbourhood which I did and received an answer saying that he would go away – however the day but one afterwards Mr Gawler learnt that Mr Smythe had only retired to the hotel at Andover five miles from where we were on this visit – and Mr Gawler sent his nephew Mr Sayers who has married his niece and who both reside with him, to Andover to ask Mr S to go away and found with him a *female* who Mr Smythe had either brought with him or she had followed him. Lord Orford had also heard that Mr Smythe was in the neighbourhood still, and having returned to Mr Gawler's wrote to Mr S insisting upon his departure and Mr S went away accompanied by this woman. We have since heard that Dorothy was mistaken for her as it was asserted that she had been *walking* with Mr S, riding with him and also that they had been discovered in a Summer House – and lastly that Dorothy went off with him in the [word indecipherable]. Do tell me if these atrocious stories are still going on and you need not fear telling me what you hear as nothing can be worse than what we have already heard and as we want to have contradiction to them it will be really kind. I have not heard from Walpole since I wrote to him to tell him of these shameful stories about his sister. She is dreadfully worried by them.

Yours very sincerely,

M. ORFORD

Dorothy's kind regards

I have been thus explicit with you Madame Disraeli for you have been invariably kind to me and mine and it would grieve me sadly if you thought ill of your once favourite, Dorothy, and Mr D'Israeli is a person of so much influence and importance and you also that a contradiction from you both would do wonders in helping my poor little daughter cast off this infamous scandal and it will really be a great relief to hear that you both give credence to my statement to clear your friend. Madame d'Israeli she was with me all our visit lasted and therefore these things are impossible. There were still worse stories circulating owing to Dorothy having met with a slight accident for just two days before the expiration of our intended stay at Mr Gawler's, Dorothy in coming down stairs fell and hurt her back and she was obliged to have leeches applied – and after we got here to Wolterton owing to having walked and rode her back again became painful and Lord Orford took her to Norwich and the surgeon where Mr Cross ordered leeches to be applied again and a warm bath every other night for a fortnight and their remedies quite cured her and we were all this time in perfect ignorance of the scandal going on about her, and had not her governess accidentally heard that a most horrible story had been inserted in one of the low *low* papers we should in all probability have still been in the dark and Lord Orford who was never told of these horrors till about three weeks ago when his nephew Lady Maria West's son came from London to pay us a visit and then mentioned to Lord Orford that some measures ought to be taken to contradict such information. Surely there never was such disgraceful proceeding for Mr Smythe when coming into the country to pay his court to a young lady of rank to be accompanied by a woman of bad character who by Dorothy being mistaken for her was caused so much *misery*. Mr Smythe has been abroad since that period. I mention he really ought in *honour* to have returned home and to have refuted these atrocious inventions – We hear Mr Smythe he is at Rome do you know whether this is the case. We are at a loss to know who Dorothy's bitter enemies can be as she is not aware of having made any. As for myself I do not know if ever that I have as I am not conscious of having offended anyone. Mr Smythe cannot deny having had a female with him at the hotel in Andover.

If you know of any news when you write do tell me some for this sad business has made me quite low and uncomfortable but I hope and trust we shall be able to make people believe that it all was a fabrication. What is Lady Clementina Villiers about? We hear she was in love but with whom I am ignorant.

My hand reports to your amiable and clever husband we shall be in London next month when I hope to see you very often. How does the Duchess of Marlborough go on I hope the Duke keeps to bed. Dorothy still talks a great deal of Mister D'Israeli. She says he is always so kind to her.

Wolterton Feb 15th 1847

Dear Madame D'Israeli,

A thousand thanks for your most kind and entertaining letter you are a consolatory person in giving me hope that the calumnous stories set about respecting Dorothy will not be believed at least by those who are acquainted with her for I have been horrified by some calling themselves friends who say that she will never recover in the eyes of the world with the dreadful stories invented by some enemy – for it can be nothing else – I shall be very much obliged to you if you will let me know whether Mr S is really in London – I presume he is come to attend his sister's marriage which will I am told shortly take place. Is this the case? as we will certainly let you know when we decide upon coming to London – and I will call upon you as Mr D'Israeli and yourself have been so invariably kind to Dorothy that I can never forget it and to his power and influence we shall I have no doubt be greatly indebted for refuting the sad story that has been set about – I never heard anything in the report you mention of Lady Clementina indeed I seldom if ever listen to scandal and *never* believe illnatured stories therefore do not deserve to have my daughter calumniated. I hear that one reason that these atrocities have been given credit to is that Mr S does not return home to contradict them. I should hardly think that he will be well received in society for it is a sad thing to have been instrumental in defaming the character of a young lady, and people who have daughters surely will not admit him to their houses – I am sure you will agree with me in this. When you are kind enough to write will you tell me what is said about him – through his conduct we have by the slander created owing to Mr S having followed D into Hampshire been made very unhappy – but I hope that now active means are taken (though late owing to Lord O having been kept in ignorance of the abominable stories about) that Dorothy will be cleared – We have warm weather today but the cold has been very severe – with kind regards to your most talented and delightful husband believe me Dear Madame D'Israeli

Your most truly & sincerely

MARY ORFORD

Lord and Lady Pollington are at Paris for a short time.

We have a family party Lord Orford's sister Lady Catherine Long and two of her daughters are here and next week Lady Maria West and her children.

March 11th, Wolterton

Dear Madame D'Israeli,

I have been anxiously expecting from my library Sharpes in Berkeley Square your talented husband's new book but alas it is not come and they say it is not yet published. Is this the case for we are all impatient to read his work all here being such warm admirers of Mr D'Israeli and his splendid talents. We shall be in London by the end of this month when I hope to have the pleasure of seeing you – by the papers I see Mr

Smythe is arrived in England, by the stories that have been set about concerning Dorothy we have been made very uneasy for though untrue some people may believe them and at all events it is always distressing to be talked about in a way so unpleasant I think Mr S must feel very sorry that through him Dorothy has been made so very uncomfortable. Have you heard that he has been well received and does he go out? We heard that the Duke of Northumberland had left Mr S a legacy of £20,000 Is this the case – and is his sister to marry Lord Sligo? Your letters are most amusing and it gives me great pleasure to receive them, so Lady Clementina is not after all to marry Lord Euston – How very cold the weather is I hope it is not quite so piercing in London as it is here. We have Lord Orford's eldest sister with us and her two pretty daughters They all leave us at the end of the week and go to London for the season. Lord Orford says that nothing is to be done in Parliament, What are the Conservatives about. Do you see much of Lord G. Bentinck What do you think of Miss Windham's marriage? Surely it is a very bad marriage for her he can have nothing as he is in debt like the Pagets.

Believe me dear Madame D'Israeli

Your most truly & sincerely

M. ORFORD

Norfolk seethed with gossip and Dorothy hated to leave the 'lunatic asylum', believing everyone was revelling in her disgrace. Surveyed constantly by her parents, she languished miserably at Wolterton blinded by her infatuation; dreaming of being with her lover. He, however, had hurried off to Europe and was satiating himself with women in Venice, Florence and Rome, whence he had written to Disraeli in December:

The [illegible, but evidently the name of some woman] followed me to Paris as I predicted and here I got helplessly and damnably entangled with another woman who gave me mortification and heart burning enough – all which I wrote in a book which will never see the light. . . . At Venice I had other affairs of debauch into which I flung myself for compensation which turned out not over much.

Lord George Bentinck wrote to Disraeli on 9 November 1847:

It is much discussed whether Smythe will be received in society after such an outrage as getting an Earl's daughter pregnant (if she is with child) and then cutting her off and refusing to marry her. This is quite a modern description of profligacy reserved for a member of Peel's government, the contagion of its political bad faith spreading into private life.

Yet when Smythe returned to attend Parliament, the gates of Society opened to his unmistakable fascination – though one may assume that, at this stage, it was rather lost on the Orfords. He succeeded five years later as the seventh Lord Strangford, and died of his excesses, hastened by potations of brandy, in 1854. He was then aged forty-one and only a few days previously had married the heiress of his father's dreams. A final claim to fame was that in the year of his death he fought the last duel on English soil – with Monckton Milnes. The combat turned to farce when a pheasant, disturbed at the moment of firing, made a terrible noise and scattered the duellists.

As for Dorothy, there was no hope. She remained in exile, but Lady Orford ventured to London for a short season. It seemed sensible for her to try to settle the Dolly saga within the family. Marriage to a relation perhaps? 'That proper young man, Mr Henry West [Dorothy's cousin], is said to be going to marry Lady Dorothy Walpole,' wrote a Mrs Hudson to Lady Elizabeth Spencer Stanhope. She was wrong. The rumours seemed to pursue Dorothy everywhere.

Mary Orford went to breakfast with the Disraelis, taking with her Reginald Nevill, another cousin, aged forty and a confirmed bachelor. Known as the 'Castle Baby', he was the grandson of the seventeenth Baron and first Earl of Abergavenny – his father being a clergyman younger son. Disraeli liked him. That summer Mary Orford, avoiding Norfolk and Dorset, took Dorothy to a house at Sidmouth in Devon where they were joined by Walpole. 'We begin to be reconciled with our residence at Sidmouth by having my dear Walpole with us. We went to some races and the place is so very secluded . . . ' Lady Orford told Mary Anne. This was the first time that Horace had seen his family since his sister's disgrace. He was followed during August by another guest – Reginald Nevill, who left only once to visit his lawyers in London. Lady Orford's nightmare was over. Dorothy was gently persuaded that marriage to this relation was a desirable connection and a return ticket into Society. In fact she was proud that she, a Walpole, should connect herself to another great family of more ancient lineage, although one Radical wit ventured that he could not trace any Nevill of distinction for over 300 years 'with the exception of a gentleman of that name whose carts carrying one of the chief supports of life [bread] are conspicuous objects in the streets of London'.

On 29 September Lady Orford wrote triumphantly to Mrs Disraeli:

Dear Mrs Disraeli,

I am happy to announce the intended marriage of Dorothy to her cousin, Mr Nevill, whose acquaintance you made at your own house when I brought him to breakfast with you. It is a charming marriage; Mr Nevill is of an ancient family (the Abergavenny family). His mother was a [word indecipherable] Walpole. Mr Nevill is a kind amicable person and particularly good tempered and has known Dorothy ever since she came out here some two years ago and Lord O and myself have been acquainted with him from a boy and added to these qualities he is rich having an independent pasture of £8,000 a year and he has a small estate in Norfolk – and I am all the better pleased as he will take more care of her than a husband of some younger years would. They are mutually fond of each other which is also delightful . . . Walpole has returned separated from Lady Walpole – they have not been on good terms for some time. She is not worthy of such a delightful person, and she never could be domestic. He has two little girls.

News of the betrothal astonished the gossips. Mrs Stanley, who had not yet got rid of Alice, wrote acidly on 30 September:

The Duchess [of Montrose] informed me of two marriages, Lady Dolly Walpole and Mr Nevill, whom she describes as a religious man with £8,000 a year, an odd choice on his part unless he wishes to practise in conversion.

Reginald had inherited his 'pasture' from Edward 'Adonis' Walpole, his uncle, a patron of the arts and a collector who possessed a magnificent library (which he also treated as a sort of bank, for on his death his nephew discovered £25,000 in notes concealed between the pages). As a wedding present Reginald gave to his betrothed a stunning trousseau and dressing box – 'the most splendid diamond rings and a string of fine emeralds and another of rubies, also a most beautiful emerald and diamond bracelet and one large gold one as thick as a cable with a large ruby and diamond heart,' Lady Orford wrote to Mary Anne Disraeli, urging her to go and view the glistening spoils at Garrard's.

The Disraelis were relieved and delighted. 'Lady Dorothy Walpole went down to Wolterton today to be married which makes me very glad,' wrote Disraeli to Lord John Manners. 'An excellent match – Reginald Nevill with a good £8,000 per annum and a real good fellow.' The marriage took place at three o'clock in the afternoon of 2 December 1847 at the old Saxon church of Wickmere, near Wolterton, prettily decorated with velvet hangings for the occasion. 'We were all Walpoles together,' wrote Dorothy in her memoirs. Her cousin, the Reverend Thomas Walpole, performed the ceremony assisted by another cousin, Algernon Peyton, who held the richest living in England, Doddington, worth £7,000 a year. They were married in the old English style: the tenantry were drawn up at the gate and the postilions wore quaint blue jackets, smart white beaver hats and nosegays. From the park gate to the church curious triumphal arches were erected surmounted by flags. The schoolchildren strewed flowers in the path of the bride and the poor of the villages crowded the churchyard. The congregation swamped the church, even the pulpit and reading desk, and clambered onto the pews in a most indecorous manner to get a glimpse of the bride. Dorothy, looking lovely, spoke her responses clearly above the din and went through the service calmly – only to break down, however, at the signing of the register and the kissing (quite unlike Rachel who had announced at her wedding that she was not at all nervous or upset as she saw 'nothing to be ashamed of in being married').

Cecilia Walpole, wife of Dorothy's blind brother, Henry, wrote afterwards:

According to my promise I write to inform you that dearest Dorothy's marriage took place yesterday and that all went off gaily and happily as the marriage bells at least as far as the bride and bridegroom were concerned but poor Lord Orford was quite overcome and could with difficulty get through the duties of the day . . . and on her return with her husband they were saluted by a temporary battery of seven cannons. The bridesmaids, the Miss Wests, were in white muslin dresses with plum coloured velvet jackets and transparent white bonnets. Lady Orford was beautifully dressed in a dove coloured silk dress trimmed with gules, a cape of old lace and a white velvet bonnet with feathers and Lady Pollington wore a rust coloured silk embroidered in the same colour, a pink silk mantilla and a pink crepe bonnet.

The guests gathered in the saloon under the Gobelins tapestries and were entertained with music. Afterwards they sat down to the wedding feast which included 'as usual in Norfolk', remembered her cousin, Henry Drummond Wolff, 'a peahen and a gosling'. The old housekeeper had been forgotten, but after dinner Dorothy rushed upstairs to bring her down, bade her eat cake and drink wine and, as she put it in *Under Five Reigns*, 'made merry with the poor creature'.

Mr Reginald and Lady Dorothy Nevill left at nine, 'and we threw old shoes at them for good luck,' wrote Cecilia Walpole. The elderly bridegroom must have been startled when his new wife dashed back and, amid much laughter, gathered up in a dirty petticoat her lizards, snakes, tortoises, little dog and other pets before setting out on the road. They spent their honeymoon at Burnham Thorpe, a house that once belonged to her kinsman, Lord Nelson – whose family, according to Dorothy, were 'all so stupid that it must be inferred that his genius came from us'.

The tenants received the couple and their menagerie in the most cordial manner, bringing the bridal couple all sorts of presents, amongst which were bowls of beautiful rich cream which looked delicious but, Dorothy wrote sixty years later,

was so infested with the taste and smell of turnips that it quite overpowered me; so strong was it that we had to eject the bowls from the house, but of course in a covert manner lest the feelings of the donors be hurt.

The strangely assorted circus spent ten days at Burnham Thorpe before returning to Wolterton, where Dorothy had been sorely missed – 'I do not know this house without her,' wrote Cecilia. They had specially delayed their journey so that their carriage could be escorted into the park by mounted retainers. Miss Redgrave had written:

Don't think it ungracious if we beg of you to defer your departure one day, and not to come until Friday, as the tenants, imagining your return was to be on that day, had prepared to meet you at Itteringham and escort you home, and it would be so great a disappointment to them and they cannot be ready before. Lord Orford, though pleased with the attention proposed for his daughter, is sorry to lose one day of your company, but he gives it up to please others. Pray be at the Walpole Arms, Itteringham, or near, about half-past two on Friday; you will come of course in your brougham and we hope the day will be propitious as before. There will be a tenants' and servants' Ball in the evening. The cart leaves here this afternoon; will you send as much luggage as you can spare by it tomorrow?

Four

Adorned in her new jewels, Dorothy sparkled at the servants' ball. Afterwards the bridal pair departed to house hunt in London, leaving a spinster Walpole cousin with Lady Orford to share the ensuing gloom. Mr Nevill soon found suitably substantial premises for his new wife at 29 Upper Grosvenor Street, opposite the Disraelis.

London was most unhealthy. Appalling fogs settled on the streets in dense patches. They were grey, orange, deep orange and sometimes black; thick, choking and full of smells. They gave people the 'spleen' – liverishness, melancholy, ill humour; sometimes they even killed. The West End was also very noisy. Small traders and street vendors cried out their wares; newsboys shouted. Worse were the organ grinders, surpassed only by the abominable horse organ with the kettledrum movement, and a hideous widow with her dreadful children who performed on a jingling pianoforte, placed on a vegetable truck and drawn by a donkey. All these plagues connived with one another, though there were welcome features too – the red-coated crossing sweepers, the lamplighters who made their rounds at dawn and dusk, their tall ladders slung across their shoulders, and the milk women in shawls, their churns suspended by wooden yokes across their shoulders.

But Dorothy could shrug off a few urban inconveniences. For the first time she had real financial resources at her fingertips. She found it a heady experience – at Webb's in the Strand, or Christie's, or some other sale room – bidding for the eighteenth-century French furniture, pastels and porcelain that since the French Revolution and the Napoleonic wars could often be bought for a song. Her father, on the other hand, had his eye on his son-in-law's wealth for subsidising his horses and, to this end, suggested they went into partnership. After the first few results, however, Reginald pulled out hastily before his fortune diminished. In his view his Walpole wife was extravagance enough.

Back at Wolterton Lady Orford could breathe a partial sigh of relief. At least Dorothy was off her hands, nicely married to a rich, indulgent aristocrat. But the family still had its problems. The wretched Rachel had gone off with her husband to Paris for Easter, and now revolution had broken out, sparking off risings in all the capitals of Europe. There the Pollingtons were, with Rachel in the middle of the barricades so frightened and nervous she had become seriously ill, so weak she could hardly walk. 'I see no possibility of tranquillity anywhere,' moaned Lady Orford to Mary Anne Disraeli; and certainly there was no tranquillity where her son Horace was concerned. He was in the adulterous arms of the Countess of Lincoln. His marriage had not been a success. There had been outrageous incidents. There was another side to Lord Walpole lurking beneath his dinner-party style which was anything but divine. When Harriet Walpole (who had a strong will and temper of her own) had accidentally surprised her husband with a woman in the Borghese Gardens, he had followed her home, battered her about the head, kicked her down the stairs and spat upon her. His fond family, preferring to believe it was her ladyship's lack of domesticity that had caused the marriage to break up, welcomed their prodigal son home, where he stayed in a small room. But like his father he was for ever restless and soon dashed off to Bad Ems. There he had an assignation with Lady Lincoln, Beckford's granddaughter and daughter of the Duke of Hamilton. She found Walpole, with his romantic charm, eccentricity and humour, to say nothing of that divine dinner-party style, the ideal antidote to Lincoln.

The lovers travelled openly with Edward Bulwer Lytton, the novelist, to Wiesbaden, Turin, Genoa and Lake Como. Here they settled into a love nest and Susan Lincoln adopted the pseudonym of 'Mrs Lawrence'. Soon they were tracked down by no less a person than Mr Gladstone himself who had taken on the job of reclaiming Lincoln's wife. He reached their hiding place and concealed himself in the bushes to establish their identity – 'Mrs Lawrence as she is called who refused two times over to see me except by verbal messages today, and who drove off from her villa between 9 and 10 at night, is far gone in pregnancy,' he wrote to his wife in London. Walpole and his swollen paramour left separately and in haste believing Gladstone to be the furious Lord Lincoln. Suzie, with Gladstone in hot pursuit, reached Vienna on 2 August 1849 and simultaneously gave birth to a son, another Horace Walpole. Gladstone, holding the proof of her identity and condition, staggered back to London. But this was not enough for Lord Lincoln, who needed further evidence. He intended to divorce his wife before Parliament. The scandal, when it broke six months later, rocked the foundations of the Establishment and provided the most celebrated divorce case of the century. The Orfords suspected it was a Whig plot to blacken the Tories and were paralysed yet again by vicious rumours involving their family. As for Lady Walpole, she certainly did not relish the affair. 'You know I presume, what is said to be going on,' wrote the Duke of Newcastle to the Duke of Hamilton, Susan Lincoln's father.

I have been told that Lady Walpole means to divorce her husband for which she possesses sufficient evidence – and lately I am assured that the child is dead. If Lady Walpole succeeded in divorcing her husband, in all probability the sequel will be the union of the criminals, which I lament and readily suppose will be by no means agreeable to you.

Quaking at the havoc that the old Duke of Newcastle might wreak in their lives, the Orfords weathered the storms and the newspapers while the lovers themselves had a delightful time in Nice and Rome, accompanied by Lytton. Walpole seems to have been quite unaffected by the brouhaha he had caused. 'We are become very intimate,' Bulwer wrote to his brother from Nice on 17 January 1850,

as much friends as I am likely to be with anyone out of my own family, he is amazingly well read – a large surface of classical and elegant information – and a charming gentleman's mind. But bad health – no ambition – and wedded to his own indolent habits.

Later, in an album annotation, he described him as

a brilliant creature thrown away . . . indolent, pleasure loving, selfish . . . In spite of all his faults, lovable.

Dorothy meanwhile was anything but indolent. Now pregnant, she occupied herself with a masterpiece of illumination, a genealogy of the Nevill family by Rowland.[1] Lady Orford could divert herself with writing to Mary Anne Disraeli about other people's unfortunate marriages: Lord Stamford and Warrington had married the daughter of his bedmaker at Cambridge, and the M.P. George Bankes had attached himself to 'the daughter of a little banker in Dorchester'. Slowly her son's affair reached its dénouement. It was reported that Noele Paovich, Lord Walpole's new courier, a native of the province of Illyria, provided the proof of the adultery. He had witnessed Lord Walpole taking off his coat and trousers and coming in and sitting with Lady Lincoln clad only in a pair of drawers, a loose dressing gown, socks and slippers. He had furthermore in November 1848 surprised the lovers in the act.

They were in a position on the sofa beside the fire. Walpole lying upon her and his dressing gown spread out over them both . . . and in his usual undress but with a very red face came to the door and collected the newspapers saying Mille Grazie, something he had not ever said to him before.

After the furore of the divorce had died down, Horace continued to live with Lady Lincoln and their love child until one night the incredible happened. He surprised her in the arms of her groom. His pride was bruised beyond endurance. He abandoned her and went home.

In December 1849, before the Lincoln divorce had been made final, Dorothy gave birth to a daughter, christened Meresia Augusta. In 1850 she was pregnant again and she and her husband looked around for a country property to accommodate the growing family and to combine their tastes. Reginald enjoyed agriculture, racing and coaching,[2] then the fashion; while Dorothy aspired to horticulture. In the event their choice was surprisingly remote – in the depths of a wild country little changed since the days of the Conqueror, near Rogate, five miles

[1] It took her four years to complete it. Ralph Nevill, in *Life and Letters* (1917), suggested it was possible that this volume was 'the most important and successful example of illumination ever executed since the Middle Ages'.
[2] 'Driving was in fashion, and sprigs of nobility used to dress as coachmen and imitate the slang and behaviour of coachmen, from whom occasionally they would take lessons in driving as they sat beside them on the box.' George Borrow, *The Romany Rye*.

from the market towns of Petersfield and Midhurst and twenty-two miles from the nearest station at Godalming. They had been stopping at Woolbeding with Lady Orford's cousins, the Ponson-bys, when they saw Dangstein, a neo-Grecian style house built like a temple in the local yellow sandstone by the architect Knowles, who had formed his tastes by visiting the monumental public works in the 1820s and 1830s and whose clients were known eccentrics. Dangstein lay in its own prettily timbered park reclaimed from the surrounding forest, encircled by a large estate of more than 1,000 acres possessing the best rough shooting in the country and intersected by the swirling Rother. They moved in six months later after the birth of Edward Augustus.

Reginald set about improving the place. He bought up large quantities of land which he drained and trenched, and underplan-ted the woodlands. Land over which he had at first only worthless rights became his freehold. His wife meanwhile equipped the house, which she felt could be far more comfortable. It was very large, with eighteen bedrooms, a fine suite of six reception rooms, a massive domed hallway with a gallery, and a ballroom beneath the basement. For heating Dorothy installed a huge furnace twenty-three yards in circumference, built rather like a great octopus with curious subterranean tentacles. It needed constant stoking, devoured annually thirty-three wagon-loads of twenty tons each, and had to burn for three days before the freezing air could be dispersed in the hall. Such a house required a huge labour force. This Dorothy partly solved by constructing in the woods an ornamental laundry-cum-schoolhouse, benevolently inscribing on the outside 'A thanksgiving for many blessings'. Here she trained girls with the help of a matron (who perman-ently wished her mistress away in London), sending those she could not employ out into the world with unhelpfully illegible references, so ill-written that a young laundress was once dismissed from an interview for producing a forgery. Dorothy hated seeing too much of her servants and blotted them out with a complicated system of pulleys, blinds and shutters that were wound up from the lower ground floor so that there was no need for the 'poor creatures' to appear after dinner. Most maids lived in terror of her strict regime, although one particularly bold one was discovered wearing Dorothy's favourite black evening dress in which she was planning to impersonate Mary, Queen of Scots being beheaded at the local theatricals. Years later, staying with the FitzClarences, Dorothy went to the theatre in Portsmouth. There she rediscovered her maid, who beseeched her patronage. Dorothy remarked that she was far better an actress than a maid.

Dorothy would have no gambling or drunkenness but was always imagining that her maids were drunk – which, considering the amount of beer brewed in the house brewery and stored tantalisingly in the cellar, was perfectly possible. Such was her paranoia that her friend the second Duke of Wellington tried to reason with her:

Your old maid opened the door for me in a dreadful state of tears because you have sent her away. She declares she was not drunk, and that smoking only made you suspect her. Drunkenness is an unpardonable offence in certain departments of men, for instance grooms, because the horses are the sufferers; but I doubt if you are correct in accusing a nervous woman . . . I don't think she drinks and dearly recommend you to retain an attached maid. It is not as if it were your butler or footman.

But the butlers drank and gambled too, or so at least Dorothy believed. There were appalling orgies in the harness room.

At Christmas, under the dome, the local mummers would act St George killing the dragon, surrounded by yapping animals. Dorothy, Reginald and the two children huddled on the stairs trying in vain to detect a faint glimmer of warmth from the subterranean inferno. The rest of the household shivered in order of precedence, grouped around the gallery.

Dangstein was still living in the old agricultural rhythm of past centuries. The only means of transport other than the distant railroad was the stagecoach, but the carrier was often tired or, like the butlers, very drunk. Either way he did not appear for hours, sometimes days, after he was due. Occasionally even his wheels fell off, once depositing in the ditch some departing guests, the future Home Secretary, Sir William Harcourt, and the artist Richard Doyle. They had to walk the last lap to Petersfield and Dicky, as he was known, sketched the bucolic scene for Dorothy.

The local postman was equally erratic and telegraphic arrangements were embryonic. One old woman, it was said, hung an umbrella on the post to go by telegraph. Another addressed a new pair of boots to her son and hung them on the telegraph wires.

The next morning she found an old pair in their place. 'God bless the lad,' she exclaimed, 'that is good of him. I never thought he would send his old pair back to be repaired.' Another poor man received a cable 'Wife and litter doing well.' He telegraphed frantically, 'For Heaven's sake how many?' and was relieved to receive the correction 'Wife and little one doing well'.

At Cowdray, the neighbouring estate, the curse of fire and water had been fulfilled with the extinction of the families of Montague, Browne and Poyntz in drowning accidents, and the burning of the house. There were numerous tales, too, of smugglers, highwaymen and buried treasure; and of how young Drewitt, the local Robin Hood, had been captured in a new pair of buckskin breeches. As the boy's corpse swung on the Midhurst gibbet, children were brought from miles to touch his lifeless hand – supposedly a remedy against the afflictions of the throat.

With its remoteness the country had retained its feudal ways. As late as 1750 there was a pressing to death in Horsham gaol and a hundred years later the stocks in Midhurst were still in use, the inhabitants enjoying the event almost as little as the incumbent. All in all it was a fanatically Tory neighbourhood, the yeomen following the Conservative politics of their local landowners – Nevill, Wyndham (Lord Leconfield's family) or Lennox (the Duke of Richmond's family). No Sussex labourer ever heard of Richard Cobden, the Radical and Free Trader, even though he had lived near Rogate at Dunford Rectory (indeed 'free trading', in the county vocabulary meant smuggling). 'Muster Cobden?' answered one to a journalist trying to find his way to Dunford; 'To be sure we all knows him. He keeps the public house at Ha'naker and rare sport he do have there at times.' On further inquiry Muster Cobden turned out to be the local hero whose sport was cockfighting. And indeed of the other Mr Cobden no one knew or even cared.

But the landlords knew all about Cobden. They shunned him and looked upon him as a usurper – the very devil in their midst – assuming he was intent on Americanising traditional institutions. There used to exist in England a great fear of traditional institutions being Americanised and Cobden was always supposed to be scheming in this direction. Old Lord Ellenborough, among others, was firmly convinced to this effect. He wrote to Dorothy in 1865 after Cobden's death:

Knowing Cobden as you did, you must feel his death very much. I never saw him . . . I confess I think they were both [Cobden and Bright] unsuited to the present constitution of this country and that they had a strange longing for something on the American model. One would think that depraved state must now have passed from all reasonable beings . . .

Cobden's policy in the end did bring ruin to the squires who for centuries had lived comfortably off their rents. Dorothy and her husband, however, never ones to conform, befriended him. He was, Dorothy found, although not exactly good-looking, fascinating and attractive – 'like a Saxon saint', George Smythe once said. In spite of Cobden's unpopularity the Nevills tried to introduce him into Sussex/Hampshire society. First they took him to Uppark. It was not a success. Old Lady Fetherstonhaugh refused to receive him, telling Dorothy persistently 'she could not bear to meet people who held revolutionary opinions'. But to the witty Bernal Osborne, M.P. for Londonderry, and Lord Henry Lennox,[1] another of Disraeli's good-looking, foppish young protégés, Cobden was more acceptable and Lord Henry and Cobden struck up a surprising friendship.

In February Dorothy, like her parents before her, would hurry up to London for the winter sessions to hear all the new speeches – particularly from fine orators like Richard Cobden and Disraeli. Since the repeal of the Corn Laws, which had caused terrible bitterness and feuds within families,[2] Disraeli had become champion of the Party of Land. He favoured protection, which sought to exploit the differences between capital and labour through a paternalistic society, ideals not far removed from Young England's. The Party of Land had returned to the policies of the Ultras and Agricultural Reactionaries of the 1830s favoured by such landed peers as the Duke of Rutland and Dorothy's father. Disraeli's rise in party status had been signalled in 1846 by two events: one was recognition by the Duke of

[1] Son of the Duke of Richmond, M.P. for Chichester 1846–85.
[2] The Duke of Newcastle became completely estranged from his son, Lord Lincoln, actually opposing his election.

Rutland, who ceased to regard him merely as a 'designing person' and invited him to Belvoir;[1] and the other was a great banquet at King's Lynn given for him by Horatio Orford, where he had addressed five hundred substantial squires and yeomen.

After the death of Lord George Bentinck in 1848 Disraeli had become Leader of the Tories in the House, and in 1852 became Chancellor of the Exchequer and Leader of the House of Commons without ever having held office before, the only individual apart from Pitt to claim this distinction. In February 1858 he was again Chancellor of the Exchequer and Leader of the House, but he was soon out of office, defeated over the Budget. Disraeli thought that his unpopularity – which he greatly exaggerated – stemmed from his Jewish origins. 'Ah, dear Dorothy,' he wrote to her, 'it is not my politics they dislike! It is myself!' The country believed his politics were inconsistent and could not forgive his betrayal of Peel, then his subsequent reversal to Peelite policies and abandonment of protection. Dorothy understood him, understood that he trimmed his sails to the wind but that he never really abandoned the early romantic ideals of Young England or his belief in government through the land and by an aristocracy. He owed his position completely to women – Lady Jersey, Lady Palmerston, Mrs Norton, and his wife Mary Anne. He found women indulgent and when they asked favours he was generally happy to reward them. When Dorothy's younger brother, Frederick Walpole, was in need of a position it was Dorothy who was delegated to approach Disraeli – not her brother Horace, his great friend. He replied by bestowing on him the North Division of Norfolk which he held until his death.

There was nothing that Dorothy loved more than to cross over the road from her house in Upper Grosvenor Street to dine with the Disraelis – dinners unusual in that they were provided by a caterer at a sovereign per head. The Disraelis were always short of money even though Mary Anne enjoyed a considerable benefit by the will of her first husband, Wyndham Lewis, M.P. for Maidstone. Disraeli, according to Bernal Osborne, loved his wife only out of gratitude. In any case Mary Anne was ever conscious of the family finances and parsimonious over small matters.

[1] Where he was received by six servants 'bowing in rows', as he afterwards described it to Mary Anne.

Nothing made her crosser than when Dorothy's brother Horace stood her up at the last minute, an event which was apparently quite normal. 'He might just as well make one throw a sovereign into the Thames,' she would exclaim angrily. The dinners were in fact surprisingly delicious but it was the men rather than the menus which made them exceptional. Disraeli believed that a constant flow of new and enthusiastic blades was the life blood of politics and he used his table to entertain aspiring young politicians, numbering in one year alone four hundred and fifty. Often he would leave his place at the head of the table to spend time with a young fellow whom he thought might be of use to future Tory administrations.

His moods would vary. Sometimes he was gay, jubilant even. Sometimes he would remain silent for hours, morose and preoccupied, allowing his wife to chatter away nineteen to the dozen while he scarcely listened – although, said Dorothy, 'he took care not to let her know it'. Certainly Mary Anne in her verbosity was capable of memorable gaffes. Dorothy claimed she once greeted the French Ambassador when he tried to kiss her hand, 'Mais Monsieur, ce n'est pas propre.' She never could remember who came first, the Greeks or the Romans, and it is said that once when the conversation turned to the subject of Dean Swift, Mary Anne had asked who he was so that she could invite him to her parties. She was only surpassed by Mrs Hudson, wife of the Railway King, Hudson, who was the Mrs Malaprop of her day. The Hudsons' parties at their mansion in Albert Gate[1] were famous. Queen Victoria was even said to have been entertained there. Everyone relished Mrs Hudson's snobbishness and vulgarity and delighted in repeating her *faux pas*. Once, while dining at the British Embassy and fearing that the conversation was unsuitable for servants, she whispered to her neighbour: 'Prenez garde que le derrière de ma chaise ne comprend pas le français.' Arranging herself before a party she would instruct her maid, 'Dress me for ten', 'Dress me for twenty'; and once she compared a guest to a pat of butter on a hot plate – 'You never knew when you had got him.'

The Reform Bill and the railway boom were combining to

[1] One of two houses designed by Cubitt and known as 'the two Gibraltars' – it was said they could never be stormed.

change the social fabric of the country. Society, according to Dorothy, had begun to cut its own throat. Mrs Hudson was not the only new, rich hostess to give parties – occasions which Dorothy with her eye for oddities hurried along to inspect. 'One half of those present', she wrote, 'seem to have been railway promoters.' For ten years this stockjobbing in connection with the railroads became a mania. It reached such a pitch that Hudson at a meeting for shareholders even delcared it quite the right thing to pay dividends out of capital – 'it only made matters pleasant.' But palatial stations and termini like St Pancras, plunder of lawyers and the formation of non-paying branch lines quickly ended the reign of Hudson (whom everyone then dropped) and caused the ruin of many aristocrats, particularly younger men who had seen speculation as some new kind of sport.

The stockjobbers had even invaded Rotten Row, the playground of Society – the fashionable place being between Albert and Grosvenor Gate. What a sight it was: dandies with blue coats, brass buttons and broad-brimmed hats, embroidered waistcoats and watchribbons; some clinging to the dress of a vanished age, some wearing duck trousers so tight that they split, their huge wide coat sleeves like gigot sleeves, which caused it to be said that the pegtops, as the full trousers were then called, were leaving gentlemen's legs and taking shelter under their arms. And how splendid the turnouts were: heavy old coaches with coachmen and horses to match – equipages that creaked out year after year with their panels revarnished and their brass work relacquered, enclosing wonderful decrepit old ladies let down stiffly from the steps of their chariots; vulgar new barouches owned by the newly rich stockjobbers, their ladies trying to be seen; mail phaetons driven by dashing blades, mysterious little broughams containing occupants about whom there were rumours, to say nothing of the scandalous Adeline Horsey de Horsey in her *vis-à-vis*, a childhood friend of Dorothy and now the mistress of Lord Cardigan. There were other sights, too: a naked horseman appearing from Kensington Gardens; old Lady Penrhyn escorted by her three ugly little pugs neatly dressed in scarlet coats and bonnets; the Marquess of Anglesey, who had lost one of his legs at Waterloo, driving out his pair of horses while his groom sat at the back, taking bets as to which of his lordship's legs was the wooden one; the ancient Duchess of Cleveland, so obsessed by the size of her feet that her whole life was passed drawing attention to her shoes, slumbering for hours on the Serpentine. Sometimes the Serpentine stank so foul that it prevented the Duchess or anyone else sailing on it, and rumour had it that the stench could kill you in twenty-four hours.

Other attractions were steamy mornings in the Fern House at Kew Gardens, or the Great Exhibition in Hyde Park, to which Dorothy was escorted by the diarist Charles Greville (nicknamed 'The Gruncher'). Almost immediately they were separated by the milling throng – never before had London seen such a mob, albeit attractive and good-humoured. Dorothy remembered:

I got caught in the crowd, and being very small would certainly have been very seriously injured by the terrible crush, had not a friendly official thrust me into a place of safety in the shape of his little pay-box.

Then, in 1852, there was the Duke of Wellington's funeral. Dorothy paid three guineas to watch it from Alabaster's, the straw bonnet shop in Piccadilly. They had to be in their places at 5 a.m., but because of the weight of the funeral carriage the flag-festooned cortège passed hours late, the horses struggling along with the car wheels sinking into the ground and all the spectators miserable because of the long wait and the gloomy occasion. 'I hate processions,' Dorothy said emphatically to Edward Cazalet sixty years later, recalling the day. 'These processions aren't worth going to see.'

Meanwhile, back in the country, there were more occasions for gloom. In 1853 a baby hastily christened Mary died after two days. The following year poor nervous Rachel expired. Her health had been failing. The disapproving Lady Stanley seems even to have pursued the wretched Walpole sisters abroad. In September 1850 she had written to her daughter from Lake Lucerne: 'Lady Pollington was at the station, surrounded by German Officers and seeming much as of old, but coarse and plain.' 'She passed away calmly and without any pain,' Dorothy told Mary Anne Disraeli. Dorothy and Reginald sailed off abroad to get away from it all, first to Ostend then on to Frankfurt, returning to Dangstein with renewed spirits. The next year was happier. Dorothy gave birth to another child, yet another Horace to add to the family collection. She wrote to Mary Anne, asking her to be the baby's godmother:

I shall be happy to show you my baby so different from her sickly poor little sister. I have begun to nurse it myself and hope I shall succeed. I had chloroform but the doctor would not give it to me strong enough to deaden the pain, although even as I had it, it was delightful.

When not nursing her babies Dorothy loved to entertain. Sometimes her dinners were physically hazardous, since she believed in including all the spoils of the countryside, particularly truffles gleaned under the beech trees from her neighbours at The Grange and motley fungi which sprang up conveniently on the lawns. In this she was advised by the Revd Mr Berkeley, described as the virtual founder of British mycology, who all but wrote off some of his friends with a noxious concoction of scleroderma which he had confused with *Lycoperdon giganteus*, both of which flourished on the autumnal lawns at Dangstein. 'Be careful,' warned Berkeley. 'Pray do not make an experiment without my advice.' Dorothy and her guests might now expect to survive her experiments; there was no guarantee, however, they would find them palatable. 'We might have eaten old shoes,' she recalled.

Tennyson bought a house on a hill nearby. It had no driveway and it was Dorothy who obtained the necessary dispensations from the neighbouring landlord for Tennyson to construct a road. This was a more successful gesture than on a subsequent occasion at Dangstein. Tennyson had come to dinner and Mrs Sartoris[1] had prepared as a special surprise a setting of one of his poems to music. Tennyson, however, was outraged. He objected strongly to the vulgar treatment of his work and ranted at the wretched Mrs Sartoris while the rest of the house retreated hastily to their rooms.

[1] Lord Leighton's 'Egeria'.

Five

In her memoirs Dorothy tells us that the Walpoles had an intense love of frivolity combined with a real liking for literature and art. In all this she was a true Walpole, a truly divided character. Nothing seemed too mundane for her and she collected around her an enormous assemblage of clutter all her life. Wherever Dorothy went, she returned with a souvenir. She bought snuff boxes, scent bottles, needle cases and travelling cases; articles of straw-work, ivory patch-boxes and counter-boxes; trayfuls of shells and brass boxes; exquisite small corset buttons (she had a name for each class); silhouettes and mementoes of her kinsman Lord Nelson and forbears Sir Robert Walpole and Horace; glass portraits, wax medallions, lockets worked in hair; anything she could lay her hands on from Strawberry Hill; dressed portraits (dress or draperies cut away from engravings, replaced with scraps of satin, silk or brocade); posy rings inscribed with 'brief poetical sentiments' – Dorothy's favourite was Lady Cathcart's who, marrying for the fourth time, had cut on hers: 'If I survive I will have five.'

There was also a lot of rubbish: old bill heads, engraved ball and concert tickets; menu cards, caricatures and cartoons; watchstands, watch papers[1] and potted meat jars; even a collection of toothpicks; anything in fact that Dorothy found curious or interesting. She had a story for them all. She collected signatures, too, in a book decorated for her by Kate Greenaway. She once sent it to Cardinal Newman asking for his autograph. Instead of writing in it he put it away in a drawer, forgetting to send it back. Dorothy, thinking it had been lost, inquired from the

---

[1] Little paper circles, elaborately ornamented and engraved. It was formerly the custom for watchmakers to put them in the outside cases of watches that came to be repaired. Dorothy possessed one with the figure of Time pointing to a dial, his scythe lying at his feet. Around the rim are simple directions for regulating the watch.

post office. The sequel was that the poor Cardinal was probed by the police, who suspected him of theft. He hastily signed it and sent it back before anything else could befall him. Archbishop Croke, on the other hand, a Roman Catholic prelate, refused to sign, saying he wanted to have 'nothing to do with her or her kind'.

She included in her collections her own 'finger-work'. There seemed to be no end to it all: the skeletonised leaves, painted china, snobbish crests of Walpole and Nevill decorating the fireplaces; shell paintings; prints and mezzotints set in satin mounts embroidered with silk and pearls and vine leaves. Then there was the filigree work – strips of rolled coloured paper gummed onto sheets of cardboard or mother-of-pearl and made into mounts, trays and even more ambitious articles of furnishing. It was delicate work, requiring infinite patience, that was popular at the end of the eighteenth century. Dorothy was the first to resurrect and the last to perfect this art.

On the one side she was frivolous and gregarious, a side she exercised vigorously in London. She needed people and collected them round her all her life, filing away her friends and acquaintances rather like curios, to show off at will. There was nothing she liked more than collecting. Edmund Gosse recalled that when Swinburne died, Dorothy was most upset; not because, so he believed, that Dorothy particularly loved his poetry, but that he had never been one of the curios. Dorothy once wrote to Gosse after meeting a very notorious individual for the first time, 'I thought I should never be introduced to him, and I had to wait 100 years but everything is possible in the best of worlds and he was very satisfactory at last.' She collected everything and everyone, turning them into possessions with which to festoon her houses, which she made into museums and theatres in which to act out her fantasies – 'Life was a spectacle for her and society a congress of little guignols, at all of which she would be seated in the front stall,' wrote Edmund Gosse. To be a satisfactory member of Dorothy's collection you had, whoever you were, to perform on the stage of life the part fate had decreed you must act – competently and if possible amusingly. 'Even a criminal might be satisfactory if he did his job properly. . . . The first principle of society should be to extinguish all bores.'

On the other hand she wanted to be serious, despising many of her female friends as 'giggletrots'. 'She is indeed curious and well adapted to open bazaars,' she said of one woman; of another, 'I supose she can just about read'; and a favourite saying was: 'Oh, any stupid woman can be sweet.' It was almost as though she was determined to justify her dull marriage in Society's eyes by breaking into a man's world. Her major contribution was in horticulture. At this time ladies were not interested in gardens; indeed, women were not supposed to be interested in anything beyond their own limited world. They played cards and the piano, did worsted and tapestry work, fashioned spills out of paper, cut silhouettes, kept the household accounts, had babies and read romantic novelettes to pass the time. These were purveyed in huge quantities by Anthony King Newman and the Minerva Press, their authors 'always finishing their heroines off by placing them in bowers of bliss and bestowing on them basketfuls of babies', wrote Dorothy in her memoirs. Descriptions were exotic to say the least:

All of a sudden the girl continued to sit on the sand gazing on the briny deep, on whose heaving bosom the tall ships went merrily by, freighted – ah! who can tell with how much joy and sorrow, and pine and lumber, and emigrants, and hopes and salt fish?

Another author depicted a fire out of which 'a horse entirely consumed made its escape, uttering terrible cries!' Another told of an unfortunate traveller who,

after being perforated with innumerable bullets by bandits and thrown into a lime kiln, where he was burnt to a cinder, had strength and resolution enough to drag himself to a neighbouring village and lodge an information before a magistrate.

Even more obscure were the popular romances dealing with fashionable life:

Having resolved on this, Lady Theresa went in search of her Bible and her 'Christian Year'.
Accompanied by Sir Arthur, she entered Lord Beaurepaire's room.
He was lying on a couch, wrapped in thick brocade dressing gown.
His small arched feet were in embroidered slippers, and a ruby velvet and gold fez covered his fine head and thickly curling auburn hair.
He was, in truth, superbly handsome, of that lofty, refined and

highly-finished style which we are wont to consider patrician or aristocratic, although perhaps the finest specimen of that antinous and chiselled face was to be found in 'the grand old gardener', in whom, after all, duke and dustman, count and costermonger, alike have their origin.

For young ladies unfortunate enough not to make matches, life held little apart from Lord Beaurepaire, to say nothing of the Grand Old Gardener. Sometimes they were expected to act as sort of high-class companions to the rest of the household, occasionally being taken to London for relief almost as part of the baggage, when the routine might be varied with a ball. Life was summed up by the Duke of Newcastle's frustrated daughters who hardly ever left Clumber, his seat in Nottinghamshire:

As usual we do little else than eat, sleep, walk. We play a little mostly in the evenings, and sometimes in the day. Somehow we are such stationary beings that we seldom move anywhere.

They would never have thought to work in the garden, usually laid out in those days in squares, cubes and triangles of different-coloured flowers, like the beds in municipal public places today. On the whole the days of follies, land and waterscapes had died with the eighteenth century and gardens in the mid-Victorian era were uninspired.

Dorothy was a pioneer of the herbaceous border long before Mrs Earle, Miss Jekyll and Mr Robinson made this kind of planting popular. From her childhood she had been whirled off to well-known seedsmen and nurseries by her father. Now, aged twenty-five, she began with amazing thoroughness to equip her own cage, starting by experimenting with the sandy loam at Dangstein. Friends such as Bernal Osborne and Robert Lowe, a future Chancellor of the Exchequer, at first treated her researches as a joke, irritated by what seemed to them to be more than misplaced energy. In their view Dorothy was fiddling in a man's world. Osborne used to declare that ladies like 'taking in scientific men by pretending an interest in subjects which were their especial study'. Sir William Harcourt was never reconciled to Dorothy mispronouncing the Latin names of plants. He thought her looks and charm enough wealth. 'Nature has done more for you than science and the arts are likely to accomplish,' he said to her. Nevertheless, in spite of such chauvinistic discouragement the gardens at Dangstein flourished, enveloping more and more forest. Thirty-four gardeners slaved away day and night scooping out dells, ponds, sunken lawns and terraces, planting magnolias, weeping holly, Wellingtonias, bamboos, pergolas and herbaceous borders. These were followed by elaborate orchid and fern houses which, like Dangstein, required huge furnaces and shifts of stokers. Almost immediately there was a terrible tragedy. Two gardeners on night watch were suffocated by the new chimneys becoming choked. Dorothy floundered in condescending anguish.

The poor men, they had been looking forward to a visit to the Chichester Agricultural Show and the tragedy had happened on the night before the greatly anticipated treat . . . It was all too dreadful. The men had been great favourites of mine, and for some time I could not bear to enter the new Fern House.

But work was resumed and over the next four years the gardens expanded steadily. Progress was astonishing. Thirteen greenhouses shot up, together with peach houses, melon and cucumber pits and kitchen gardens planted with apples, pears, vines and plums fanning out over the sunny walls. There were huge underground heaters and rainwater tanks, with arches like Roman aqueducts. Not a drop was wasted. Rainwater dripped from roof to tank to farmhouse, orchid house and conservatories, until finally it filled the pond in the bamboo-infested dell at the bottom of the garden. A pinetum was planted with California redwoods, Wellingtonias, monkey-puzzle and all kinds of fir trees, bordered by oaks and ilexes; aviaries were constructed for breeding lovebirds and choughs that strutted proprietorially round the gardens. Friends would send Dorothy exotic crates full of strange creatures: mice, half-brown, half-white, that Dorothy said got up in the middle of the night and danced and danced; lion dogs of China, bred at Goodwood by the Duchess of Richmond; a Kurdish sheepdog sent from Turkey by her brother, Horace, which cost her £40 for its passage; a demoiselle crane dispatched from the Crimea by Sir John Mitchell which terrorised the chickens and ate their eggs; Siamese cats, a beautiful dun colour, specially bred by the King of Siam, so delicate they rarely survived long (although one of them, Mrs Poodles, lasted long enough for

Dorothy to show her at the Crystal Palace and duly won the gold medal); and some storks which ate everything. These eventually died and a post-mortem revealed crops bursting with slates, bricks, brass buttons and a varied collection of ironware.

In part of the garden Dorothy made a cemetery, a sort of garden of remembrance, for the ever-increasing pile of non-survivors: her horses; Shuck, a favourite dog named after the spirit haunting the Norfolk lanes; a most irritating barking collie given her by Sir Edwin Landseer, the court artist; pug-like dogs usually depicted beneath the wheels of carriages; and the various mongrels that it was fashionable to purchase from vendors outside the gates of Rotten Row. The graves had stones and inscribed epitaphs composed by visitors such as Lowe, W. H. Mallock (author of *The New Republic*), and the Duke of Wellington. It was one of the minor ways Dorothy selected to exercise her guests. One memorial to a favourite dog reads:

ON TOPSY

Where art thou now, little wandering
Life, that so faithfully dwelt with us,
Played with us, felt with us, fed with us,
Years we grew fonder and fonder in?
You, who but yesterday sprang to us,
Are we for ever bereft of thee,
And is this all that is left of thee,
One little grave and a pang to us?

Not to be outdone by her heroine, Marie Antoinette, Dorothy embarked upon a model farm whose inhabitants were goats, donkeys and pigs. It was at the time that graveyard and church at Rogate were in the process of being restored. Dorothy, with her eye for the eccentric, seized upon piles of engraved memorial slabs as suitable material with which to build pigsties.

In just four years Dorothy's schemes achieved public recognition. Her gardens were noticed in the *Gardener's Chronicle*. Dorothy confided the glad tidings to Mary Anne Disraeli and two days later they were even gladder. The notices had reached illustrious ears: 'Sir William Hooker of Kew has written to propose himself to Dangstein. We are getting on well in the Botanical World.' It was a great compliment that the seventy-year-old Master of Kew was prepared to make the arduous journey. In fact Hooker had already met Dorothy several times and escorted her round the Fern House and gardens at Kew.

Dorothy's letters were instruments of friendship: hastily misspelled missives written generally on scraps of different coloured paper; pink and blue and snuff brown, violet and green and grey; stamped with patterns like a napkin, or frilled like a lace handkerchief, or embroidered with forget-me-nots like a child's Valentine. She sometimes had tricks of timesaving, putting '1' for 'one' and 'x' for 'cross'. 'I did not care for any of the guests,' she confided in a letter to Gosse. 'We seemed to live in a storm of x questions and crooked answers'; or, 'I am afraid my last letter was rather x.' The second Duke of Wellington once wrote to her: 'How eloquently you express the want of breath, the exasperation resulting from heat, by leaving out the h in "exhaustion"!' Dorothy, alternately whimsical and anxious to please, then petulant and demanding, even tyrannical, would one moment be scolding her friends for being negligent, the next waxing apologetic: 'Your humble style is the devil's favourite voice, the Bride that apes humility,' wrote the Duke again.

To Edmund Gosse, having forgotten he was coming to tea, Dorothy wrote:

To think that every hour since you said you would come I have repeated to myself – Gosse at 5, Gosse at 5, and then after all to go meandering off and leaving you to cuss and swear on the doorstep, and you will never come again now, really. No punishment here or hereafter will be too much for me. Lead me to the Red Hill Asylum and leave me there.

Often in her letters, Gosse tells us, 'she pretended to be, supposed herself called upon to seem, passionate and distracted', showing the remarkable contrast between their general tone and her real disposition, which was placid, indulgent and calm. She never let her friends or acquaintances, once caught, off the hook. She played them like small fry, caught them, netted them, threw them back into the water, only to be fished out again some other day. With her older more serious friends she feigned the mouse playing in front of the lion, often pretending to be herself one of the 'giggletrots'.

Very soon Dorothy was writing to Sir William Hooker, besieging him with a stream of botanical demands – could he send *begonia boliviensis*, patchouli, pampas grass, melon seeds and goodness knows what else besides: 'May I petition you for a few seeds of the gourd you mentioned to me as well as the anchusa?' She seemed to view Kew rather like a philatelist does a competitor's stamp album; plants were there to be swopped. Vain, Dorothy's head gardener, resplendent in his top hat, would struggle up to London and prowl round the Botanical Gardens hunting for duplicated specimens as yet missing at Dangstein. In return the new Dangstein fern house supplied Hooker with some samples.

I fear you will be terribly bored of my request [continued Dorothy] but I hope you will forgive me, I was reading in Curtis Magazine a description of a plant called Costus Afer – I see it is at Kew and if it is not too much to ask I should be so grateful to you if you could allow me a few seeds of it as it seems a curious plant just in my line.

A few days later she was writing again:

I trust you were not horrified at my impertinence in asking about the plant, but I am very forward where anything of botany is concerned . . . I fear you will think I am always teasing you for something but I hope for your forgiveness . . . by this time you will regret having made my acquaintance.

Hooker, however, was doing no such thing and on 30 March dedicated to Dorothy Volume 82 of the *Botanical Magazine*.

Meanwhile everyone feverishly prepared for Hooker's visit, proposed for summer 1856. 'I feel you will find us in some confusion for we shall then be building a new conservatory and gardener's cottage and adding to our own house,' Dorothy explained to the anticipated guests as twenty-two gardeners worked busily against the clock, scything the lawns (a job which had to be finished before their mistress rose for breakfast) and tending the herbaceous borders. At last the Hooker party arrived, bumped and tired, and were met at the Drover's Arms in Rogate by a Nevill carriage. They were then drawn sedately through the new white gates and up the avenue of magnificent trees and the new pinetum before being deposited under the massive columns of the portico. Inside, the hall was bright with floral arrangements, pots of weeping ferns and orchids. Dorothy's table decorations were always ravishing. She designed them and they were executed by Mr Vain, always in his top hat. It was said he never got his fingers dirty.

All in all the visit was a grand success. Sir William's son, Joseph Hooker (by then Sir Joseph), writing in 1906, said:

I knew Lady Dorothy very well and had many invitations to her hospitable home. Her narrative does not do justice to herself. She was not the frivolous character she paints. She was thoroughly interested in the rare plants of her noble garden. Her exertions in the hopeless endeavour to establish a silkworm culture were earnest and long continued, and her efforts to improve donkey breeding and other interests of a like nature were as intelligent as useful.

The Hookers loved the extraordinary establishment and were so impressed by the plants that they ordered many rare specimens for Kew. They had hardly set foot on home ground before Dorothy was pestering Sir William Hooker for a portrait to add to her gallery

I hope you will not think me very grasping but I so wish to have your portrait to hang up amongst my friends in the little sitting room. If you would kindly give me one with your autograph underneath I would esteem it very highly.

Very shortly he was hanging in the little sitting room. Dorothy, at thirty, had achieved the position of a serious botanist in the eyes of Sir William Hooker, who from now on considered her as a colleague, referring botanists to her and sending down his gardeners on annual visits to observe Dangstein's progress. He wrote conspiratorally:

You will smile at the application of the Premier King of Siam for a plant from our garden, the Lombardy Poplar, which would neither bear the voyage, nor grows with their awful heat. I believe he expects a full grown one – I must claim to myself something of the prophetic spirit in dedicating that particular volume of the Botanical Magazine to you which contains the figure of the Aralia papyrifera thereby indicating that you also would soon have the honour of flowering it. When I penned the little dedication I knew you deserved the trifling compliment but I am much more conscious of that now I have seen Dangstein. And what I admire in your ladyship more even than your love of plants is your great desire that others should partake in the pleasure of seeing these beauties of nature's creating, improved by the art of man.

Six

Dorothy's botanical successes were soon eclipsed by family worries. Both her mother and father had fallen ill while she herself was again pregnant. 'This is a sad bore but it can't be helped,' she wrote to Mary Anne Disraeli. 'Boys are such a nuisance.' But a boy it was – William, born in March 1858. Then, eight months later, Horatio died. 'You will be grieved to know of my dear father's death. I loved him so intensely,' Dorothy wailed to Mary Anne. As for Mary Orford it was practically the last straw and Dorothy and her brother Horace took her off to Great Malvern Spa to try to recruit her health. But nearly a year later matters had not improved.

The following September, soon after Dorothy had six teeth pulled out, suddenly there were alarms for William ' . . . suffering from acute inflammation of the lungs'. Dorothy, reporting this new calamity to Mary Anne, added inconsequentially:

Where do I get Mr Disraeli's photograph as am beginning a book and want his portrait as a fit beginning to so worthy an undertaking?

Sure enough William, not yet two, died at the beginning of February 1860, and was buried next to his little sister in Terwick churchyard. Now, relentlessly, it was Mary Orford's turn. Again Mary Anne Disraeli heard the bad tidings:

I have had so much sorrow with the death of my little baby, and called up to see my poor mother who died yesterday morning. I go away tomorrow and am so busy today that if I could I should like to see you for a few moments . . . [several days later] Mother's funeral today, I feel so upset and am not able to do anything. I am so fearful should I come to see you anyone might see me even the servants, and then they might accuse me of not feeling what has been the grief of my life.

Dorothy assuaged her grief in therapeutical pursuits. She learnt to illuminate skeleton leaves. It was Sir Harry Parkes who had drawn her attention to the Japanese art of illumination, dispatching from China a *Ficus religiosa* for her hothouse. These made particularly fine tracery. First they were macerated, coated with isinglass – a glutinous substance usually prepared from the air bladders of a sturgeon – then illuminated minutely by Dorothy herself. She sent some to Dr Hooker who thought so highly of them that he placed them in his museum at Kew. He told her:

You have excelled at preparing skeleton leaves, and I have seen I think some foliage in the early stages of the operation in vessels of soft rain water to remove by a putrefying process the pulpy substance. A lady friend of mine wants to know the further process of removing all the decaying matter and leaving the Ficus in the beautifully clean state when the operation is finished. Is it chloride of lime or some other bleaching fluid?

This made Dorothy so enthusiastic that she finished her own vegetation and had to send to Dr Hooker for some more. Such was her skill that a ficus leaf she illuminated for Disraeli was considered so beautiful that it was carefully cherished and returned to her upon his death. 'You pick your leaves,' she explained to E. F. Benson fifty years later,

vine leaves or what not, and put them to soak in some chemical muck that eats off the green part, but it can't tackle the ribs and fibres. Then you wash them with a bit of fixin' in the water, and dry them and set them up in bouquets . . . very pretty they used to be reckoned, and keep a girl out of mischief.

She compiled also an elaborate, snobbish album of country parties. She grouped small photographs the size of visiting cards in house parties, arranging the guests around the houses themselves. Thus Blenheim, Belvoir and Bretby were to be themselves crowned by family insignia, illuminated with coronets and crests. Next she painted her own family tree, planting it round photographs which had been executed in the fern house by huge, clumsy equipment. Here is Reginald looking like Lady Chatterley's lover, finely bewhiskered in his shooting clothes; Dorothy herself three-dimensioned, reflected, vastly crinolined, looking into a mirror; Meresia gay and plump in riding habit; Teddy disagreeable in bumfreezers; Horace playing with his toys; and, in place of the deceased William, she painted cupids ascending, and on another page copied out a rather sickly epitaph:

He is not dead, the child of our affection,
But gone into that school
Where he no longer needs our poor protection
And Christ himself doth rule.

We will be patient and assuage the feeling
We may not wholly stay
By silence sanctifying not concealing
The grief that must have alway.

Day after day we think what he is doing
In those bright realms of air,
Year after year his tender steps pursuing
Behold him grown more fair.

Yet she was still distraught. Mary Anne Disraeli tried hard to entice her to London.

Town is going to be very gay, at least the Palace. Comte Persigny comes here as Ambassador very soon, to our party's great dismay. Duc de Malakoff very sorry to go – kissed Lord Malmesbury on both cheeks!

But Dorothy preferred to travel, and once again Reginald took his wife abroad to recover her spirits. She returned fortified, needing something new to exercise her energy. Dr Hooker had sent her news of a new hardy kind of Chinese Ailanthus silkworm which titillated both her imagination and – since she dreamed of achieving something useful for the country – her patriotism. In fact she had already been through a disastrous episode with these creatures in Upper Grosvenor Street. She and a friend had started their own farms and had advertised for mulberry fodder. Immediately they were inundated, postmen and porters staggering to their doors with enormous branches. Soon whole cellars and rooms were bursting with foliage and Reginald returning from White's was exasperated to find the hall vanishing in verdure. Frantically the ladies telegraphed the newspaper to stop deliveries, and Dorothy transported her silkworms to Dangstein where they were kept in the house. But here their manners left much to be desired. They strayed about and crawled up the gentlemen's trouser legs. So they were banished to the garden, where a special silkworm farm was laid out and kept under constant observation. At first all seemed well – 'I am happy to say a great many seem good and some have already come out and paired and laid eggs but I do not know what they are feeding on,'

Dorothy had written to Sir William Hooker. But all except one eventually came to a sticky end and were eaten by the tits.

The Chinese Ailanthus silkworm, which had already been successfully introduced into Western France, had a double bonus. Not only was the silk said to be durable, to bleach and wash well, but the worm's diet was *Ailanthus glandulosa*, the Japanese varnish tree (the Tree of Heaven), which it was hoped would not only sustain the larvae but also produce the precious varnish so esteemed in the East. Dorothy immediately prepared against her new venture, planting out in the sunniest part of her garden rows of rapidly spreading Ailanthus (whose leaves were so odoriferous that even the marauding rabbits and pheasants would not touch them). Next she wrote round to her friends to try and find the worms themselves; and it was through Richard Cobden abroad in Algiers that she eventually succeeded. He wrote back to her, at the outset somewhat discursively – describing the vigorous orange trees, custard apples and dates, and how Moorish women walked about enveloped in white muslin with only holes for the eyes.

If one of these were seen walking near Dangstein the country people would think that a newly-buried corpse had escaped from the church-yard . . .

When walking in the country the other day I plucked a little wild flower like a larkspur, with leaves resembling parsley, and remarked to my wife, 'If we had found this in Lady Dorothy's conservatory, how we should have admired it.' . . . The hedges are made of cactus and aloes, and they would puzzle the foxhunter to go through them.

At last he came to the main news:

Having called at the Jardin d'Essai and spoken with the intelligent Director, he tells me he has only about 100 cocoons of the kind of silkworm you alluded to and that he obtained them from Paris where he advises me to apply . . . I give you this address, but know you are impatient to possess these animals, and to send them before I get to Paris; otherwise if you will be so good as to express the wish I shall be delighted to execute the commission for you on my way to Paris.

Finally, it was arranged with the President of the Jardin d'Acclamation, Monsieur Guérin-Méneville, that the eggs be dispatched at the beginning of June.

It was all very exciting, not the least of it being that she had won in a capacity where the Hookers had failed – 'I feel myself a superior being for though small as I am in every way I have succeeded better than you have with your official capacity,' she teased them, announcing her success with Guérin-Méneville, 'the real father of the worms'. It seemed to her that this really might become a new branch of industry, an object of utility to the country, a source of riches to Great Britain. Her dream, it seemed to her, was really shaping up nicely. A first crop was hatched in June, not without casualties. Some expired from heat, several from disease. Then again the wasps and the birds took a fancy to them and they had to be hidden in a large oak tree. Next, through inexperience, too many worms were crowded to a tree so they descended in search of more foliage, many perishing on the way. But the survivors made their cocoons as required in the Ailanthus, to say nothing of some cabbage plants nearby.

No sooner were they removed than the trees burst forth twice as strongly as before and a second crop was hatched 31st August and doing well until the second week of September when the fine days brought out the wasps and the fruit having been gathered, they seized the worms sucking them up until nothing was left but the skin.

Disaster again. Undaunted, however, Dorothy translated, abridged and annotated M. Guérin-Méneville's pamphlet on the silkworms, hoping thereby to inform the public where to buy the plants and eggs and to establish a market for the produce. She created silkworm studs across the world, sending the little beasts to South Africa where a family called Cloete sent her bottles of Constantia wine in return, to parts of Australia where they became a pestilence, and to Stratfield Saye to the second Duke of Wellington – 'her Duke' – who became an enthusiast. He wrote to her on 22 October 1867:

My love is most unlucky if it is silkworm love for I have a fourth moth come out and a female. No Gabriel. I fear we are doomed to virginity . . . [Later.] I have to 'faire part' of the birth of a litter of our children. Most of our eggs have been since the moment of their production deposited in the cellar, but the gardeners kept out 20. They have produced worms which ravenously eat the leaves of the Evergreen Oak.

The remnants of the stud at Dangstein ate on but were destined for failure. All deterrents such as nets and scarecrows proved powerless against the birds, which regarded the worms as an irresistible gastronomic treat; and the weather, the ants and the wasps – not to mention the gardeners forgetting to put leaves on the eggs – all took their toll.

Eventually Dorothy was forced to abandon the scheme after spinning enough silk to make one dress – a crinoline gown which in 1865 proved as accident-prone as the worms. That year the Easter party was made up of its usual guests – Lord and Lady Airlie, Mr and Mrs Sartoris, Mr Hamilton Aidé and Lord Leighton. After dinner the ladies had assembled in the sitting room to admire the gallery of portraits, under the aegis of their hostess who was wearing her foulard crinoline, a most unwieldy creation. To illustrate just how unwieldy a crinoline was she tells us in her memoirs that when Dr Fuller was summoned to remove a fishbone from the throat of Frances Anne, Lady Londonderry, he was obliged to remove the lady's clothes before he could reach her mouth. Here is the scene: Dorothy, posed in the middle of this enormous contraption, was just pointing out Richard Cobden when she burst into flames. None of the other ladies dared go near her for fear of igniting their own cages. They shrieked hysterically, hands outstretched towards their blazing hostess, who with great presence of mind rolled herself into a tiny ball and put herself out. Luckily she had recently read a remedy for burns in a newspaper – one applied common whitening to the afflicted parts. This done she returned, suitably plastered, to entertain her guests downstairs.

Unlike her father Dorothy actually encouraged the railways, realising they would facilitate her schemes. For years she had been pestering her friends, and particularly Disraeli, to vote for a direct line from London to Portsmouth which stopped at Petersfield. In 1850, much to her delight, the line had arrived. Now, with transportation of exotic material becoming simpler, her building became wilder and wilder. A Gothic cottage appeared with intricate dogtooth tiles and slits for shooting arrows, together with aviaries and pigeon lofts, grandly marked 'Dorothy Nevill 1861', a huge tropical palm grotto, and an orchid house (to say nothing of the rain water tank for 11,500 gallons) for which wagon-loads of different sorts of coral toiled up from the station. As usual the fern house was a major feature, this one being decorated with coral and conch shells set in flint. Dorothy loved it there. She would sit emblazoning and painting china cups and saucers, compiling her snobbish albums, drinking whisky and smoking a cigar, gazing out over her increasingly eccentric demesne. She encouraged visitors, who would be conducted on a grand tour, stopping amid the tropical palms to drink tea which had to be transported a quarter of a mile from the house by panting maids. After this would come the laundry, complete by now with a nice new matron. Not content with ordinary birdsong she had sent off to China for whistles something like small organ pipes made out of gourds, all playing different notes, which she attached to her pigeons' tails – to such good effect that a flight of doves could reasonably be mistaken for a squadron of Aeolian harps. The guests, hot from the palm grotto and the laundry, tended to be astonished by this heavenly music and the sight of their bewildered faces afforded great amusement to their hostess, who loved her little games and secrets. 'No one but myself has organised such a winged orchestra,' she said proudly, and the Duke of Wellington told her:

I kept the secret of your whistling pigeons religiously, and again lied through masonry denying it; to my horror I found you had imparted the secret to scores of other dear friends.

Everyone was discussing them just as they were meant to. Professor Owen of the British Museum wrote:

Far from forgetting you it was yesterday I was describing your music of the air, and somehow it decided me thinking such ephemeral visits with glimpses of your paradise must soon pass away from the memory of the mistress, creative genius of the place.

There was nothing, it seemed, that Dorothy did not hope to include in her paradise. She wrote to Lady Airlie:

. . . I long to begin a co-operative shop. 'Dorothy Nevill licensed dealer in tea, tobacco, snuff etc.' will sound well. The poor people are so needy that I should be glad to help if I can.

Occasionally the Nevills managed to tear themselves away to stay with friends, to shooting parties at Petworth, for example, with 'His Majesty The King of West Sussex', Lord Leconfield, who had been very shocked by Dorothy sitting on a rug made from the skins of foxes which had been caught in a trap. Foxes, in his view and according to sporting convention, were to be hunted, not shot or trapped. But Dorothy's approach to foxhunting was eccentric, like her father's. Lord Hastings had written to his neighbour, Horatio, before the start of one season: 'Dear Lord Orford, We are beginning to hunt foxes – Will you help us?' Horatio replied: 'Ten to one I kill more foxes than you do'; and although Lord Hastings killed thirty with his hounds, his rival shot more.

Sometimes there were Goodwood picnics with the Duchess of Richmond, surrounded by hampers and fornicating lion dogs. Sometimes Dorothy would ride across the county on her mare, Black Bess, to call on her neighbours, such as Sir John Hawkshaw, the great engineer, who lived at Hollycombe, or 'Soapy Sam', Samuel Wilberforce, Bishop of Oxford, at Lavington. She would ride right up to their doorsteps and pull the bell from the saddle. As she grew older she began to dislike riding and resorted to a pony chaise, so fashionable in the 1860s, controlling the pair of ponies with a whip which cleverly combined to make a parasol. She loved to make the ponies perform dotty antics in the road, making them rear and shake their heads in a manner startling to the passers-by. Her children remembered being driven out somtimes in their mother's barouche for miles to make courtesy calls; it was the custom to drop your card on your social inferiors and Dorothy would be praying she would find the neighbours out.

Travelling was still a lengthy procedure and staying away a laborious and expensive business. It was usual to take in several houseparties on a progression round the country. The tall, deep-voiced Maria Marchioness of Ailesbury (the 'Evergreen Marchioness'), notorious for her multi-coloured toilettes, corkscrew ringlets, extraordinary headdresses and lofty young footmen, all of whom were required to be over six feet, declared she would go to no country house unless she could stay a fortnight, 'as otherwise it would not pay me'. Visits to Belvoir seemed to have been a bad bet: several times the Nevills were obliged to turn back because the Duke of Rutland, their host, had suffered some terrible fall out hunting. The place was anyway a potential incendiary bomb. Dorothy recalled in her memoirs the Duke showing her into the lamp room – full of gigantic barrels of oil for lighting the lamps, in whose service six men were constantly employed.

Lord Warwick (later husband of the celebrated Daisy) remembered that aged twenty he found himself with Dorothy in a crowded railway carriage. She was travelling in the best of spirits with a bundle of game – pheasants and a hare. Although the meat was on a high rack high above their heads, the carriage was hot and the stench became unendurable. Dorothy, however, seemed oblivious. At last Warwick persuaded her to let him tie the stinking corpses to the exterior door handle. 'Unfortunately the game was in an even more tender condition than we thought and by the time Paddington was reached there was nothing on the door handle save the heads and the string.' Dorothy was furious.

Often Dorothy would go alone to stay with the Duke of Wellington at Stratfield Saye. He was brilliant and witty, Dorothy's favourite companion. Sometimes his tongue could be mordant. Once when Henry Irving was dawdling after lunch, hoping to stay on, Dorothy overheard the Duke say, 'Mr Irving the day is hot, the horses not yours, you had better go; and when Dorothy had excused herself from visiting he expressed his irritation forcefully:

You have deranged at least 10 things and at this moment I do not know what the Duchess has agreed with you to do . . . It is a great pity you had previously not arranged with Lady Chesterfield or that you had not sense of honour enough to abide by an engagement which you had yourself offered. It is not the first time you have done it. Pray let it be the last, for it is most inconvenient.

Although he had none himself he loved children, particularly Dorothy's, who often accompanied their mother to Stratfield Saye. The Duke would conjure up all sorts of tricks and games and compose riddles and poems; for instance one epitaph for Horace:

> Here lies the Smasher:
> He broke his Aunt in little bits
> And then forthwith expired in fits
> Of mirth; Meresia he defied
> And gave Mum comfort –
> When he died.

or mottoes for Dorothy's sundial:

> I stir with the morn, and work all day
> Nor cease but with the light.
> If man would practise what I say
> He'd not be poor at night.

and a poem to Dorothy's greedy dog, Trip:

> Devouring spectacles is not
> The way to become wits;
> The lawyers do not feed on tomes
> Or dine on parchment writs.

Visits were so frequent that they furnished the gossips' tongues. 'It is to be hoped that the Duchess will take alarm and forbid your being asked so often – you clearly like attracting sententious Dukes, all go down,' wrote Bernal Osborne to Dorothy. There is no doubt that the Duke loved Dorothy but the Duchess need not have worried – the relationship was purely platonic. The following verse was found in the Duke's handwriting amongst Lady Dorothy's clutter when she died:

FROM ANACREON

> To love is one of human ills
> And not to love is tedious pain,
> But Fate the bitterest cup distils
> For him who loves, and loves in vain.

The house was run as a sort of museum to the Iron Duke. Dorothy remembered 'her Duke' standing by the fireplace beneath the portrait of his father, the same strong aquiline profile. They looked exactly alike. There had never been much sympathy lost between father and son in the Iron Duke's day; he had once even refused to meet Lord Douro, as the second Duke was then called, when he called to visit his regiment at Dover, because Douro had failed to leave his card. Yet on his death 'Dorothy's' Duke began a cult to his father's memory, even taking the utmost trouble to find a suitable epitaph for his charger, Copenhagen. He sent Dorothy two to choose from. The first:

> Here, full of honour and great memories,
> Wellington's war-horse Copenhagen lies.
> Spare empty praise to me so tried and true –
> These words suffice: Peace – Victory – Waterloo.

The second:

> God's humble instrument, though coarser clay,
> Should have his meed on that heroic day.

She chose the first. The Duke wrote back that she was 'no judge of epitaphs' and decided on the second – though later altering the last line to 'should have the glory of that glorious day'.

Dorothy remembered, too, the hilarious inauguration of the statue by Marochetti of the Iron Duke, the strong chiselled figure perched atop a high column, where it is still to be seen outside the Park. On that occasion, in 1865, Disraeli was in an unusually gay mood and made a speech. Dorothy wrote to Lady Airlie:

> It would have made you laugh to have seen the Duke, Dizzy, Lord Stanhope etc. dancing a new dance which consists of running in a ring jumping and singing 'What have you got for supper Mrs Bond? Ducks in the larder, geese in the pond, etc.'

Stratfield Saye however was most comfortable to stay in. They dined in a cosy, low passage room off a dinner service painted with views that had once belonged to Napoleon. The walls around them were plastered with illustrations cut out of Boydell's Shakespeare. After dinner the Duchess played on the harp, an entertainment which was unfortunately lost on Dorothy's ears though she enjoyed the brilliant company who gathered to listen – Lady Chesterfield, Lord Wolseley, 'Flea' Fleming, General Hamley, Mr Escott, Mr Arnold, owner of the Lyceum Theatre, and the Revd Mr Gleig who, before entering the Church, had carried the regimental colours at Waterloo. After the ladies retired to bed the gentlemen would retreat to the servants' hall for smoking,[1] balancing on plain wooden chairs. To special guests on their departure the Duke would offer lengths of goat hair, culled from his own herd of cashmere goats. 'But I must confess that the coat I had made of it was so stiff that it really could not be worn,' wrote Dorothy. 'One might as well have put on a coat of stout cardboard.'

To those around her Dorothy's life seemed unworried and idyllic. 'Ah, you have no worries,' Mr Delane, editor of The

---

[1] No gentleman ever smoked in public or in the presence of ladies until after the Crimean War. The Duke of Sutherland was the first to astonish Society by actually smoking in Rotten Row.

Times, told her. 'Your path is strewn with rose leaves and those carefully ironed out.' When not planting, emblazoning, painting and breeding, she was corresponding with her friends. There was a constant traffic of mail which flowed to and from learned men on all manner of subjects – discussing dragons and pterodactyls with Professor Owen or mushrooms with the Revd Berkeley. Botanical specimens poured in from all over the world. Sir Ivor Shepstone dispatched a new kind of cotton asparagus from America; the Duke of Wellington sarracenias and China grasses in return for donkeys, bantams, dogs and dandelions, no less; Sir Roderick Murchison, specialities from Mozambique; while the Duchess of Teck sent her gardeners from White Lodge, Richmond, to see what they could pick up. Both a plant and a child were named Dorothy Garcinia after her by a swindling botanist.

Festering packets of game went to the Hookers and particularly fragrant strawberries, for which Dangstein was famous, to Disraeli. 'We have 1000 pots of strawberries in force so D. can look forward to a good stuff,' Dorothy told Mary Anne. Disraeli wrote most politely on receiving them.

You have made me not only the most graceful but the most magnificent of presents. I have never feasted on my favourite fruit in its entirety before; they were not only too plenteous, but really without precedent, superb. Two nights after the House of Commons, and today after a long council at the British Museum your delicious strawberries, as absorbing as yourself, have refreshed and renovated me. When are you coming to town? And how do your conifers and all their graceful companions flourish? I envy you in your exotic groves.

. . . I am always your affectionate D.

Recognition by the *Gardener's Chronicle*, her friendship with the Hookers and her rare plants, particularly the orchids and insectivorous plants which were part of Dorothy's serious research, bought her in contact with the most famous botanists, scientists, geologists and explorers of the day: Huxley, the zoologist and man of science ; Professor Richard Owen, anatomist and Superintendent of the Natural History Museum; Professor Mivart, the biologist; Sir Roderick Murchison, explorer and geologist; and even Darwin himself. Controversy was raging over Darwin's book, *The Origin of Species*, published in 1859. He argued that all species including mankind had evolved from base forms of life, challenging the theory that species were immutable productions, separately created. The stir caused by his theory of evolution (the transmutation of the species effected chiefly through the laws of natural selection) is difficult to imagine. As with the Reform Bill and the railways people realised that nothing ever would seem the same again. Darwin was reviled from the pulpit. Could religion ever be reconciled with science? Darwin himself, confirmedly agnostic, thought it could, believing that the theory of evolution was quite compatible with a belief in God; 'but you must remember that different persons have different definitions of what they mean by God,' as one member of his family wrote. And Darwin himself, when pressed, explained:

Science has nothing to do with Christ, except insofar as the habit of scientific research makes a man cautious in admitting evidence . . . As for a future life, every man must judge for himself between conflicting vague possiblities!

He used to tell the story of a pious professor, ever seeking to reconcile biology with the mastodon by saying that the door of the Ark had been too small to admit it.

Lady Airlie wrote to Dorothy:

How far does Darwinianism enter into you – does it disturb your old beliefs or not? I think the mind of the real Naturalist is sometimes so bent upon each fact and each discovery as never to generalise and so they manage to keep the two things separated in their mind. That is the real way, I think, and if men have faith in God, no facts however startling will make them doubt, but as Arnold said, they will wait before the greatest doubts with the same patience and belief as they did in the old days when all dogma seemed safe.

Dorothy was unperturbed. Her beliefs, rather like Darwin's, were agnostic. She did not deny the existence of God but she was superstitious in a sort of mocking eighteenth-century sort of way, 'as Mme. du Deffand might have been,' wrote Gosse in his portrait of her. She constantly said, and frequently wrote 'D.V.' after any project, even of the most frivolous kind. 'The idea was', observed Gosse, 'that one should be polite all round, in case of any contingency.' When on the Riviera she heard that the Prince of Monaco had built and endowed a handsome church at Monte

Carlo. 'Very clever of him,' she said, 'for you never can tell.' She had a horror of feasts of the Church, particularly Christmas – 'Christmas pains and penalties,' she would moan with December looming, probably resenting most of all the disturbance of her social engagements.

W. T. Stead, the radical journalist, who was very fond of the occult, once took Dorothy to a seance. The medium was a young girl, Julia, who tore her handkerchief to bits in a sort of frenzy and told her she had never ever seen anyone so surrounded by spooks. Dorothy thought the seance a complete waste of time. Stead was drowned in the *Titanic* tragedy of 1912. Dorothy commented in *My Own Times*: 'What a pity Julia or some other spook did not warn him against setting out on his fatal journey.'

She was also much interested in the theories of evolution herself, studying and practising with the rare plants in her garden. Not only this, she had for some time had an eye on Darwin as a member of her gallery. She did not have long to wait. In 1861 Darwin was preparing a book on the intercrossing of plants, the fertilisation of flowers by insects, using *The Fertilisation of Orchids* as his treatise. After observing the behaviour of fifteen genera of British orchids he turned to the great exotic tribes that ornament tropical forests. But where could he obtain them? It was Dr Lindley, the author, previously Assistant to Sir Joseph Banks and now Secretary of the Horticultural Society, who gave Darwin a letter of introduction to Dorothy. He wrote to Sir William Hooker.

. . . Lindley from whom I asked for an orchid with a simple labellum has most kindly sent me a lot of what he marks rare and rarissima of peloric orchids, etc., but as they are dried I know not whether they will be of use. He has been most kind and suggested my writing to Lady D. Nevill who has responded in a wonderfully kind manner, and has sent a lot of treasures.

Darwin kept the treasures in a small glass lean-to behind the kitchen. Dorothy, always trying to justify herself as usual in the eyes of her friends, was delighted to be of use to the great man and grabbed the opportunity to put him in the bag. Her whole correspondence with Darwin is an interesting illustration of her approach, at times rather forward and aggressive:

Dear Sir, I have been a long time meditating whether I dared ask and make the request I am about to do, but even if you cannot grant it I hope you will take it as a compliment rather than in other light. I would so like it if it were possible that you would give me a photo or lithograph or any other portrait of yourself to hang up in my own sitting room. Sir William Hooker and many more have done so, and it is such a pleasure to have near me the resemblance of friends to whom I am indebted for so many pleasant hours in reading their works and listening to their conversation . . . I shall enclose with this a list of orchids now in bloom that you may see whether you want any.

Sure enough this had the desired effect and she soon had Darwin's portrait hung up to show off to her friends – opposite, as, she told Darwin, 'my esteemed friend Sir William Hooker'.

Darwin's book on *The Fertilisation of Orchids* was finished in 1862 and had provided him with one of the finest of all test cases for the theory of evolution. He showed first that the contrivances by which orchids are fertilised are as varied and almost s perfect as any of the most beautiful adaptations in the animal kingdom and that these contrivances have for their main object the fertilisation of the flowers with pollen brought by insects from a distant plant. Here is the description of the wonderful and weird construction of the flower of the orchid coryanthes given to the Linnaean Society in 1865.

Large Humble Bees, noisy and quarrellous, are attracted at first by the smell of the flower; but the smell probably only gives notice to the insects, the substance they really care for is the interior brim of the labellum which they gnaw off with great industry. They may be seen in great numbers disputing with each other for a place on the edge of the hypochile. Partly by the contest, partly perhaps intoxication by the matter they are indulging in, they tumble down into the bucket (epichile) itself full of the fluid secreted by the horn-like organs at the base of the column. Then they crawl along the interior inner side of the bucket where there is a passage for them. If one is early on the look-out, as these Hymenopters are early risers, one can see on every flower how fecundation is performed. The humble-bee in forcing its way out of its involuntary body has to exert itself considerably, as the mouth of the epichile and the face of the column fit together exactly, and are very still and elastic. The first bee that is immersed will have the gland of the pollen masses glued to its back. The insect then generally gets through the passage and comes out with this peculiar appendage, and returns immediately to its feast, when it is generally precipitated a second time, passes out through the same aperture, and so inserting the pollen masses into the stigma, while it forces its way out, and thereby impregnating either the same or some other flower. I have often seen this, and sometimes there are so many of these humble-bees assembled, that there is a continual procession of them through the passage specified.

The correspondence was resumed some years later, in 1874, when Darwin was investigating and preparing a work on insectivorous plants, sixteen years after his first observations. While resting near Hartfield in Sussex he had come upon two common species of drosera, the sun dew. He noticed that numerous insects had been entrapped by the leaves.

Fortunately, a crucial idea occurred to me [he wrote], that of placing a large number of leaves on various nitrogenous and non-nitrogenous fluids of equal density; and as soon as I found that the former alone exerted energetic movement it was obvious that here was a fine new field for investigation.

Whenever time permitted, Darwin pursued his experiments. Meanwhile Dorothy, at Dangstein, was particularly fascinated by her insectivorous plants, practising on her nepenthes (pitcher plants), dionaea (Venus fly trap), utricularia and different species of drosera, making observations such as how the leaves of *Drosera capense* closed over the meat and when quite consumed relaxed to their ordinary state, and tempting these singular monsters with all kind of delicacies: 'They had I remember curious tastes, manifesting a violent repugnance to cheese, and were not at all adverse to alcohol,' she tells us in her memoirs. In August 1864 Darwin had resumed investigating the digestive system and behaviour of the drosera and the dionaea – an insect had only to touch one of these and the trap snapped shut 'with quite a loud flap', he observed. He wrote to Dr Hooker on 30 August:

Now for your letter you are very generous about Dionaea, but some of my experiments will require cutting off leaves and therefore injuring plants. . . . I could not write to Lady Dorothy . . . I think I am now on the right track about Utricularia after wasting several weeks in fruitless trials and observations. The negative work takes five times more work than the positive.

Hooker spoke to Dorothy of Darwin's need for specimens. Although frightened that Darwin might not take her seriously, she took up her pen:

Some years ago you were kind enough to refer to me on some question referring to the fructification of orchids. I have been most deeply interested in your last investigations with the carnivorous properties of certain plants and Dr Hooker has told me you would much like a plant of Dionaea. Alas, ours is too small to be of any use to you but we have plants of Drosera Dichotoma and we could send you some of the different kinds of Sarracenia. I am sure we possess numerous plants which would interest you. Would you but come and see them.

Darwin replied that he had never seen *Drosera dichotoma* and that he would very much like to make an examination of it. 'I have so often heard of the beauty of the gardens of Dangstein,' he wrote, 'that I should much enjoy seeing them; but the state of my health prevents me from going anywhere.' The drosera was duly dispatched with full instructions for its maintenance.

We keep the Drosera in a house with a north aspect and hardly any heat and damp. The Gardeners say you must syringe it, and that will produce the dew on it – in a short time; it does not stand in a saucer of water.

Dorothy then offered Darwin five small plants of *Utricularia montana*. He was most grateful for a fine specimen. This particular species of utricularia was not aquatic like the European species but grows in South America among the moss and debris on the branches of trees. Darwin discovered it could not digest but absorbed decaying matter. On 18 September he wrote to Joseph Hooker excitedly,

I have had a splendid day's work and must tell you about it. Lady Dorothy sent me a young plant of Utricularia Montana, which I fancy is the species you told me of . . .

On the same day he dashed off the news to Dangstein:

. . . the great solid bladder-like swelling almost on the surface is a wonderful object, but are not true bladders. Those I found on the roots near the surface, and down to a depth of two inches in the sand. They are as transparent as glass, from 1/20 to 1/100 of an inch in size, and hollow. They have all the important points of structure of the bladders of the floating English species, and I felt confident I should find captured prey. And so I have to my delight in two bladders, with clear proof, that they had absorbed food from the decaying mass. For Utricularia is a carrion-feeder, and not strictly carniverous like Drosera. The great solid bladder-like bodies, I believe are reservoirs of water like a camel's stomach. As soon as I have made a few more observations I mean to be so cruel as to give your plant no water, and observe whether the great bladders shrink and contain air instead of water; I shall then also wash all earth from all roots, and see whether there are bladders for capturing subterranean insects down to the very bottom of the pot. Now shall you think me very greedy, if I say supposing the species is not very precious, and you have several, will you give me one more plant, and if so please send it to 'Orpington Station, S.E.R., to be forwarded by foot messenger'. I have hardly ever enjoyed a day more in my life than I have this day's work; and this I owe to your Ladyship's great kindness . . .

It was all very gratifying that she was being so useful. Dorothy immediately dispatched another utricularia complete with bladders, but apparently bladders were not enough to tempt him so she tried a new line – in cats.

I see in your interesting work of animals and plants on the cats you make no mention of the Siamese breed, of which I possess the only specimen. He is just like an otter with a brown fur coat and a beauty. I am not much in L [London] during the winter and if you will do me the great pleasure of calling on me I would bring him up and show him to you.

But Darwin seemed to prefer bladders to cats:

The large swellings on the roots on rhizomes certainly serve to store up waters and it is wonderful how long the plant can exist in quite dry earth, these swellings or tubers gradually yielding up their water. But the minute bladders have interested me most. I have found in four of them on your plant minute decayed animals, and in the dried bladders of plants from their native country a much larger collection of captured creatures, commonly mites.

The bladders are lined with quatrified processes, consisting of most delicate membranes; these are empty and transparent in the bladders which have caught nothing; but are filled with granular spontaneously moving protoplasm in those which have lain for some time in contact with decayed animal matter. Therefore I feel sure that the plant is adapted for catching live animals, and feeds on their remains when decayed . . .

But at the end of this letter the longed-for meeting seemed in sight. 'When in London during the Winter I hope that I may be so fortunate as to have the honour of seeing Your Ladyship,' wrote Darwin. Dorothy wrote off excitedly to Lady Airlie to boast of her success:

Mr Darwin has expressed a desire to see me; I hardly dare hope for such happiness . . . I am sure he will find I am the missing link between man and the apes.

As for Darwin she was determined not to let him off the hook.

I am coming up to London [she wrote]. I whould so extremely like and appreciate a personal acquaintance with yourself though I much fear you will find me dreadfully wanting – for I have to mix so much in a frivolous world but though my delight is in studies like those you undertake yet I cannot give very much attention to them. Therefore if we do meet I hope you will make full allowance for my shortcomings and blandness – I have begun to read your son's articles in the Fortnightly Review but it appears to me though so very interesting abstruse – perhaps later on I might understand it.

As luck would have it she missed him when he called

I am more grieved than I can say at having missed you but I do hope when you come next time you will give me due warning. I will willingly drive to you for an hour, if you are ever willing to receive me, but perhaps you are too busy.

At first there was a suggestion that Dorothy might stay a few days with the Darwins at Down, Beckenham, Kent. This nearly gave Mrs Darwin apoplexy – such a visit from a frivolous society lady was the last thing she needed. She had heard it said that those who lived in London Society were accustomed to find their country visits enlivened with all sorts of sports and practical jokes. She believed that tossing people in blankets had become highly popular as a diversion. 'I am afraid we should hardly be able to offer you anything of that sort,' she wrote unenthusiastically to Dorothy. Her ladyship set off undaunted for Down but she found Darwin laid low from a violent attack of sickness contracted during his voyage on the *Beagle*. She still had a most interesting afternoon, managing between Darwin's pangs and paroxysms to discuss their researches – the drosera, its monstrous machinations, bladders and all. Darwin's work was published in July 1875 just after Dorothy's visit, revealing the important discovery that a plant should secrete when properly excited a fluid containing an acid and ferment, closely analogous to the digestive fluid of an animal, and proving that the higher species of insectivore plants subsisting by such diversified means are admirably adapted for capturing aquatic or terrestial animals. Darwin presented Dorothy with an autographed copy. She wrote in reply:

How seldom things in this world dovetail in nicely – A wet day and the receipt of your interesting book was however all I could wish. I have been reading the Droseras with the greatest attention and am going thoroughly to digest every part.

Although he never did get to Dangstein Darwin paid Dorothy several visits at Charles Street and their researches continued into the nastiness of vegetable matter. Specimens of orchids, earthworms, vegetable snails and bladders, packed in Wardian cases,[1] streamed from Dangstein to Down, where Darwin was engaged in researching for a larger edition of his *Fertilisation of Orchids*, and a work on the 'Formation of Vegetable Mould through the Action of Worms and the Power of Movements in Plants', experimenting with seedlings representing the whole plant kingdom dispatched from Kew, South America and Dangstein. Dorothy sent 'some very curious monsters' of seeds of a plant he thought was 'allied to Medicago or Medicks'. He wrote:

I am much obliged for all the trouble you have so kindly taken. One of your references relates to the Apocynaceae catching Diptera, and this is the most gratuitous case of cruelty known to me in a state of nature, for apparently such creatures are of no use to the plant, and assuredly not to the wretched butterfly, or moth, or fly.

Also there is much suffering and cruelty in the world which seems to us both meaningless and unnecessary, but after all human intelligence is but finite and in all probability everything is designed for the best.

[1] A kind of close-fitting glass case for transporting delicate ferns and other such plants – or for keeping them indoors. So named after Nathaniel Bagshaw Ward (1791–1868), the inventor.

Seven

Lady Palmerston had abdicated and the new leaders of Society were Lady Waldegrave and Lady Molesworth, both of low birth. Frances Waldegrave, who pulled off the grand total of four marriages, was the daughter of 'Old Braham', the famous tenor. She was not ashamed of her origins: 'I am a true – Jewess I love curiosities and I love Dukes,' she once told Disraeli; and if doubtful-looking strangers were seen among her guests she assumed people would say they were 'some of my vulgar relations'. She had inherited Strawberry Hill through her second husband and had spent more than £100,000 in ruining the house. When Dorothy saw the heavy gilt furniture all covered in coronets and the galleries of bad paintings of Lady Waldegrave's friends, horribly executed by Sant, she sighed for the shades of Horace Walpole. She had been to the first sale at Strawberry Hill, in 1842, and saw it much as Horace Walpole left it, with the rooms very small 'like little cabins'. She remembered the Grand Gallery; the full-length portrait by Van Somer of Lord Falkland dressed in white which suggested the incident of the picture walking out of its frame in *The Castle of Otranto*; and the lovely portrait of Laura Walpole, Duchess of Gloucester by Reynolds, which sold for £735. Now it seemed to her that Victorian art had drifted to the lowest ebb imaginable. Arsenic green paint everywhere made people sick. Dorothy was pleased to cite as the most execrable example of bad taste the lifesize statue of Lord Dudley's favourite Newfoundland dog costing nearly £4,000. This sculpture stood on a cushion of richly veined Siena marble, a metal snake with diamond eyes glistening between its legs, the whole positioned on a marble pedestal enriched with mosaic and ormolu. The animal, fashioned from statuary and Derbyshire black marble, had mother-of-pearl claws and eyes of oriental topaz lined with sardonyx. The monument was meant to imitate nature as closely as possible. Luckily the guests were more palatable than the decorations. Lady Waldegrave liked artists and mixed them up with politicians and the *beau monde*. Indeed all kinds of new people could be seen at her house: editors of newspapers, writers, publishers, lawyers and judges, even the Irish Party; yet members of the medical and dramatic professions were still barred. There could be exceptions to this rule, for example Mr Alfred Wigan and Miss Helen Faucit (famous for their acting), and Sir Henry Thompson, the physician and photographer, credited with killing Napoleon III. 'Everybody belonging to the Liberal Party met there as well as large numbers of the Opposition,' wrote Dorothy in her *Reminiscences*. Lady Waldegrave's entertainments were very catholic and cosmopolitan.

Lady Molesworth entertained in a small house in Eaton Place. Her parties by inference were more select. Although Lady Waldegrave was the cleverer of the two, Lady Molesworth wielded greater power and enjoyed the more success. While the guests at Strawberry Hill were mainly Liberal, Lady Molesworth's were more Conservative. Either she would invite fifteen to twenty or gather together carefully six or eight of the best brains in London: 'I believe if the King of the Cannibal Islands were to come to England, within twenty-four hours he would be dining with Lady Molesworth,' Samuel Wilberforce once remarked to Dorothy. Lady Molesworth's strength lay in an extraordinary power of bringing out people and making them talk, a talent which it seems Lady Waldegrave could not match. Dickens is a case in point. Lady Waldegrave had persuaded Bernal Osborne to bring this great lion to dine, in itself an accomplishment since Dickens was allergic to fashionable society – and with good reason, as there he was faced with a number of very modish people 'all agog to see how amusing he was going to be', and anticipating all kinds of intellectual somersaults. But Dickens refused to perform, uttering only a few commonplace remarks. Bernal Osborne said afterwards: 'I feared this, once he imagines he is being trotted out he won't say a word!' How different it was at Eaton Place. The week after Dorothy and Dickens were invited to one of Lady Molesworth's sextets

Dickens simply bubbled over with fun and conversation, talking in a way that resembled nothing so much as some of the best passages in his own books [Dorothy wrote in *Reminiscences*]. He laughed and chaffed telling me I remember that he had a great scheme for writing a cookery book, and I believe the poor man really meant it, but alas! his death, which occurred very shortly after, prevented the realisation of the subject.

Now Dorothy began to model herself on Lady Molesworth. At no. 45 Charles Street, a middle-sized house at the end of Berkeley Square and opposite the Running Footman, a busy public house, she entertained a small salon which was soon noted for its field of intelligence. She was always at home for the tea hour. To be a successful political hostess this was one of the sacrifices required: 'One had to be at home at the same time every afternoon.' There is no doubt that she was possessed of a singular energy that could be radiant and magnetic. 'You held out your hands as if to be warmed,' said Gosse, describing Dorothy as 'like a household blaze on a rainy day'. Her guests were a hybrid lot, linked only by their admiration of their hostess. Among them might be Robert Lowe, escaping from the duty of nursing a semi-invalid wife and playing billiards with the children; Sir William Harcourt, brilliant young journalist and barrister; old Lord Ellenborough, coming to recite Dante; the Duke of Cambridge, for whom Dorothy always kept 'the soldier's chair' – 'I have business enough for ten little bodies like me and all to meet the Duke of Cambridge,' she once moaned to Blanche Airlie. But the most exalted visitor was Disraeli. He had discarded his foppery now, his elaborate waistcoats, gold rings and chains; only his long black ringlets remained. And clearly he was delighted with his hostess. He once scribbled in a character sketch:

The Walpoles were a very strange family. Lord Walpole's character drawn prophetically by Horace Walpole in one of his letters. Lady Dorothy Nevill, his sister, a very clever woman; equal to Professor Hooker as a botanist, without doubt the finest pinetum and conservatories and collections of rare trees in the world – all formed and collected and created by herself at Dangstein – introduced the silkworm on acanthus or something – and wrote a very good pamphlet in advocacy – the finest and most fanciful emblazoner in the world – and without absolute beauty, wild and bewitching.

Their relationship remains an enigma. There is nothing in their correspondence, which treats mostly on horticultural and house-hold matters, to suggest more than a close friendship. But Mrs Colin Davy, Dorothy's great-niece,[1] was brought up to believe that Dorothy's younger son, Ralph, born in 1865, was Disraeli's. To her this was a fact – 'He looked like him as well'; and Virginia Woolf, staying at Hatfield not long after Dorothy's death, questioned the assembled company: 'And didn't Lady Dorothy have an illegitimate family?' Could she have been referring to George Smythe or Disraeli? Ralph had decidedly Jewish looks with a massive nose utterly unlike the Nevills. He appeared to be the cross between his grandfather, Lord Orford, and Disraeli. Lord Lytton described Ralph as looking like 'an over-cooked snipe', though very amusing. Certainly there would have been plenty of time during the tea hour. Mr Nevill and his wife were often separated, the former finding agriculture a good excuse not to accompany his wife to London. Yet Disraeli was turned sixty, very scruffy, usually dressed in an old shaggy coat and generally considered very ugly. Not by his wife, however, who once said, 'You think he looks ugly but he is not. He is very handsome. I should like them to see him when he is asleep.' As for Dorothy, nearly fifty years later she was to turn to Edward Cazalet, a young Etonian, and with a twinkle in her eye confide: 'Why I have seen Dizzy in his night cap, I have known him ill, I have known him in every possible way.'

Whatever experience he may have had of her more private skills, Disraeli considered Dorothy the 'finest and most fanciful emblazoner in the world'. He told her the best words he had ever uttered were part of a speech delivered to the Manchester Athenaeum in 1844:

Knowledge is like the mystic ladder in the patriarch's dream. Its base rests on the primeval earth, its crest is lost in the shadowy splendour of the Empyrean, while the great authors, who for traditionary ages have held the chain of science and philosophy, of poesy and erudition, are the angels ascending and descending the sacred scale, maintaining, as it were, the communication between man and heaven.

Dorothy emblazoned it for him, and he was so enchanted with her work that he signed it.

[1] Daughter of Colonel Walpole, of Heckfield Place; granddaughter of Lady Lincoln.

After Lord Palmerston's death Disraeli became Leader of the House and Chancellor of the Exchequer. Now no. 45 Charles Street was a salon of influence. Many of Dorothy's admirers were scandalised by the new Reform Bill, believing that the new enfranchisement would impair the security of possession which had been the foundation of prosperity and wealth. 'We shall see some strange candidates and strange men, perhaps in the House of Commons,' warned Lord Ellenborough. Three years later Lord Derby resigned and Disraeli was 'at the top of the greasy pole'. 'It is all well and good now I feel my position assured,' he replied to Dorothy's congratulations. Yet success did not bring happiness. Mary Anne now showed the first symptoms of stomach cancer. By December Disraeli was again out of office and Dorothy's reign as confidante of the Prime Minister was curtailed. The Queen offered Disraeli a peerage, but since he was anxious to stay in the House he asked if she might not grant it to Mary Anne instead. Society at large still considered Mary Anne absurd, her sayings so notorious they were known as 'Maryannery'. The Queen was advised against it. Yet to honour Disraeli she created her Viscountess Beaconsfield. Disraeli meanwhile retired to Hughenden, struck down with bronchitis, asthma and gout.

Eight

Dorothy seemed as tough as a nut. She appeared very formal, never bothering much about Christian names. Her husband was always 'Mr Nevill', Meresia was usually referred to as 'Miss Nevill' and Ralph 'The Master'. To many she seemed uncaring. Never being sick herself she could not understand indisposition in others; to her it was merely a good excuse and, worse, it interfered with her social diary. She was also capable of sharpness – 'She carried a bow and shot at folly as it flew,' wrote Gosse. Marie Belloc Lowndes remembered Dorothy unkindly lampooning one giggletrot: 'Mrs — spends her time crawling about on her stomach before God and before countesses for she is deeply religious, as well as very snobbish.' Yet that was the only time Mrs Lowndes heard her say a malicious word: 'Her arrows, though they were feathered, were not poisoned,' explained Gosse. The kernel penetrated, Dorothy was kind and affectionate; even her dislike of illness evaporated after a set time and she would then become genuinely concerned for the sufferer. Nothing then was too much bother. Her generosity was spontaneous and unobtrusive and she expected no reward. She lent money to the bankrupt novelist, Ouida, which she knew would never be repaid; she invited the poor, shy artist Kate Greenaway to the theatre 'to take her out of herself'; she went to Paris to nurse a grieving friend back to normal; she helped young people going out into the world to obtain posts; she kept for forty years on the top floor at Charles Street the German nurse who had never saved a penny from her wages. 'I can only say I am indeed a true friend. My religion is always to try and mend up any wounds others have made and be sincere,' she informed Mrs Cazalet. When Oscar Wilde went to prison Dorothy was almost alone in feeling compassion. After Frank Harris had announced to a startled dinner table he would prepare for Wilde's release with a party, only Dorothy had the guts to ask if she could be included because she felt sorry for him. She liked to think of Wilde as 'that brilliant writer over whom I think it is best to believe a dark cloud of insanity settled'.

As a mother she was hardly maternal. She was just as interested in her plants as in her children, and when returning home she found it difficult to choose which to visit first. The nursery was supervised according to custom by French governesses and German nurses, who fought continuously amongst themselves – the squabbles reaching a high point with the French reverse at Sedan in the Franco-Prussian War. Dorothy was of course much too busy to be in the nursery all the time. Meresia, Teddy and Horace were all healthy, so there was not too much to worry about and they had plenty of children to play with, let alone their mother's menagerie. But what Dorothy did find time to do was to encourage their early education much as her father had done – reading and showing them her books and trying to ensure they heard good conversation. Her primary concern, however, was to instil in them a sense of reverence for the family. In an age of hero worship it was customary to idealise hero figures. Apart from Marie Antoinette Dorothy's were her own eighteenth-century forbears – Charlotte Atkyns (née Walpole), a delightful actress who spent her time and fortune trying to spirit Marie Antoinette and then her son, Louis the Dauphin, out of prison; and Horace Walpole and his father, Sir Robert. She took on the role of her old governess. Ralph's first memory was of a jolly, corpulent, bewigged figure in eighteenth-century dress placed above his bed. His mother then intoned it was 'Sir Robert'. On discovering who Sir Robert was, Ralph was horrified to find there was at least a school of thought that he had got all his money from robbing the Exchequer, in the light of which his mother's reverence seemed most misplaced.

It was Ralph who aroused Dorothy's maternal feelings for the first time. Dorothy was thirty-nine, her husband nearly sixty. Ralph, the child of old parents, Disraeli's or not, appeared puny. Remembering her two sickly children that had died, she worried dreadfully. The doctor was always in the house prescribing fresh medicines, and Ralph was under constant supervision. With Dorothy's encouragement he was soon absorbing *Childe Harold* and *Paradise Lost* as well as *The Origin of Species*, running about asking people their opinion of Darwin. He was very much abashed when Dorothy's friends told him he had no business to want to know – evolution was an unsuitable subject for a little boy. His favourite book was *Don Juan*, from which he learned long passages by heart, although his mother tried to place it out of reach.

She also introduced him to her friends. To A. H. Sayce who was peering at one of Ralph's teeth mounted and pinned to her bosom, Dorothy said:

Ah, I see you are interested in my brooch. He inherits the blood of the Walpoles and the Nevills and might be a credit to them, so I am taking care to make him see as much of men like Darwin and Tyndall, and to know what sensible conversation means.

She would take Ralph with her whenever she could: in her brougham to drop cards on her neighbours, or up to London where she always muffled him up and forced him to wear a respirator to combat the 'pea soupers'. Medicine at this time was somewhat rudimentary. Dorothy's doctor told her that if her son ate too many chocolates he would surely die. Ralph, feeling perfectly strong, never could understand what all the fuss was about and to prove his point ate a whole box of them; whereupon Dorothy, realising he was not so weak as they thought, duly packed him off to a Dickensian boarding school in Portsmouth. From there he went on to Eton, where he survived one unhappy year (oddly, he was to write a book entitled *Floreat Etona*) before being sent to a tutor in Slough.

Dorothy in fact disliked being a woman. It stopped her from being accepted in a man's world. She was very annoyed, for instance, not to be able to join Sir Henry Thompson's exclusive male gatherings; he told Dorothy she would have to wear trousers if she came. It was a challenge she often felt like taking up. 'You are your brother in petticoats,' was how Lord Lytton bade goodbye to her after their first meeting, and this was to Dorothy the highest compliment she could be paid. She regarded most females as stupid, although some of her great friends were women. Lady Airlie, in particular, appealed to Dorothy in spite of her different political tenets. A fine-looking, intelligent matriarch,

Blanche Airlie was the granddaughter of that disapproving Lady Stanley, and a worthy inheritor of her grandmother's mantle. Alarming and dictatorial to some (her grandchildren even had to hide their bicycles from her deprecating eyes), she enchanted others, while ruling her husband, her family, her Scottish estate workers and their families with a despotic benevolence to do justice to the creed of Young England. Lady Cork (formerly Lady Emily de Burgh, Canning's beautiful and witty granddaughter), Lady 'Chattie' Dorchester (daughter of Byron's friend, John Cam Hobhouse), Lady Chesterfield, her daughter Lady Carnarvon and Marie Belloc Lowndes were other favourites. Intellectually they were the '*crème de la crème*'.

Dorothy's disappointment with the majority of her sex dampened her interest in the suffrage movement first suggested in the mid-Sixties. The second Duke of Wellington wrote:

I know you are radical enough to advocate Women's Suffrage. It is charming that the writers don't know that in the possessive case plural the apostrophe is after the s. I hope the women will learn better before the vote.

Dorothy in fact came near to signing a manifesto in favour of votes for women at this time, saying when remonstrated with, 'What does it matter? The whole thing is a nonsense . . . in the long run things will go on much as before.' Along with others she poked fun at suffragettes such as the Countess Kisseleff who, although very rich, very gay and well advanced in years, was so noted a stickler for women's rights that at her grand entertainments in Paris her husband had to wait for an invitation, often in vain.

In 1871 Dorothy had her only daughter, Meresia, presented at court. The social scene had been somewhat penetrated by the daughters of rich Americans who were viewed by Dorothy at first with a certain distaste. Dorothy's attitude displays very well her divided mind. On the one hand she wanted to be scientific, tolerant, progressive; on the other she was prejudiced deeply by her previous conditioning. She was deeply suspicious of foreigners and new ways: 'We rather dreaded the social influence of a people we did not know,' she observed haughtily, 'and wished the Americans would take away their girls and their tinned lobster.'

The American invasion was the result of the Franco-Prussian War. With the defeat of the French and the fall of the Second Empire the American mothers who had infiltrated their fresh-complexioned daughters into the French court, hoping to hook a member of the European aristocracy, transferred in strength to London sporting the latest Parisian fashions. The father having made the fortune was usually left behind in America, being considered too uncouth to be seen 'eating out loud'. But even the mothers and daughters were at first inclined to be looked upon as strange abnormal creatures with repulsive accents, nasal twangs and eating habits on a par with John Jacob Astor, 'who ate peas and ice cream with his knife' and then wiped his hands on the sleeves of his neighbour's coat. 'I never thought you were an American' was one of the best compliments you could be paid. 'I cannot see why people go over to America,' remarked Lady Chesterfield, 'the changes from heat to cold are so sudden it does not suit an English temperament.' But for all the snobbish strictures it did not take very long for the American mothers to trap the titled. The latter very soon saw it was beneficial to have the money to invigorate their heritage and mend their roofs. Lord Randolph Churchill was a pioneer in the domestic field with his marriage to Jenny Jerome. At least her father, Leonard Jerome, seemed to behave like an aristocrat.

Meresia, although Disraeli's favourite girl child, was hardly as attractive a bait as a pretty, rich American heiress. Nor did she have the exuberant vitality of her still youthful mother, who was inclined to overshadow her. She preferred politics to balls. Nevertheless she endured a round of junketings which could have been taken straight from her mother's diary of 1846: 'We returned from Belvoir and had 40 dinners and dancing every evening,' Dorothy recorded. While at the end of the London season the metropolis became a perfect desert, the country was bursting with eligible bachelors. Meresia and her mother trailed from house to house: 'Only give a sensible woman thirteen wet days in a country house and she'll marry her daughter to anyone,' one lady was heard to say. And when a young man remarked what a beautiful place hers was, she replied disagreeably: 'It is indeed, but remember my daughters don't dance with the house.' Poor Meresia, she hated it all: the dancing, the flirting, and particularly those interminable games of croquet so fashionable for courtship.

Meresia's coming out was concluded quite in the Orford vein by a trip abroad, taking in the battlefield of Sedan, continuing to Switzerland, then on to Paris where Dorothy managed to acquire some souvenirs from the previous year's siege. Dorothy had never been able to forget the uncomfortable journeys of her youth and reserved for foreigners some of her father's contempt. Now she was somewhat mollified by the delicious food which luckily bore no trace of last year's horrors. She wrote to Lady Airlie:

The French I think are improved, not so childish – how refined their manners and talk and how dirty their habits. Morality and decency they know nothing of, but yet with benefit we might exchange a little of our morality for some of their cooking virtues.

Dorothy's attitude to food was usually unrefined. Whenever she was in Norfolk she would gorge on Cromer crab. But she liked to experiment with food (to wit the truffles and mushrooms) and twenty years later she tried out guinea pig on her guests. The Duchess of Somerset had given her a basket of the little animals together with a book of a hundred different recipes for cooking them. In the middle of lunch she divulged what the chicken they thought they were eating really was. One guest rushed out and fainted on the spot. Frederic Harrison never forgot the occasion, writing to Dorothy in July 1901:

You, I suppose, have been in the shock of recent earthquakes in the radical party? I expected to hear that you had given Asquith a luncheon party and had asked T. P. O'Connor and the King to meet him. You might have given him guinea pig ragout as you gave George Russell on a famous occasion which makes me laugh every time I think of it.

Dorothy seems also to have given gastronomy lessons to E. F. Benson:

Guinea pig, there's a tasty dish for you, but it was always a job to make your cook do it. They want bakin' same as the gypsies serve the hedgehogs. I tried eatin' donkey too but I had to stop that for it made me stink.

Fifty years later Gosse overheard her at a gathering of fine ladies, all discussing their favourite delicacy. 'What I like is a blow out of tripe n'onions,' cackled Dorothy, scattering the assembly.

Dorothy returned from abroad to find clouds gathering on the horizon. Poor Mary Anne Disraeli was seriously ill although she and Disraeli refused to admit it to one another. In April 1872 she managed to struggle to Manchester for one of Disraeli's greatest triumphs – his speech at the Free Trade Hall. Here he declared war on Gladstone, likening the Liberal leader and his front bench to a 'range of extinct volcanoes'. He spoke for three-quarters of an hour, during which time he sustained himself with white brandy and water, consuming, it is said, two bottles by the end. Robert Lowe taunted Dorothy: 'I hope you were proud of your hero's Bacchanalian feats last night.' The trip to Manchester was nearly the last straw for Mary Anne. Two months later she fainted in the middle of a royal reception and by the end of the sessions was too ill to move to Hughenden. Disraeli took her for drives to the London suburbs: 'What miles of villas! and all sorts of architecture! What beautiful churches! What gorgeous palaces of Geneva!' he wrote, making notes for a letter he never sent to the Queen. On 26 September he wrote to Dorothy:

Yes, we have been here the whole summer. Such a thing has never happened before. It tells our sad tale, but I rejoice to tell you that absolutely this morning we are going to Hughenden. There has been of late a decided improvement in my wife's health and she now fancies that change of air will greatly benefit her. I am sorry we are to make the experiment in the fall of the leaf in a sylvan country but we could go nowhere else. Home alone could insure her the comfort and ease, which an invalide requires.

Mary Anne died four months later, urging Disraeli in her will not to live alone but to remarry. He was shattered; it was the supreme sorrow of his life. Mary Anne's dowry ceased with her death, so he had immediately to vacate Grosvenor Gate where they had lived for so many years. Fortunately he had been the beneficiary of the will of an eccentric lady from Torquay, Mrs Brydges Willyams, to the extent of £30,000. But he had always been careless about money and now he had to live in a hotel, which added greatly to his sense of isolation and loneliness. He could not even be persuaded to Dangstein in spite of Dorothy's attempts to reinvigorate him: 'We will take you to Our Lady of Uppark[1] – and do our best to enliven you.' But he could not be moved:

[1] Lady Fetherstonhaugh.

I am a prisoner and prostrate from one of those atmospheric attacks, which the English persist in calling 'colds' . . . but to tell you the truth I am still not equal to an enterprise of such magnitude. I can just dine out with friends, but after that I feel distrait and embarrassed and am glad even to escape to my homeless home. Perhaps in happier times you will not forget your old friend, D.

Disraeli gradually recovered. Over the next few years Dorothy was of tremendous support and Charles Street again assumed an importance when he became Prime Minister once more in 1874. Dorothy congratulated him:

I was told a few hours ago that you enjoyed relaxation with a good portion of folly, so I venture to disturb you at this important epoch – to say how happy I am at your great success – the only drawback to you must be that Lady Beaconsfield is not here to see it and hear it.

But Disraeli was exhausted:

Power has come to me too late. There were days when on waking I felt I could move dynasties and governments but that has passed away.

It was not just Dorothy's confidence and sympathy that Disraeli valued, she was undoubtedly an influence. Writing to her on the sudden death of her brother Frederick in 1876,[1] Disraeli said:

Your note last night was another offering to the altar of our friendship . . . I will say nothing now of the public consequence of his untimely death other than to express my hope that nothing may be done without your advice and sanction, and that the name of Walpole may always be connected with the county of Norfolk. Ever your devoted friend, D.

To cheer him up she sent him the delectable strawberries. He acknowledged them with:

The most charming deputation I ever received. They faithfully represented, in their fragrance and brightness, the dear friend who sent them to her attached.

She also sent him books, including *The New Republic*, written by a young friend of hers, W. H. Mallock. In it friends were gathered in a country house to discuss problems of religion and society in the manner of Plato's dialogues. Disraeli concurred that the book was brilliant:

[1] The Member of Parliament for the North Division of Norfolk.

Wish all its characters were for Hughenden . . . Very witty and rather wise and almost unrivalled as a first effort. The writer, I fancy, will take an eminent position in our future literature.

And, chastened by her bookplate 'Stolen from Dangstein', he concluded: 'Here is the lost book.'

Back at Dangstein there was much to worry about. A series of commercial disasters had struck the country and the worst sufferer was agriculture, hit by wet summers, new machines, freight charges and the Civil War in America. Cobden's policies had finally brought ruin to the farmers; the consequences predicted by the protectionist aristocracy had materialised. And there was worse – grave fears for the life of Mr Nevill who for three years had been suffering from cancer. Lady Chesterfield wrote to Dorothy:

I fear you are very uncomfortable about Mr Nevill. Why do you not take him to town, I have little confidence in the skill of the country doctors – one so seldom meets with a clever one.

But nothing would induce Reginald to budge. As his condition deteriorated he became even less sociable, caring only for his family and the estate workers whose future he worried about acutely. The bad harvests and his illness made him quite intolerant of his wife's friends – the liberal-minded politicians whose company he had once enjoyed but whose hypocrisy and devious methods now disgusted him. The last straw was the Hare and Rabbits Bill introduced by his friend Sir William Harcourt, which caused consternation in Tory households. It provided the occupier of land with equal rights to ground game and protected them from its ravages. Sir William, during a stay at Dangstein, had lectured Reginald on his lack of rabbits – how they did no damage to the crops. Now merely to mention Harcourt's name to Reginald was enough to induce apoplexy.

To distract herself from this depressing world, Dorothy threw herself into a number of expensive diversions: breeding donkeys and ponies; filling large tanks with axolotls and fish lizards, following the craze for aquariums; dragging trunks of wood, green with decay and covered with fungus, from the forest, hacking them into bookcases, mantelpieces, tables, boxes and picture frames, then finishing them off with silver and ormolu mounts. She filled the emptiness of her life with more clutter, beginning to collect old Sussex iron work: calivers, falconets, andirons, plough shares, spuds, and other obsolete implements and ornaments discarded as rubbish and covered with rust from the fields and outhouses. She was always rummaging around the ruins of Cowdray, and she even purchased the leg irons of William Carter, a local boy hung in chains for attempting to rob the customs house at Poole.

There was also Disraeli to look after. She managed sometimes to escape from Dangstein by chaperoning him on his visits to his passions, Lady Chesterfield and her younger sister, Lady Bradford. Mary Anne had charged Disraeli to remarry and Dorothy records in *Under Five Reigns* that he actually proposed to Lady Chesterfield, and she would have been inclined to accept if her daughter, Lady Carnarvon, had not prevented it. Lady Cardigan also claimed that Disraeli had proposed to her but that she could never face his malodorous breath. Dorothy countered that there was certainly no truth in the matter – it was more likely to be the other way round. Anyway, it was hardly less gloomy chaperoning Disraeli. He seemed so morose and bored – even on the weekend with Lady Bradford at Weston when they were celebrating his earldom. Dorothy wrote:

Dizzy very preoccupied and more difficult to get on with than usual. He sat each day at dinner between Lady Bradford and Lady Chesterfield and except an occasional meteor of intellect he never uttered but I think he is delighted in being Earl. There is a great deal of worldly leaven in his nature, and in spite of his genius he dearly loves high persons and high places.

But by November 1877 poor Mr Nevill was iller than ever. It had been another wet year and the price of wheat had dropped to 56s. 9d. a quarter – and was to drop steadily thereafter. The family income was affected. What a dismal winter it was. Dorothy's brother Horace lay ill in Norfolk, her best friend, Blanche Airlie, seemed near to death in Scotland. Mr Nevill was to linger on for a year. It was all very harrowing, and she could invite no one to stay to cheer her up. She could not even go to Charles Street in July when Disraeli returned from his triumph over the Treaty of Berlin. She wrote to him:

I know you will grieve for me when I tell you Mr Nevill is now most dangerously ill. His own doctor from London who is here gives us no hope whatever. He has been so long an invalide that I have been prepared for the end coming sooner or later.

Reginald died surrounded by his family on 17 September 1878: 'He suffered so at the last that none of us could wish him to stay where there was no rest . . . and we have the comfort of knowing that all that skill and loving kindness could do was done,' wrote Dorothy to the Hookers. He was carried through the park to Terwick churchyard by six of the oldest estate labourers dressed in smock frocks. A stone cross inscribed 'Peace at Last' marks his resting place. From then on Dorothy rarely spoke of her husband outside her own family. It was almost as though she had never been married. Marie Belloc Lowndes, who knew Dorothy well, only recalled her mentioning Reginald on one occasion: 'He was so very kind to me,' said Dorothy. 'When he died I wondered how I could go on living without him.' Then she added joyfully: 'But you see, I have!'

Nine

The economic regression followed by the agricultural depression had eroded the Nevill fortune. Furthermore Reginald had seen that Dorothy could not squander what was left. He had left the assets in the hands of trustees, providing for Teddy, Horace, Meresia and Ralph separately. Dorothy's friends were all greatly exercised as to her well-being and the subject of Mr Nevill's finances was the topic of much speculation. Disraeli wrote to Lord Derby:

Mr Nevill's property was mainly personal, but that is always a mystery. The origin of the fortune was a cadet of the House of Walpole who was a Lombard Street banker in the days of Mr Pitt and left Mr Nevill, who was his nephew, £200,000 – no slight sum in those days, but in the present about the figure with which the Rothschilds cut off their rebellious offspring.

In fact he had only left his wife with an annuity of £800 a year, which effectively put a stop to extending the exotic groves. The depression was worsening, the price of wheat this year had once again fallen, to 46s. 5d. a quarter. The trustees counselled Dorothy to sell everything, yet she hesitated. The children were against it, feeling the depression might be shortened, and she did not want to leave her garden which now housed the finest collection of plants outside Kew. She hated to sack the bailiffs, gardeners and estate workers, who relied on her; yet she could no longer afford them. At last she took a deep breath and pretending to herself she had always hated the house, decided to sell the estate in lots. The plants were to be sold separately. Dorothy asked Sir Joseph Hooker to 'puff the collection . . . and make the country come down handsome'. She had seen Sir Stafford Northcote, the Home Secretary, who had promised to spend money out of public funds to acquire some of the specimens – 'but of course,' she wrote to Hooker, 'the money and the thought alike melted.'

Her second son, Horace, a pillar of support and the financial brain of the family, sailed off with the 60th Rifles to fight the Zulus, leaving Dorothy alone with Meresia to struggle with the chief trustee, Mr Talbot. The sweltering conditions in the bush would have been enough for Horace without financial lamentations from his mother, which got through intermittently. Talbot was as much the enemy as the Zulu king, Cetewayo. Horace wrote to his mother:

I am so afraid of Talbot not making the most of it . . . as according to Talbot we shall scarcely get what poor Papa paid whereas with railways etc. it was supposed to have nearly doubled in value.

Poor Horace, steaming in the bush, which he likened to the South Downs, doubted the wisdom of selling Dangstein at all, and warned his mother they were making a great sacrifice. He reported that everything was incompetent in the bush, added to which the campaign was 'horrifying, harrowing and monstrously ill-run', with a certain general even telegraphing for a 'certain condiment' which he thought more important than his campaign. Altogether the struggle was humiliating and disastrous. Something that everyone thought would soon be over dragged on and on. 'When you in London laugh at the Zulus,' he wrote, 'you have no idea if reports speak true about what they are really like.' Certainly Dorothy had no idea; the only Zulus she knew about were in the Westminster Aquarium.

Horace's tribulations continued. He wrote:

Please give Edie [his sister-in-law] my fondest love, and thank her very much for her advice on dysentery but tell her that at the time I write the sick were lying under the wagons in the open, and there was neither milk nor arrowroot, or in fact anything to eat but trek ox and hard biscuit, and nothing to keep the dew off but a single blanket . . . One of our men who was sick was being embarked for Durban when he began struggling and making a noise. The Doctor said he was shamming and ordered some soap and water to be squirted up his nostrils upon which the poor man expired.

He tried through his mother to get a transfer:

Urgent Private Affairs must be my plea. You must recollect that the ways of the War Office are horribly crooked and one's only chance is to meet them with like weapons.

Dorothy meanwhile was also having a miserable time. The frightful weather postponed the sale of the plants and how was she going to dispose of tropical palms and tree ferns, some of which had reached thirty foot and were exceedingly difficult to move? She tried to be philosophical about the whole thing, writing to Sir Joseph Hooker that she had no doubt

they will sell for nothing, still it will be a comfort to get rid of the expense which is ruinous. I never expect anything good, so can never be disappointed.

How right she was. Another dreadful day ruined the sale. The house itself went for £53,000, but other prices were disappointing. Some of the larger plants did find good homes. The King of the Belgians filled his greenhouses at Laeken, his palace outside Brussels; the Prince of Monaco surrounded with tropical palms the Temple of Chance in his public gardens, carried thither in a large steamer chartered from Southampton. Some of the plants, notably her orange grove, of which she was particularly proud, found their way to Charles Street, where true to style she was building a conservatory. The rest were packed up and driven in three van loads to Stillians, a house in East Sussex which she had leased from Dr Hodge, a scientific friend. Here Dorothy resettled herself, in Marie Antoinette style, with her menagerie, including 'the dear pony who walks in and out of the drawing room and dining rooms', goats, donkeys, dogs, fish, lizards, axolotls and dancing mice. Room had also to be found for her peculiar collections, which now included her children's teeth, leg irons, Soyer's cookery books,[1] hatpins, unusual bonnets and buttons, watch stands, and green fungus furniture. They made a new obstacle course for the servants. Dorothy wrote to Sir Joseph Hooker:

A most comfortable house, and I shall have enough land for ourselves and our animals . . . but I have been scarcely able to survive with all the wants of those real plagues of life, the servants, they must each and all of them have their wants and wishes attended to at once, and I find myself a maid of all works to my dependents. If ever I survive these worries I may live to enjoy the place.

[1] Soyer had been chef to Lady Blessington, then chef at the Reform Club. The inscription on his tombstone in Kensal Green reads 'Soyer Tranquil'.

By September 1879 the family were reunited: Ralph from Eton, where for some unknown reason he was known as 'Betsy', Teddy and Edith over from Trotton, the house they had retained on the Dangstein estate, and Horace. At last the brave Cetewayo had been hunted like a wild beast to his capture and Horace's sickly battalion summoned home, the conditions and climate having added at least ten years to everyone's looks. Horace was his mother's son. His spoils included Zulu assegais and knobkerries which added to the clutter in his mother's house. He had even tried to buy Cetewayo's meat dish but was outbid by General Wolseley, who seemed to have similar collecting tastes to Dorothy.

Stillians was in country even more remote and primitive than Midhurst. Streams ran everywhere, overgrown with boughs and brambles and filled with trout. The inhabitants hardly ever moved from their own villages and viewed any region out of a one-mile radius as frightening and foreign. Families made their living in cultivating hops, making trugs and ropes, roof shingling, higgling or chicken fatting. Heathfield was the chicken fattening centre and as the industry increased, fatters were compelled to employ 'higglers' who went far afield to bring back inexpensive fowls which were then cruelly crammed by means of a sausage machine turned by labourers.

Dorothy was always poking nosily in the labourers' cottages, seeing how they lived if not rummaging around their outhouses to see what clutter she could find. She was pleased to note the cottages were clean and neat inside, but, she added despondently,

such quarters were not always comfortable, the brick front generally damp and uneven, the ceiling formed of massive oak beams, strong enough to support a church and heavy enough to pull it down.

The only place free from draughts was the inner corner of the huge open chimney.

Every cottage had its beehives and whenever a member of the family died it was the custom to tell the bees. It was also the custom in those parts to place food in the coffin (later, in 1893, a labourer was buried with a tin of salmon and an opener). There was also a local legend that the Devil had appeared to St Dunstan in the guise of a beautiful woman. Recognising him, St Dunstan had tweaked his nose with his tongs and the Devil had run off across the Weald dripping blood into the streams – which consequently to this day turn red. The actual tongs were supposed to be at the Mayfield Convent with the nuns. In fact the rusty red current was derived from the ore deposit in the river bed, Stillians being at the centre of what had been the great Sussex iron-producing area. Heaps of scrap in the farmyards indulged Dorothy's endless scavenging. 'What, more rubbish?' her friends would say as she returned with her spoils,

but having gone patiently on my iron way rejoicing, I have been rewarded by knowing that not only has this pursuit given me great pleasure (for what is life without a pursuit?) but that I have wasted neither time nor money.

She even received some ironwork from a Mormon woman setting out for Utah. Dorothy had tried to stop her leaving, telling her her husband would have twelve wives instead of one when they arrived at the City of the Saints. Unconvinced, the woman presented her before leaving with a particularly fine seventeenth-century fireback with a border of apples encircling Neptune with a trident, drawing sea monsters.

Dorothy next added black sheep to her menagerie which were more like deer than sheep. She turned them out like ordinary sheep under the impression that they never strayed, but they jumped hurdles and fences with ease, one or two escaping nightly and causing havoc. Then she introduced consignments of crayfish from France into the streams, but the experiment was, as so often, a failure. Water rats devoured the crayfish, defying the gratings that were supposed to protect them.

Predictably, Dorothy embarked on a new garden: wilder, smaller, less formal, needing less upkeep. She enjoyed some badinage with the local nurserymen. One near her sent her a 'Gladstone apple'. Dorothy insisted it should be rechristened 'Lord Beaconsfield', even though the man said he was as true a Tory as herself and only grew it that he might devour it. 'It has cost me something in orders, but the man promises not to transgress again,' she told Lady Airlie, now restored to health, who understood the importance of Dorothy's gardens.

People like yourself and Mrs Somerville, some more some less, I am not putting you quite with Mrs Somerville, so do not say I flatter, but people of your sort have a little kingdom of delights to which they retire after the rubs of the world, and where they sit aloft and commune with nature and laugh at the disturbing elements below which make the happiness and sorrow of the stupidest parts of mankind.

Dorothy's gardens were the 'green spots' of her life, where she turned when bothers assailed her. 'They are always sweet and grateful for attentions,' she told Lady Airlie. On the whole she was very happy, her peace only shattered by Ralph brandishing a gun, 'aimin' at everything, hittin' nothing'. She was doing her best to economise, leaving, for example, her equipage in town. This could sometimes cause problems. The Duke of Wellington arrived and insisted on attending a bee show some three miles distant. They drove there in a farm cart, balancing on two chairs precariously placed on top, Dorothy up on one, the Duke on the other, dressed quite extraordinarily in an old soft hat, goggles and goatskin cloak, stiff as cardboard. The villagers mistook him for a local character, 'Old Bobbles', a centenarian labourer.

Dorothy remarked that her old friend was beginning to lose some of his faculties. His hearing suffered and his eyesight began to fail. This made him even gruffer. One of his eyes had to be removed. Before the operation he terrified the surgeon:

Now, Sir, pray understand that I don't fear death but I abominate pain. If in your endeavours to spare me the latter you introduce me to the former, I would, should we meet in another world, freely forgive you; but if you let me suffer, and I remain in the flesh, God help you.

The operation was a success and the Duke joked with Dorothy about his eyes. In answer to an inquiry he replied: 'Thank you, one of them is in excellent spirits in Harley Street'; and to a friend who was bewailing his financial straits he said: 'Take this tip, go to your club and bet as many as will take you on that you cannot name the distance between the Duke of Wellington's eyes.' The answer was the distance between Apsley House and Harley Street.

His charm however, was still effective. He even persuaded Dorothy's bigoted sister-in-law, Cecilia, that the Lord would not mind if she made up a four of whist on a Sunday. This was considered a great feat. Dorothy considered him kind but his behaviour could be outrageous. Dorothy remembered the old boy driving her to a donkey show where he refused to be moved from a patch of ground reserved for the judges. An official approached him. 'Sir, may I ask are you a judge?' 'A judge of what?' thundered the Duke. 'Of donkeys,' came the reply. 'Certainly I am, and', looking very hard at the man, 'a very good one too. Leave me alone.' When the Duke's identity was finally established, they deferentially asked him to judge. Assenting, he went off to find Dorothy to sit with him, and together they judged the show, the Duke delighted by the success of his tactics. Dorothy, to her credit, was at least embarrassed. But it has to be said that the behaviour of some of her friends was not infrequently churlish. One sometimes wonders what a return to government by the 'benevolent aristocracy' would have implied.

As soon as Dorothy had established herself in the country she moved to London. As an attractive and vivacious widow of fifty-three she was very popular in Society. Figures such as Bernal Osborne who had dominated the conversation had now disappeared from the scene. With their disappearance everyone was much more relaxed. Disraeli, too, had retired exhausted and bent. Dorothy believed it was his early struggles and financial worries that had worn him out. Whatever it was he departed for Hughenden and Dorothy saw much less of him: 'I wish I ever saw you but the sun seldom shines on me now,' she wrote to him, faithfully remembering to send his presents of strawberries. She sent him other surprises: musk plants to generate ozone in his room; Athenian laurels, 'an appropriate present for the Hero of Cyprus'; a swan from Wolterton, 'for the author of Endymion, not in life – but an end and cure for gastronomic delights . . . ' Disraeli lived just long enough to learn of the success of *Endymion*, dying on 19 April 1881. Dorothy wrote to Lady Airlie:

It makes me more than ordinarily sad for it reminds me of my early married days. For 21 years we lived near each other and much happiness and brightness we had then. Now all my dear ones are gone – and what a blank it all is – I am a philosopher, but yet I must feel deeply this blow for tho' I have not in later years seen so much of him when I did see him he was always the same, nice and kind, and for us all we have lost the chief almost the only barrier who defended us from the mob and dangerous classes. You will not think this, but it is true, and we may even live to see it.

Her elderly admirers were now dead: her husband, Disraeli, Bernal Osborne, Lord Ellenborough. The gruff old Duke of Wellington was the only survivor. Clearly her court was wanting. She needed replacements; her vanity demanded new flatterers. In the event she chose three men, each brilliant in his different field, and drew them into her confidence. All were to stay faithfully by her side for the rest of her life. First there was Edmund Gosse, poet, critic and man of letters, the son of devout Plymouth Brethren. He was about thirty-two years old, fair with piercing blue eyes, a fine forehead, and a curious walk – suggesting both eagerness and caution. But 'he could be as touchy as a housemaid and as suspicious as a governess', and was quick to take offence. He was polished, discriminating and a voracious reader. Up to the age of seventeen he had been forbidden to read anything except religious tracts. Apart from his portraits his great contribution, yet to be written, was *Father and Son*, the story of his restricted upbringing. Gosse loved the aristocracy and embraced the paradoxes of his childhood. Dorothy fitted nicely into this category. She was invited to meet him at a country-house party. He was at once delighted with her and recorded their abandoned conversation. They first talked of Zola's novels; and of how he wrote about sex. Dorothy said:

He takes the varnish off rural life, I must say; oh these horrid demons of Frenchmen know how to write. Even the most disgusting things they know how to describe poetically. I wish Zola could describe Haslemere with all its shops shut, rain falling and all the inhabitants in their cups.

Dorothy was very well known for her wide reading of French novels. About one she wrote excitedly:

It is very beautifully written, but very improper so much so that Hachette won't sell it in the railway stores! Need I say on hearing this I immediately ordered it . . . if only somebody would write a readable English novel we should not be driven to bad French ones 'pour charmer nos ennuis'.

Her choice of reading shocked some of her guests. A young Oxford prig seeing *La Bête Humaine* on her table remarked that it was not a book for a lady. 'It is just the book for me,' retorted Dorothy.

Then there was Sir Garnet Wolseley, the hero of Tel-el-Kebir, who discovered in Dorothy identical tastes of horticulture – to say nothing of collecting clutter, for it was he who had snatched King Cetewayo's meat dish out of Horace's grasp. He was the leader of a group called the 'Wolseley gang', whose hard work, efficiency and determination to change an army unaltered since the eighteenth century appalled old fogies such as the Commander-in-Chief, the Duke of Cambridge, who liked nothing better than parades and addresses: 'H.R.H. delights in oratory,' Wolseley wrote to Dorothy. 'I squander all my time inspecting cadets and watching them drill etc.' It is a tribute to Dorothy's tact and skill that she always remained on the best terms with both the Duke and Wolseley. (Dorothy, incidentally, never could remember how to spell his name: 'Wolsey, Wallesley, Wollesly, Woseley,' were her variations on the theme.) He was soon an habitué.

I hope your knocker and your doorbell have not suffered from the violence of my efforts to obtain a hearing on Sunday week when I called at 45 Charles Street by appointment. I soon gave up the bell and took to the knocker holding onto which I was found by Lord Barrington, who passing by was attracted by the funny position. I then gave it up as a hopeless affair, assuming that you were closeted with some crowned head or some radical fellow who is anxious to cut off every head that wears a crown.

Maybe Dorothy was hiding her third admirer, Joseph Chamberlain no less,[1] who was interested in both French novels and horticulture – orchids being his speciality. He always wore one in his button hole and his orchids at Highbury, Birmingham were famous. At forty-eight he was tall and handsome; monocled and elegant; civilised, sophisticated and urbane. He was also very clever. According to Dorothy he never in his life took any exercise. There is no doubt that Dorothy knew how to make someone feel good. She flattered him, telling him how Disraeli had admired him and how the prospect of their meeting had cheered him up. Her first two conquests had been conventional, and eminently eligible to be her admirers, but Chamberlain was not acceptable. Because of his radical views he was believed by the Conservatives to be highly dangerous. Radicals were unwelcome in Society, being considered likely to produce uncomfortable changes that would undermine the way of life.

[1] The new President of the Board of Trade.

'Oh dear, oh dear, where will it all end?' wrote Dorothy to Lady Airlie.

But it is useless continuing a topic on which we are so divided but it is all too shocking to think of. I must own I have made Mr Chamberlain's acquaintance and like him very much, as he allows me to tell him wholesome truths; but I don't think he is up to working the revolution he has taken in hand.

Nevertheless she proceeded to invite him to her salon. 'It is very brave of you to run the risk of inviting me to your home,' wrote Chamberlain, 'and I shall have the greatest pleasure in concealing my hoofs and tail so as not to alarm your other guests.' Dorothy's friends were scandalised. Was she now turning into a revolutionary? She left the copy of Chamberlain's speeches prominently displayed round her room: 'I shall not expect you to read it as life is too short for such tasks,' wrote Chamberlain to her, 'but I will put "with kind regards" on it and it will serve thus to alarm and disgust your Tory friends when they see it on your table.' Only the gruff old Duke of Wellington showed a remarkable lack of prejudice:

The devil is not as black as he is painted [he wrote to her] and somewhere it is written that it is well to make friends with righteousness, therefore I shall have pleasure in meeting Chamberlain; besides I think him a sensible man and sensible men go on reasoning and reforming opinions all their lives.

Other members of the Establishment viewed her salon with much distaste. Old Lady Chesterfield wrote disagreeably:

I am glad to hear you have had Sir Stafford [Northcote] to entertain you, had better have young Curzon whom you met here instead of all those radicals more particularly Chamberlain who is a blackguard and would like to be Prime Minister in order to turn the world topsy-turvy.

Every three months she would send Dorothy a turkey. This time it did not materialise. Thinking it had been mislaid Dorothy wrote off to Lady Chesterfield to inform her. It was not mislaid, it was withdrawn. 'I hear you have had Mr Chamberlain to lunch,' replied Lady Chesterfield. 'I therefore cannot send you a turkey to feed such a democrat and I am angry at your seeing him so much.' 'You are wrong,' Dorothy retaliated: 'Sir Stafford Northcote has been my only political guest of late and I promise if you send me the turkey nothing but a Conservative tooth shall touch it.' The turkey duly arrived.

Ten

No. 45 Charles Street was decorated in the Nevill colours; painted crushed strawberry, multi-crested even down to the knocker in the shape of a bull sitting on top of a coronet. You entered through the rose-red front door. Dorothy's drawing room was on the right, which you came into announced by an odd contraption of bells which jangled over the door as it opened. It was cluttered with Victoriana: beaded shawls, antimacassars, glass domes encasing dried flowers; her own ormolu-mounted fungus objects mixed with the fine furniture that the Nevills had saved from attics, and wood scrolls pilfered from the panels at Wolterton, since abandoned by Horace Orford; silhouettes, including profiles cut by Princess Elizabeth, daughter of George III, and one of Mrs Jordan in a hat profusely plumed; a favourite Meissen bust of Frederick the Great bought by Dorothy's father; the watercolours executed by her old governess depicting their travels, and a set of plates telling its horrors; a fine Rose du Barry tea service, once possessed by Marie Antoinette, bought from Webb's in the Strand, displayed in French cabinets; a favourite willow desk that had once belonged to Pope; Louis XVI sideboards from Forrest, the celebrated dealer, who had been so worried about the cholera epidemic that he rushed to the country to hide (to no avail for the epidemic pursued and killed him even there); then mementoes of a new hero, Disraeli, and the heroines, her beloved Queen and Charlotte Walpole. Dorothy had hung a plaque beneath the frame of a print depicting Charlotte Walpole in the role of 'Nance', inscribing on it: 'Elle poussa le dévouement jusqu'à l'héroisme, et le courage jusqu'à la témerité'. The tables were littered with piles of improper French novels, dangerous speeches, yellowing photographs curiously framed by Dorothy, and old *Morning Posts*.

The staircase was a gallery of famous faces – all the old acquaintances Dorothy had acquired and all the new people too: Samuel Wilberforce, Disraeli, Lord Ellenborough; Lord Chief Justice Cockburn, Bright, Darwin; Lord Randolph Churchill, Chamberlain, Ellen Terry. On the first floor was the dining room, a little more formal, painted primrose yellow to show off the beautiful pastels by Perroneau and Rosalba that the Nevills had collected. The centrepiece by Watts was the youthful portrait of Dorothy under which she presided, looking essentially the same, as her guests were pleased to comment. Next to the dining room was her boudoir into which the sun flooded and which was suitable for her work. It looked over the Running Footman, the public house, so she could inspect the swaying populace and watch out for a drunken butler or maid. In her boudoir Dorothy might be rolling paper, pasting in her scrapbooks, or writing missives on curious paper, refusing to be interrupted if disturbed, relentlessly carrying on with her industry. Meresia and Ralph, now grown up, contributing to the household, had their own rooms; Meresia's cluttered like her mother's with old prints, political paraphernalia, addresses. Dorothy's bedroom was extremely Spartan. She never had a fire and slept with but one blanket, always rising at the same hour for breakfast. Wherever you were dogs bounded around and canaries and love birds swooped and darted, so even the dining room lost its formal look. Edward Cazalet, twenty years later, recalled his first visit. Dorothy was sitting there amidst numerous dogs and birds.

They have the most extraordinary house I have ever seen. Oh! so dirty. Everything was covered with dust. She will not let the servants touch anything so that everything gets dirty.

Dorothy's dress was quaintly episcopal in character. It had nothing of Victorian convention about it. Her friend Kate Greenaway painted adorable eighteenth-century women and children. Dorothy seemed like one of her enchantresses. Clothed in black vestments with an undulating auburn wig, she now affected to 'dress old' which only accentuated her youthfulness. She looked neat and dainty, 'coquettish and quakerish together', wearing innumerable ropes of amber and amulets and Egyptian beads, let alone her children's teeth and a skull made from her posy ring fixed round her neck with a ribbon. On special occasions a sort of enamelled gate-like structure swung on her neck in emeralds and rubies, designed like the crested door knocker and emblazonings. She seemed made to measure for the house. When she went out she protected herself from the 'kipperin'' effect of the sun and wind with masses of veils crowned by a straw bonnet, decorated with clusters of artificial fruits all seemingly unripe – 'including the greenest of redcurrants, which even a starving bird would not peck at,' wrote Lady Galway in *Past Revisited*.

For the next twenty years there were two important salons in London. Mary Jeune, later Lady St Helier, entertained on a grand scale in the evenings. Lady Dorothy Nevill, *à la* Lady Molesworth, selected eight or ten guests generally for luncheon. She was notorious for her mixtures: scientists with soldiers; artists with politicians. Sir Squire Bancroft, the actor manager, remembered in *Empty Chairs*:

One met everyone worth knowing and heard pretty well everything worth listening to. There assembled men of all opinions and every class and calling, honey gathered from many a hive.

It was said that all London had passed through Charles Street, that even a criminal might be invited if he was interesting. There is a well-known story of an explorer penetrating into a wild and hostile region who had been captured and bound to a tree preparatory to being roasted and eaten. As the fire burned the savages' chief appeared: 'I know your face,' he said. 'We have met at my friend Lady Dorothy's, and so instead of dining off you I shall ask you to dine with me and tell me all the London news.'[1]

Dorothy's children were a disappointment to her. All were without doubt intelligent, but none of them was making the mark she had expected in the world that mattered to her. She had given them a handle which they had no wish to turn. Perhaps they were the victims of maternal pressure. The two elder boys in particular were unambitious, and Teddy was retiring, like his father. Many of Dorothy's friends did not even know that Teddy, her firstborn, existed. He lived at Trotton, the dower house of Dangstein, unsold in 1879. The youngest boy,

[1] Some sources attribute this tale to Lady Molesworth's table.

'The Master', was tiny, snipe-like, ill-favoured but very amusing, with a challenging if hardly distinguished literary talent – he once wrote six books in one year. He regarded Charles Street merely as the launching point for his delightful dissipations in Paris. He would dart off there, enjoy himself, then return to base to support himself by writing another book. Meresia, now Dorothy's companion, was another problem. The pretty, plump girl had become manly with a deep, gruff voice and hated going out in Society. Already she was suffering a little from St Vitus's Dance. Rather overwhelmed by her mother, she seemed to prefer politics and her woman friends. Physically there was no resemblance between any of the children and their attractive elfin mother. Dorothy looked as if she had been born on another planet, with Meresia appointed to guard her. Yet all the children served their purpose as everyone must on Dorothy's stage: Teddy looking after Dorothy's rural interests; Horace, the stockbroker and financial adviser, ensuring continuity of the lunches and the family tree, producing grandchildren for Dorothy; while for Ralph the principal purpose was in the future. For the moment his wit sufficed, Dorothy delaying his debauches by obtaining through her friends several minor diplomatic posts abroad for him. Poor Meresia, treated like the secretary, forbade her mother's excesses and assisted in the role of hostess. She was in effect a partner. Dorothy called her 'my sheet anchor and rudder'. They were an eccentric team. Lady St Helier wrote:

Lady Dorothy was cosmopolitan to her finger tips, in curious contrast to her daughter, who was nothing if not an uncompromising Tory. She did not follow her mother in her social wanderings, but steadily adhered to her own opinions, and drew a relentless line at many of the acquaintances whom Dorothy delighted to make but whom Miss Nevill never recognised.

And later:

All her friends were *dans le mouvement* and she knew everything that was going on. Cabinet Ministers in moments of *épanchement* confided their secrets to Lady Dorothy, she knew the latest scandal and the latest story, and her information was most comprehensive and accurate.

Her dinner table was now in a sense her garden. She used her guests to renew her energy and vitality, which was to last all her life. She applied that energy to her political luncheons. She needed to feel powerful. About this time she had a conversation with Henry Mayers Hyndman, the Marxist, which he thought summed up the attitude of the cleverest aristocratic class in the world. Dorothy scolded him:

You are making a very great mistake, Mr Hyndman, in devoting yourself to Socialism. We believe you to be honest in what you are doing because we have offered you all a man can hope to get in this country and you have not chosen to take it. But you will never succeed anyway in your own lifetime. We have had an excellent innings, but I don't deny that for a moment: an excellent innings and the turn of the people will come some day. I see that as clearly as you do. But not yet, not yet. You will educate some of the working classes, this is all you can hope to do for them. And when you have educated them we shall buy them and if we don't the Liberals will, and that will be just the same to you. But now remember thirty years have past and you have another generation to deal with, to stir up and educate, while if I venture to say so you yourself are not so young. Nor quite so hopeful as you are today. Not yet, Mr Hyndman. Your great changes will not come yet and in the meanwhile you will be engaged in a very thankless task indeed. Far better throw in your lot with men whom you know and like, and do your best to serve the people whom you wish to benefit from the top instead of from the bottom.

Dorothy was interested in manipulating people, drawing them around her like a magnet, and she used Meresia to organise the appointments and arrangements so that all she had to do was enjoy herself. Those were not auspicious days for the Conservative party. Since Disraeli's retirement in 1880 the leadership had fallen jointly to Lord Salisbury and 'The Goat', Sir Stafford Northcote. To the go-ahead members of the party their leadership seemed altogether ineffectual. Now the Fourth Party was formed, a rebellious movement led by Lord Randolph Churchill, Sir John Gorst, Henry Drummond Wolff, and Arthur Balfour, to sting the party out of its inertia. No one felt the need for a creditable performance more than Dorothy. Ralph wrote in *Life and Letters*:

She felt the need of regulating her hospitable rites so that they should rebound to the credit and advantage of the Tory Party. She would invite to lunch on Sundays certain leading Conservatives and people not entirely out of sympathy with the Party's aims, especially the Fourth

Party. It was in a sense the spirit of Young England all over again, in that those who met in her house were rebels and looked to a new England and a regeneration of the Party. Dorothy knew their aversions, weaknesses and foibles, and how to control their outbursts. Although a clever talker she knew how to keep silent at the right moment. She was also discreet, so they were relaxed occasions often running late into the afternoon with a great deal of laughter and joking at the expense of Salisbury and 'Old Goaty', as well as Gladstone, no one failing to be amused at his clever methods of extrication from awkward predicaments.[1]

The Fourth Party was an odd bunch. Lord Randolph Churchill was frank, egotistical, often rude and indiscreetly outspoken. He could be unbelievably difficult when he chose. Yet those whom he admitted into his intimacy found him brilliant, exciting and very attractive. Dorothy called him 'The Dolphin'. Generally, lounging in the conservatory under the orchids and orange trees, he was the life and soul of the party, although difficult to placate. Like Lady Chesterfield, Lord Randolph paid great attention to the guests Dorothy entertained. 'I was looking forward to dining with you but dear . . . is too much for me. How can you have such a person,' he remonstrated. 'I heard of you keeping dreadful company – Joseph Arch,' he wrote again after Dorothy had entertained the founder of the First Agricultural Union, the new Radical member for North Norfolk, a former ploughboy. Finding guests to suit Lord Randolph was proving difficult. She wrote to him:

We had no choice – or even any souls at all for luncheon – I feel I have no one left you would care to meet. Next Sunday we have the Kendalls – a pretty American actress Miss Calhoun, Lord Kenmare, Mr G. Russell. I fear this might not suit the Dolphin.

In her correspondence with him she both flatters and soothes him. Certainly she did not dare to tease him.

I did indeed live yesterday in the happy hunting ground of the Liberals, Mr C – [Chamberlain] came in the morning and talked with the most affectionate regard for you. He delighted my heart when he spoke of you so tenderly – In the evening I not only met the GOM [Gladstone] but Lady Breadalbane made him take me in to dinner – and I must say I succumbed to his pleasant converse and I did this time make him laugh and was flattered when Mrs Gladstone said 'W is much better for his

[1] Gladstone's defence of the Land Act 1881 for instance. When it had proved an obvious failure he said: 'We do not admit that the measure has been a failure, but admit that its success has been incomplete.'

dinner and pleasant company.' He mentioned you several times and in most flattering terms said you had great aptitude, immense ability and a great deal more which my poor waggly head cannot remember – The Liberals are clever enough to appreciate you. It is only those jealous block-headed Tories who run you down – but never mind – you must rise whatever happens.

Sir John Gorst, a sincere social reformer, was not such an animated conversationalist as his colleagues but had a peculiar knack of saying the most incisive things in a soft and flute-like voice. He provided, too, an encyclopedic knowledge of public affairs and was, as a contemporary put it, 'a pointer to find game for Lord Randolph to run down'. Sir Henry Drummond Wolff was Dorothy's first cousin, eminently diplomatic; and the fourth was Arthur Balfour, Lord Salisbury's nephew, who was the last regular of the visitors. He was not happy in his role; his family loyalties clashed with his political ideals.

On the whole they were Conservative teeth that tackled her lunches. Joseph Chamberlain afforded a notable and continuing exception. Hostess and guest each sought to change the other. Dorothy's motives were primarily selfish, to do with saving herself. They were like her father's who resented any innovations which were likely to change the old feudal manner of life. What is more, Dorothy blamed her own class for fresh inroads:

These horrors [the Radicals] are so clever and we are so stupid; but then look how well they [the middle class] are educated, while our children learn nothing but how to spend their parents' money.

Just two years before she died she was still complaining about the upper classes after a visit to the Victoria and Albert Museum:

Just a few sprinkles of legs, for I am sure they looked too frivolous to have bodies and souls attached to them, but what softened the sight to my eyes were two little Japs poring over each article with a hand book . . . our bodies of course giggling and looking at nothing. Still worse, not one soul of the higher class visible; in fact I never heard of one knowing the place.

Chamberlain's impulsions were essentially middle-class and idealistic although he was cynical too. One of their main issues between them was education. Dorothy's belief went along with the general view that education would make the working classes

143

less loyal and more discontented with their lot. Some people went as far as to say that if Englishmen were taught to read or write they would lose their ancient courage and become timid. Dorothy, too, was horrified with the idea of public libraries – 'Much better to feed the poor and destitute.' Chamberlain, who had himself taught in the Birmingham Sunday schools, believed that education must be compulsory and free.

Another issue was land, on which Dorothy held staunchly conditioned views. She was terrified of the effects of the new Agricultural Union founded by Arch. Chamberlain on the other hand had wanted reform. Protection of private interest over the common good was what he disliked. 'I ask what ransom will property pay for the security it enjoys?' he wrote to Dorothy on one occasion, and again:

We have been so long a peer-ridden people and I hope you will say to them that if they will not bow to the will of the people they shall lose for ever the authority they have so long abused.

In 1880 Henry George, an American, published a very successful book called *Progress and Poverty*. He perceived that land speculation was locking up vast territories to the detriment of the labouring classes. Everywhere he saw there was an effort to corner land, not for use but for profit. Chamberlain's view was that the only way to counter revolution was to take notice of George. He wrote to Dorothy:

I am sorry to hear that your friends are so angry with what I say. I laugh at them and they abuse me. One day they will discover what a good friend I have been to them and how I have saved them from the wrath to come.

Confiscation was the topic on everyone's mind. 'The Duke of Bedford', Dorothy told Chamberlain, 'is selling land at any price.' Chamberlain replied:

I sympathise with the poor Duke of Bedford. At least I should do so if he had not been mean enough to ask for a Lord Lieutenancy before he announced his conversion. I suppose that he is dreadfully straitened, not more than £300,000 or £400,000 a year left. I do not understand however what he is going to invest in. Does he flatter himself that the Radicals will be satisfied with confiscating land? I advise him to emigrate to the United States which will soon be the only country where a rich man will be safe.

Their correspondence at this time is infused with tones of banter.

No doubt China is a very nice place [wrote Chamberlain] but it has its drawbacks, for instance there is no hereditary peerage and I do not see how life is possible without a House of Lords. I have always thought that the present government, based as it is on the moral law, was destined to triumph over all its enemies. We are so good from the Prime Minister downwards that providence has evidently blessed my efforts and those of the Caucus.[1] Political affairs are very quiet, so they ought to be during the early days. We shall have to invent something before long which will stir the surface – something in the way of destruction and confiscation.

How Dorothy enjoyed it all: 'If you have a moment to dispose of, waste it on a poor creature who is really improving under your tuition,' she wrote. 'Your paper is admirable,' he replied. 'It is I think of the colour known as '*Bismarck malade*' and it seems to me most appropriate for the present conditon of the Tory party.'

After three years the Fourth Party grew restless and were no longer content to remain in their powerless role. Lord Randolph Churchill wanted no less than control of the whole party machinery. In 1883 he was elected Chairman of the Council of National Union. This provided a useful weapon with which to fight the central leadership. At the same time the idea of a new society was conceived beneath the Perroneaus and Rosalbas in the yellow dining room. The morning of 19 April 1883, the second anniversary of Disraeli's death, Mr Cave, the attendant at the House, gave Sir Henry Drummond Wolff a primrose buttonhole, thought to be Disraeli's favourite flower. At lunch on Sunday they all discussed the idea of forming this new sort of *corps d'élite* of young, democratic, militant Conservatives fed up, like members of the Fourth Party, with the existing party organisation. The aim was 'to instruct the working men and women how to answer the arguments of the radicals and socialists and the atheists in the workshops and on the street corners'. Sir Henry suggested it should be called the Primrose League and its motto was 'to support an Empire built on Liberty'. From then on the Primrose League movement turned out to be a cult led by Disraeli, which was celebrated every year on what the Liberals were pleased to call St Beaconsfield's Day. All the trimming smacked of Young England

[1] A conglomeration of constituencies in and around Birmingham held together for the Liberals by Chamberlain.

and the society was launched on a grand banquet in the yellow dining room where primrose salads were served at tables, and outside the railings and window-boxes were dressed with flowers. London was inspired: businessmen wore primroses in their button holes; bouquets were sold at street corners; cabbies decorated themselves, their horses and their harnesses. Yet it is not at all certain that the Saint's favourite flower was the primrose. Queen Victoria's wreath bore the inscription 'His Favourite Flower', but this could have meant the Prince Consort's. Primroses abounded in the woods around Hughenden. A search through Disraeli's novels reveals only two mentions of the primrose. In *Coningsby* a dish of ham and eggs is likened to a bouquet of primroses, and Lord Jerome in *Lothair* exclaims: 'Primroses, I think, make capital salad.' So perhaps Gladstone was right after all. He and Disraeli never met socially. One rarely referred to the existence of the other. But Gladstone, sitting near to Dorothy at dinner at about this time, asked her: 'Did you ever hear Lord Beaconsfield express any fondness for the primrose?' Dorothy admitted she had not. 'The glorious lily I think was more to his taste,' sniped Gladstone.

The Primrose League was different from any other society, mainly in one particular. The year after its foundation it amended its membership to include women. This in a sense was a blow struck for women's suffrage. It was the first time that women were given a political voice. Lydia Becker of Women's Suffrage welcomed it as a unique stepping-stone towards the enfranchisement of women; while Mrs Fawcett, a personal friend of Dorothy's, and a leader of the Women's Emancipation Movement, declared that the opportunities for political work by enfranchised women in political parties short of the vote itself was 'one of the most important political weapons which can be possibly put into our hands'.

Non-members poked fun at the 'Primrose Dames' as the ladies were pleased to call themselves. But they were not simply to be useless ornaments. Ladies were to provide free concerts in the poor districts, to speak in vans with magic lanterns attached, to turn out millions of leaflets and to do individual canvassing. Some women even became Dame Presidents of Habitations, as the different Primrose League zones which spread round the country came to be called. The Primrose League was to rally people round the throne through the agency of a free aristocracy; to create fortresses of strength in urban districts until now occupied by the Liberals, and to maintain Conservative power in rural districts at a time when manorial fidelity to the squire was in doubt. It was to rejuvenate enthusiasm for the Empire at a time when the newly enfranchised working class threatened to dominate the scene; and for the throne, unpopular since the Queen's seclusion and reported scandals concerning the Prince of Wales. The League was to provide an effective bulwark against revolution and was to bring to life politically half the nation. It dissipated the bleakness of late-Victorian life in the country. There was dancing on the green, there were dances with low admission charges; punchinellos, pierrots, ventriloquists, vying for favour with orientals, marionettes and microscopic exhibitions. Few of the working- class villagers were proof against reverence for the great families, and of course the Primrose Dames knew exactly how to use this for political ends. There was no entertainment all the winter except, possibly, for a concert given by the parson. The wives and daughters of the agricultural labourers were finding time hanging heavily as machinery eliminated their work in the fields. In the Seventies the National Agricultural Union had offered women as well as men a centre of community life, but now the Union had collapsed leaving a real social void. The entertainment provided by the Primrose Habitations was of course like a magnet, though the Dames were left wide open to criticism. A weakness for double-barrelled names was cited and there were dark references to 'aristocratic hangers on and needy relations'. Dorothy's friend Mr Labouchere, the proprietor of *Truth*, once said: 'I trust that we Radicals will never teach the people to confound their politics with a donkey or a negro entertainment'; and he quoted from a Primrose handbook: 'Primrose Day, Primrose Day. Don't forget the Grand Negro Entertainment.'

Eridge, near Heathfield, was to be Dorothy's Habitation in the country. Eridge Castle was the seat of her cousin, Lord Abergavenny, and one of Dorothy's favourite places. Not everyone was as delighted as she with the family or the place. Edward Cazalet, when only sixteen, criticised both in his diary:

The family are all very nice but very stupid . . . Really, inside it is quite the most hideous place I have ever seen. The family arms are a rose and a bull and these you see everywhere. On one ceiling there were at least three hundred.[1] The top of every lamp is a bull with the flame coming out of its mouth. Really I might have been looking at the house of some nouveau riche or parvenu. The family pictures . . . have been so varnished they look like linoleum pictures.

His lordship, known as 'The Tory Bloodhound', was the terror of the Liberals. He was so frightening that Gladstone, staying at nearby Frant, refused to visit Eridge saying 'I will not enter the Lion's den.' When at home he would open the windows after breakfast and bellow. The gardeners would gather round and he would throw them all the eggs and bacon left over from breakfast. Another democratic gesture was to sit his butler to eat beside him at his birthday celebrations.

The lawns and terraces surrounding the castellated castle, built in Strawberry Hill Gothic style, formed a perfect amphitheatre for the Primrose League; beyond it deer grazed, and there were rocks, hills and vales, grand trees, rivers and waterfalls, stretching to the horizon. In the summer Lord Abergavenny would give an annual fête in aid of the Conservative cause. The entire Nevill family would turn out to buy votes and raise money, headed by booming Lord Abergavenny, with drooping moustache, eccentrically dressed in violent checked tweeds. He, his tall handsome children, Dorothy, clad like a cardinal with the quivering bass-voiced Meresia, all took turns to pilot the Nevill van, equipped at the family's expense and decked out in their colours. It was not necessarily the speeches which attracted. There were delicious teas, beer and numerous sideshows. Under the cedar tree there were jugglers and nigger minstrels. Once a whole ox was roasted in the park. Balloons rose over the lake where swimming races were held; meanwhile, hardly noticed by the labourers, the double-barrelled gentry read speeches from the terraces. The Habitation was a great strength to the cause in raising money and votes – the beginning of Conservative Party machinery as it is today – and the labourers came away thinking there was nothing like the Nevills and the old manorial way of life.

[1] Probably this would have appealed to Dorothy. Excessive use of the crest seems to have been a family failing.

The first meeting of the Ladies' Grand Council took place in the drawing room of Lady Glenesk. Dorothy and her daughter were founder members and others among the Council of Fifteen included the Duchess of Marlborough, Lady Jersey, Lady Randolph Churchill, Lady Charles Beresford, and Lord Salisbury's daughter, Lady Gwendolen Cecil; an aristocratic gathering who swore to maintain the imperial ascendancy of Great Britain and to obey all orders emanating from the constitutional authority of the League. Finally Dorothy had found a niche for Meresia, organising with her friends that she should be elected Treasurer of the Rotating Committee of the Grand Council. Her services to the Primrose League were eventually rewarded in 1907 with the Diamond Star of the Order. Dorothy wrote:

Though one of the first members of the Ladies' Grand Council I am sorry to say that I have never manifested anything like the activity or power for organisation displayed by my energetic daughter.

Soon Meresia became a good speaker. She had been coached by the Duke of Wellington who had summoned her after breakfast to his study in the presence of W. H. Mallock. She stammered and stuttered over a few hastily prepared notes and he simply ordered her not to speak as if she was saying her prayers. An oil painting depicting the Founding Ladies hung in Meresia's Executive Room in Victoria Street:

In bonnets and bustles posed in stiff clusters Duchesses and Countesses gravely hand papers to each other. In the foreground two solemn King Charles spaniels squat on richly flowered carpet at their feet forming a kind of pediment to the carpet. Sitting on the platform at the Albert Hall they look the apotheosis of the innumerable dames who sat on draughty village school platforms presiding over home-made entertainment.

After all this activity everyone retired to the country for August, Dorothy and her daughter to make their usual progresses: a tour of Rothschild houses, to Aston Clinton and Mentmore, then to Haddon and Bretby. She ended by Bayham and Eridge with 'polo, lawn tennis and cricket, and although these were not the fields of glory in which I care to dwell, yet the fine weather etc made it all very pleasant'. She returned home to Heathfield to hear of the death of 'her Duke'. Dorothy's friends wrote her letters of condolence just as if she had lost her own husband. Lord Lytton wrote:

And who will inherit the wit of your departed friend and preserve amongst us the features of the hero of Waterloo? . . . Oh dear, why do we grow old? It would be so much nicer to grow younger and die at last in the arms of the wetnurse in the bosom of innocence.

For twenty-three years [wrote Dorothy to Blanche] he had more or less been my constant companion and correspondent and I cannot yet realise that I shall never see his kind face again . . . he was always so happy here and joined us in all our innocent amusements and pleasures. It is all too sad.

Dorothy's life was dull, surrounded by women – 'Short women, tall women and all very tiresome,' she told Gosse. There was nothing to enliven her days except for 'one pleasant episode of a drunken housemaid'. She had her sister-in-law Cecilia staying. On Sundays Cecilia attended as many services as possible and expected Dorothy to go with her. Dorothy mistrusted those who developed an excessive zeal for churchgoing, but she complied, writing to a friend:

My dear, a church to Cecilia is like a public house to a drunkard. She simply cannot pass it. [And to another] We are here living in the odour of sanctity as my sister-in-law is here, very good in every sense of the word, and my old governess and her sister, and they never have yet come out of the Garden of Eden. I am bursting with goodness. It will be quite a relief to see or hear something to the contrary.

She was growing increasingly restless in the country. 'Oh, I am so longing for the fleshpots of dear, dirty old London,' she wrote to Gosse on 23 September signing her letter 'Your recluse D.N.' Then suddenly Tina, a favourite dog given her by the 'dear Duke' died, giving her something else to think about. She grieved to Lord Lytton:

She has just departed from this land of X questions and crooked answers – after living with us seven years. She was an idiot but a graceful one . . .

She now exercised herself composing inscriptions for tombstones; appealing to the luckless Lytton:

But I write to ask you who have written such charming poetry if you could ever write me 4 or 6 lines as an epitaph . . . I shall place it in everlasting remembrance of your goodness and dear Tina's qualities by inscribing it myself on a china tablet.

The Earl was nearly at a loss. He wrote to his friend the Revd Whitwell Elwin: 'The only words that occur to me are "Poor Bitch".'

By October Dorothy was nearly frantic. She wrote to Lytton on 7 October: 'Six weeks in unadulterated peace in East Sussex has done for me.' Her salon now was definitely her top priority.

Eleven

The Primrose League had gone to such strength that even a French Primrose League was started. Dorothy on one of her trips to Scotland was staying with the Glenesks in Aberdeenshire amid beautiful scenery and 'killing of all kinds':

We had indeed all sorts and conditions of men on this occasion at Invercauld which was just like a vast hotel with no trouble and nothing to pay. Madame Albani came over for 3 nights and sang beautifully. Queen Victoria came to tea, and Wolff the great vionist played.

Dorothy met here the Comte de Paris. He had conceived the idea that some organisation like the Primrose League might be formed to promote Orleanist influence in France and to combat atheism and the radicals. Dorothy talked to him about it and put him in touch with Meresia. Consequently the White Rose League was formed, its badge in the form of a gilt rose with all the same veneer as the Primrose League. The Countess nominated two lady superintendents – 'But France manifested little enthusiasm to breathe new life into Royalist circles,' recorded Dorothy.

By 1885 there were 11,000 members of the Primrose League and in 1886 100,000. Foreign affairs (Egypt in particular), the franchise, land and Home Rule were other controversial issues of the day. Dorothy knew as much about Home Rule as she did about the local labourers. She was Unionist to the core and regarded Home Rule as her father would have done. It might have been the French Revolution. So controversial was the subject that it produced deep rifts in families. The Duke of Marlborough was so astonished by his son Lord Randolph Churchill's view that he could only think he was drunk from all that claret and champagne. Dorothy's own views were verging on paranoia. She was terrified that separatism in Ireland would involve the splitting up of the Empire and what the Primrose League stood for. Being a Primrose Dame, at least in her case, did nothing to broaden the political outlook. When she went to Ireland, which she did frequently, all she ever saw was from the windows of the Viceregal Lodge and Dublin Castle where she had stayed as the guest of successive Viceroys, Governor Generals and Commanders of the Armed Forces, her friends. She did not see the battering rams, the evictions, the hunger, the poverty and the dying. In fact she knew many of the absentee landlords who were causing the misery; and she liked to think they were maligned. But occasionally from inside the Castle there were moments of reality. Once the beautiful Maud Gonne, the friend of Yeats, who devoted her life to the Irish National cause, came to dinner at Dublin Castle dressed in verdure. After dinner she stood up and much to the embarrassment of all sang 'The Wearing of the Green'. Dorothy found it all very distasteful and added she was never asked again.

Both parties were in disarray. The Liberals were still in power, and though defeat seemed likely, 'You see after all they are again doomed to disappointment,' wrote Chamberlain, 'and that the Randolph-Salisbury ministry is postponed for the present.' Chamberlain described his own Government as being

like Mr Pickwick's cabhorse of which the cabman says he was in the cab on account of his weakness; 'We bears him up werry light and takes him in werry short so as he can't werry well fall down.'

The Government, defeated on 8 June 1885, resigned. Lord Randolph Churchill was so excited he jumped on the green bench and stood there waving his hat round and round, cheering. No man had done more to weaken the Liberals in Parliament or to rouse the spirit of the Conservatives in the country. His claim to a place in the new Cabinet could not be ignored, and when the Ministry was formed it was seen that the concessions made by Lord Salisbury to the Leader of the Fourth Party were of the most substantial kind, one of which was official recognition of the Primrose League. Randolph's principal stipulation in accepting office was that Sir Stafford Northcote should retire to the House of Lords, and the Leadership of the House of Commons be transferred to Sir Michael Hicks Beach. So it was done. 'The Goat' was removed to the Upper House; Sir Michael was made

Chancellor of the Exchequer and Leader of the House, and 'The Dolphin' became Secretary of State for India.

In the election that followed land reform was part of the Liberal manifesto. Chamberlain's henchman, Jesse Collings, Mayor of Birmingham and a great friend of Dorothy, introduced a new slogan: 'Three acres and a cow'. Chamberlain was optimistic for the outcome and could not feel that the Primrose League would offer any threat. 'I saw the account of your meeting,' he scoffed at Dorothy on 17 August following reports of Primrose League festivities at Eridge:

The speeches seemed to me very dull and I hope that Olsilly the Juggler and the performing dogs made some amends. . . . I am concerned that I have been too moderate hitherto; I shall try and develop my view about the Aristocracy and the landowners. The revolution progresses, but it must be quickened a little before the General Election. I see that both Liberal and Tory candidates are advancing their bids. The last example is Sir R. Temple who began by telling the labourers that they had no right to the land and could do no good with it. They broke up his meetings and he now offers to compel their landlords to give them an acre apiece. The result is that they only carry amendments now and do not refuse to listen. Before long he will offer 3 acres to a cottage.

On 7 October he wrote to Dorothy again:

Routledge is just going to publish a volume of my speeches, so I shall send you a copy to put on your table and to irritate the ordinary company. By the way is Lady Maidstone a friend of yours, she is a charming specimen of the shrieking sisterhood to whom some idiots want to give votes.

I am glad that you are beginning to have confidence in my predictions, but it is rather late in the day. Remember that I told you a year ago that we should get the agricultural labourers who are not as stupid as you – who have lived among them all your life and who consequently know nothing about them – have supposed. We are going to sweep the country with my programme. The Salisbury Churchill combination will try to cut the ground from under us. But they are too late for this election and by the next one I will take care that we are as far ahead as ever.

Dorothy replied several days later:

Many grateful thanks for quite an historical souvenir which I hope may descend to generations not yet begotten. As for me I know full well the heinous crime I am committing yet I follow your criminal career with the deepest interest. I think you are overconfident about the Elections. Mrs

Grundy is furious about Disestablishment and nearly all the parsons are coming soon over, and in many places. Hodge don't see how he is to work for us and farm his acres. All the labourers near us in West Sussex want to have protection and will vote for the Tory – in East Sussex the same – they believe as my Bailiff tells me Land means ruin. We have E. Grinstead quite safe although you predicted its fall . . . I saw the Duchess of St Albans, who says Ireland is quite awful, and as to rent that is a thing of the past.

Chamberlain had completely misunderstood the strength of the Primrose League, to say nothing of Meresia's organisation. The Conservatives won. He wrote to Dorothy on 4 December:

The elections have been most interesting. They have not gone as I expected but they are not on the whole bad for us i.e. the Radicals. Six weeks ago I thought we were safe of a quiet majority but the latest information before the polling makes us doubt. The 'Cow' has done very well and could have done much better if the Whigs had not been such asses, and had not done their best to discredit this admirable cry. London was an awful disappointment to me . . . Meanwhile I am not at all anxious to have the Tories out, I like a weak Tory Government much better than a Whig one, and I will not lift a finger for a Ministry of the regulation Hartington Goschen sort with a sprinkling of Radicals who are expected to be filled with submissive gratitude.

Indeed Chamberlain was right; so weak it was that it hardly lasted two months. On 1 January 1886 Dorothy wrote to Lord Randolph:

What is to happen to us? Certainly your people do know how to keep silence – I hope it will be all for the best. The yokels in Dorsetshire and some parts of Norfolk are already beginning to smell a rat instead of the Cow . . . All the Prince of Wales' tenantry and labourers voted en masse for Arch.

In the event it was Jesse Collings who brought the new Government down with an amendment to obtain compulsory powers over land. Gladstone once more assumed the leadership and committed himself to Home Rule. Dorothy now referred to him as 'the arch villain', his followers as Gladstone's 'convicts'. Chamberlain was unhappy at the direction his party was taking,

not caring to lead a party so careless of the national interests as to sacrifice the unity of the Empire to the precipitate impatience of an old man careless of the future in which he can have no part . . . The party is going blindly to its ruin and everywhere there seems to be a want of courage and decision and principle, I shall win if I can; if I cannot I shall cultivate my garden.

Dorothy's friends looked at Chamberlain with interest and suspicion. It seemed for the moment that his garden would get him. Two months later he resigned. The Home Rule conspiracy resulted in splitting the Party. It also scattered the group of Radical Land Reformers which had gathered round the Agricultural Labourers' movement. Henceforth they were in opposing camps – Arch and his associates adhering to Gladstone, Collings and his associates to the Liberal Unionists. The effectiveness of both groups was destroyed. In Chamberlain's view it was altogether a pitiable spectacle, and he went off abroad on a two-month holiday: 'If the GOM is still alive when I return I shall go into a monastery,' he wrote to Dorothy.

After all that the Home Rule Bill was defeated. Lord Salisbury again became Prime Minister. Chamberlain wrote to Dorothy:

I see the Daily News says that Lord Randolph is to lead the House and heard yesterday that Hicks Beach says he was only put there to be a warming pan for My Lord. I believe in Lord Randolph. It is only the dodo lot of Tories who hate clever young men.

At last Lord Randolph had reached the number two position in the Government, becoming Chancellor of the Exchequer and Leader of the House. But his position went to his head and he became more difficult and arrogant than ever. At Hatfield he was so rude to his hostess, Lady Salisbury, that he had to apologise, and soon, believing he was indispensable, had a disagreement with Salisbury himself, and resigned, imagining that public opinion would sweep him back into office. He was utterly astonished when it failed to do so and Goschen was appointed Chancellor of the Exchequer. Lord Randolph's expression 'I forgot Goschen' is well known, but Walter Long, present in the Carlton Club where Lord Randolph was when he heard the news, told Dorothy the correct version: 'All great men make mistakes,' he had explained. 'Napoleon forgot Blücher, I forgot Goschen.' And in everyone's view it was very good for Lord Randolph. Dorothy reported to Lady Gregory that 'he was very low but she wishes he would resign every day, he is so gentle and pleasant'. Sir

Fitzjames Stephen gave Lord Randolph a great rating in her presence and he took it very well and said that if anyone had spoken to him like that before, he would never have resigned.

From the beginning of the Fifties it had become fashionable to go to the European watering places in August, the object being not so much pleasure as to restore energy after the wear and tear of the London season. It was said that in these places there was the greatest amount of calculating economy in the world, for early in the season a number of German Jews made it a practice to send one of their number with the symptoms of various diseases so that he might report back to his coreligionists the exact treatment of their case and thus save expense. In 1887 Dorothy set out for Carlsbad, 'laughing and sneezing a dozen rounds like a *mitrailleuse*'. Socially it was dull.

The place is full enough [she wrote to Chamberlain], but chiefly of Jews and Jewesses – the yellowest and longest nosed in Europe . . . Also Lady Augustus FitzClarence and her daughter – the latter a most formidable maid – with a fist, a nose, a chin and a will of the sternest.

She went on to Bad Homburg, which was more fun – 'Homburg, I am glad to say rather giggletrotty – but yet a few sober moments.' Here, as in London, there were coteries of Unionists and Home Rulers and opportunities for argument. Dorothy relished these holidays. She wrote again:

We are here enjoying lovely air; plain living and German romances. I read nothing else to try to improve my German. We have the Duke of Cambridge but he is much taken up with his love, Mrs Vyner . . . The Roseberys are here and the Spencers and Mr F. L. Gower, a happy family of Home Rulers. Sir A. Bolitho, Sir R. Knightley[1] etc. are the opposition.

We have had a most charming tour. We were ten days at Homburg, and I am ashamed to own I liked it very much. The World – The Flesh – really the Devil was left out – lots of friends – and yet life made so easy for they did not bother me. The P of Wales most amiable. We dined and had luncheon with him and he walked us home. He often spoke of you [Chamberlain] and said he would give me a red sheet to write to you. From Homburg we came on to this oasis amongst the glaciers and the chalets and a happy and primitive people – who have but little

---

[1] Sir Rainald Knightley, whose well-known weakness of unrestrained pride in his long pedigree prompted Sir William Harcourt's couplet:
'And Knightley to the listening Earth
Relates the history of his birth.'

government to tease them and no Ireland and no GOM to mar the even temper of their ways. They live among the glorious mountains and waterfalls such a peaceful life making their butter and cheese . . . We walk about seven miles every day – amongst the most lovely scenery stopping at times to take a draught of goat's milk.

The character of the gatherings now at Charles Street had altered, with Lord Randolph out of office, Chamberlain sent on a mission to Washington and Drummond Wolff posted to Tehran as ambassador – taking 'The Master' as secretary to deliver him from the fleshpots of Paris.

H. Wolff seemed to be doing very well in Persia [wrote Dorothy to Chamberlain], but the description of the whole system of Government seems deplorable and even the Persians themselves ask when the foreigners are coming to deliver them from their rulers; every office is to be bought – and their idea of medicine is swallowing a vellum sentence from the Koran – never was such a state of barbarism. They want some Birmingham administration.

No longer was there much political content at lunch. Other gimmicks had to be sought. Certainly the attitude towards money was becoming a reality. All values were beginning to be translated through economies and the American heiress was being viewed as a positive asset. Actresses, Jews and bankers were now accepted in the first circle – the Prince of Wales's Marlborough House Set, which was decidedly fast. Indeed Jews and bankers were the only people who could afford to entertain him. Conversation on the whole was more spontaneous but less witty and considerably less entertaining. So hostesses had to provide other sources of entertainment – singular specimens, a talking point for their guests. This was known as 'lionising'.

Even actresses were acceptable now. Horace had contributed to the excitement by marrying a star player, Annie Rowe, and had obligingly appended a mini-lion to his mother's table. Annie Rowe had the added glamour of being mentioned in the newspaper columns for her performances: 'It is an immense advantage when a lady has a Lady's part,' cooed the critics, praising her acting in Bulwer's *The Lady of Lyons* at the Olympic Theatre.

For tender and refined sentiment, for a certain nameless charm and grace, Mrs Horace Nevill's 'Lady of Lyons' was quite remarkable . . .

Indeed Mrs Horace Nevill was poorly supported all round which makes her success the more notable.

For Dorothy, her daughter-in-law opened up another world – the world of Henry Irving, the Beerbohms, Wyndhams and Trees. The theatre was far more sophisticated than the days when you risked being burnt alive in your seat. Now there was the Gaiety Theatre managed by the Bancrofts, and Irving's spectacular, rich world at the Lyceum. Dorothy had a box there which was beautifully illuminated with gas footlights throwing up a soft and mellow light. You expected to be received at the theatre as if you were in your own home; programme sellers wore parlourmaids' aprons. Dorothy would attend as many of Sir Henry's performances as possible: Richelieu, Louis XI, Charles I, Macbeth, Richard III, often asking him to dine with her afterwards. She loved particularly the first nights and the lavish parties afterwards, prepared by Gunter's and given on the set:

Everything most beautifully done while singers and musicians made the moments glide away swiftly. The stage on which they were set was highly illuminated, and the weird light emitted by the footlights produced a very strange and impressive effect, indeed the whole scene reminded me of some Eastern Festival such as might have been given in the now deserted Halls of Persepolis.

Her favourite performance was Ellen Terry impersonating Nance Oldfield, whom she watched over and over again – 'sliding off the sofa so gracefully as only she could do it'.

There was never a dull moment: visits to her rival, Lady Jeune, where one met Robert Browning and Lecky, Fitzjames Stephen, Whistler and Oscar Wilde; to Lowndes Square where it was rumoured that Lady Haliburton, renowned for delicious food, could even herself prepare a dinner without cooks; to Lady Rosslyn, mother of Daisy Brooke (soon to become one of the fastest members of the Marlborough House Set), and Lady Maud Warrender, who remembered being sat out of earshot far from Dorothy's risqué conversation. Then there were lunches at Raffaelovitch's, the fashionable restaurant, with Lady Gregory and Robert Browning, once at a table so crowded that Browning called out to Dorothy: 'You look like Napoleon on St Helena as if you wanted elbow room'; and he at once folded his arms and imitated the Emperor most absurdly. Everyone thought that very funny. There were garden parties at Holly Hill, home of the philanthropic Lady Burdett-Coutts and at the White Lodge[1] in Richmond Park, where the charming, impecunious and enormous Princess Mary Adelaide, Duchess of Teck, sister of the Duke of Cambridge and mother of Queen Mary, stumbled about dispensing hospitality she could ill afford. Dorothy was even invited to go round and gossip with their old invalid mother, Princess Augusta, a daughter-in-law of George III, who lay bedridden in St James's Palace – the more surprising since her niece, Queen Victoria, did not receive Dorothy at court.

Whenever Horace Orford was in London Dorothy paid him a daily visit. He lived in Cavendish Square in seclusion, surrounded by his books. In contrast to his early life, he liked nothing more than to be invited everywhere and to go nowhere. He was now protected from the world by Carlo, a formidable Italian butler, whom few people managed to get past (the Prince of Wales was one). Once when some ancient kinswomen had called and were told his lordship was out, Carlo allowed the ladies to enter the hall and write a note. Just at this moment Lord Orford appeared at the top of the stairs shaking his fist at Carlo, who bellowed in Italian: 'Take care, Milor', the hags are still here and writing.' Happily his dislike for his relations did not extend to Dorothy and together they would sit reading from Horace Walpole's letters and the classics. Meanwhile his wife from whom he had been separated for nearly forty years led Florentine society. She was an eccentric lady dressing in the style of the Fifties, alternating cigarettes of caporal tobacco, which she rolled herself, with long, rank cigars in the evening. Her hair had turned a reddish grey, very thick with age, and dripping white patches of flour which she used as protection against the Italian sun. Thus attired she would drive about Florence in an old shandrydan 'with all the stuffing showing through the cushions and foxes wobbling at the horses' ears to keep off the flies'. She would entertain the intelligentsia on Sunday nights and get very drunk, suffering attacks of delirium tremens and lavishing money on anyone who excited her pity. Lord Orford and Dorothy would discuss how to prevent the passionate spending. Ouida reported:

[1] Dorothy had helped create the gardens.

Wolterton Hall

Mannington Hall

Dorothy, aged twenty, by Richard Buckner

Horatio, 4th Earl of Orford,
Dorothy's brother

Harriet Walpole
with her daughter Dorothy

A page from one of Dorothy's albums

Dorothy

Reginald Nevill, aged five, Eridge Castle in the background

'The Tory Bloodhound' (seated, with stick) in front of the Eridge cricket pavilion
Standing, sixth from left, the author's grandfather, 4th Marquess of Abergavenny

Dorothy with her three eldest children, c. 1858

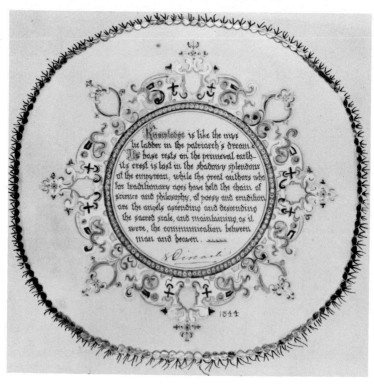

Disraeli's favourite speech, worked by Dorothy

Dangstein

Dorothy in her Charles Street drawing room

Edward Cazalet and Dorothy at Fairlawne, 1911

Shooting party including Horace Nevill (bearded, kneeling)
and his wife (hand on his shoulder), the actress Annie Rowe

Poor Lady Orford is in a terrible state. Worse than I know. A lady related to her found her and her house in indescribable filth, while the man Cesare makes her bed, her broth and her medicine. The trustees found £10,000 spent for which she will give no answer and there is no remedy unless Lady Dorothy will consent to declare her incapable – *non compos mentis* in fact.

Mercifully Lady Orford decided the issue, dying in 1886.

Certainly Lord Orford was just as eccentric as his wife. Feeling himself cheated in his father's will, he had sold Ilsington, angrily closed up Wolterton, having removed all the contents, and chosen to reside most of the time at Mannington, the smaller medieval moated manor house next door to Wolterton. On his inheritance Horace had prepared a most extraordinary tomb for himself in the nave of the ruined church, open to the sky, in the sacred grove at Mannington, engraving on it a glum Latin inscription. Being of unusually cynical mind he thought that nobody else would bother to remember him. For forty years he used to visit his own tomb and Dorothy reported in *Mannington and the Walpoles* that he was once nearly struck down in it when an old family retainer accosted him there, demanding money and brandishing a pistol. He remembered, too, the loves of his life. He erected a pillar to his mother – 'Matri Dulcissima Horatius Filius'; and another to the young Catholic princess whom religion forbade him to marry and who had died young. Now he was rather lonely. His two married daughters lived abroad, brought up almost as Italians, having married Italian grandees and dukes; so his only company was occasionally his natural son, Colonel Walpole of Heckfield Place, and his housekeeper who were nearly driven insane by his reading to them continually in Latin. His routine otherwise included a weekly visit to Aylsham in a closed carriage to see his doctor, followed by a game of whist which he expected the doctor to play. He loved exercising his decorating tastes, pilfering rare old panelling from Norfolk farmhouses and churches to adorn his house. He had even indulged his classical fantasies on the masonry, gloomily inscribing 'Morituro Satis', which Dorothy translated as 'This house is big enough for one who has not long to live'. The eccentricities even extended over the entrance door where there was a nasty testimonial to his wife and Lady Lincoln:

> What is worse than a tigress? A demon.
> What is worse than a demon? A woman.
> What is worse than a woman? Nothing.

Yet there is nothing to suggest that he gave up sex. On the contrary, his will suggests that he practically exercised the *droit de seigneur*, leaving money to housekeepers and to women with children about the Norfolk villages. Not surprisingly he was now known as the Mad Earl, not least because he became – horror of horrors for a Walpole – both a Jacobite and a Catholic, a conversion quite in keeping. However, toasting the King across the water was one thing; entertaining the Prince of Wales quite another. The Prince often went to see the old libertine and sometimes coincided with Dorothy there. She nicknamed him 'J' – for Jupiter – and her forthrightness and odd behaviour interested him. Soon she received invitations to Marlborough House and Sandringham, which were, unfortunately, commands. One could not refuse: 'I am sure I always feel as my scullery maid does in my presence,' wrote Dorothy to Gosse. Yet 'basking in the sunshine of royalty', as she liked to put it, suited her very well. She felt quite at home talking about dogs with the Princess of Wales or eating oysters with her knife. The Prince of Wales sent off to Dorothy a parcel of oyster knives with a note: 'In memory of your criminal tendencies.' Every August he provided her with grouse which she countered with a clutch of pheasant eggs, a most extraordinary present for one whose shoot was the best in England. Yet the Prince always replied, thanking her gracefully. Once he wrote to her on paper and envelope embossed with red devils. Dorothy often met him at the watering holes and pursued him all over the world with little misspelled missives: 'I directed the letter to him Marienbad, Deutschland, and he says he must send me a map of Europe that I may learn geography,' she wrote to a friend. (Indeed even Dorothy's local geography was at fault. No matter how many times she was told she always addressed the Duchess of Teck's letters to the White Lodge, Hampton Court instead of Richmond Park.)

Charles Street was one of the Prince's favourite venues for lunch. A typical party invited to meet him would be the Brookes (Lady Brooke – Daisy – was his future mistress), Bram Stoker (author of *Dracula*), Baron Hirsch, a Jewish friend of the Prince's,

Henry Irving and the ravishing Ellen Terry. Yet Dorothy was by no means sycophantic where royalty was concerned. She once asked the Prince to stay on after lunch and warned him that he was not fit to be a King; that, rightly or wrongly, his conduct was giving him a bad reputation in the country. Her beanfeasts, moreover, did not always proceed as planned; the servants tended to play up. She told Lady Gregory:

These wretched servants! I ordered what he [the Prince of Wales] was sure to like, boiled beef and chicken and bacon and beans, but I told them to bring up the bacon and chicken together, and they thought they knew best and brought the beef first and he said, 'No, I am going to have chicken,' and he had to wait until it came. Then he always liked bacon and beans that I ordered for him, though of course there are only flageolets to be had now, but he liked them on separate dishes, and that wretched cook squashed them on the same dish.

It was not everyone who enjoyed her parties. There were some people who thought them dull. They thought that, too, of the hostess. Vernon Lee[1] wrote of one gathering:

John Morley was naturally *accaparé* by Lady Ponsonby, so I talked with Lady Dorothy, Pater and Lady Airlie, who didn't interest me much. These women have, whatever they are, a charm of ease of manner.

As for Meresia, she appeared to Vernon Lee 'crop-headed and frumpy, all black and quivering with political fervour'. Another time Dorothy promised her 'to get her stupid Duchess' if Vernon Lee would bring along Cotter Morison, the writer and chief of the Positivist Circle. For Dorothy it was fruitful trading. Vernon Lee did bring Cotter Morison, and – though he lived only until 1888 – he became a great friend and introduced Dorothy to other Positivist thinkers, such as Frederic Harrison. But sometimes her lionising was less successful, and once brought a stinging rebuke from G. F. Watts. She had invited him to lunch to meet the specimen of the day – a famous beauty.

Many thousand thanks. I am pleased to meet remarkable people especially those from whom I can profit; and I delight in beauty but I have little interest in those who become famous through accident. The

[1] Pseudonym for Violet Paget (1856–1935), authoress. 'Vernon Lee was by far the eleverest person I ever met,' wrote Maurice Baring. 'Her culture was shot with imagination.'

amusement you so kindly offer me in this case would be in the indulgence of curiosity, not a nice feeling to be encouraged towards anyone who wears a crinolette, so please give me another opportunity of so pleasurably paying my respects to you.

Dorothy's method of entertaining did not change over a lifetime. The more horrifying the topic the more she enjoyed it. As she grew older she grew more outrageous. She entertained such notorious characters as Oscar Wilde[1] and Frank Harris.[2] She even tried to get Verlaine, the most decadent of the French symbolist writers and a homosexual. When he was in London to lecture in 1894 Dorothy was insistent that Gosse should bring him to visit her. She said – 'I think,' wrote Gosse, 'under some illusion' – 'Verlaine is one of my pet poets; though not of this world.' Gosse was obliged to tell her that neither Verlaine's clothes, nor his person, nor his habits admitted of his being presented in Mayfair, and that indeed it was difficult to find a little French eating-house in Soho where he could be at home. She then said, 'Why can't you take me to see him in *this* eating-house', meaning that Gosse should bring him to Charles Street. Gosse had to explain to her that 'of the alternatives that was really the least possible'. Dorothy was furious.

You can detect strains of the sensational even in her philanthropy. She had always been interested in freaks of nature such as General Tom Thumb, the Dwarf, and members of Mr Farini's circus in the Westminster Aquarium. Every week she would trot off to the London Hospital in Whitechapel, one of the most densely populated parts of London. She travelled there in whatever third-class conveyance was available, chatting with the conductors and passengers, quizzing them as to their lives and salaries. Then she would bustle into the office of the formidable matron, Miss Luckes, who found her a great source of strength. Twenty years later, on Dorothy's death, she wrote the following letter:

Her welcome visits have been a joy to me and her welcome insight and quick understanding sympathy. She has so often left me feeling quite brightened up by just coming in touch with her personality.

[1] Robbie Ross wrote on 7 April 1894: 'Oscar was just in the mood that I like him – very 1880 and withal brimful of intellectual themes and anecdotes of dear Lady Dorothy Nevill.'
[2] Lady Warwick claimed that it was the Prince of Wales who first introduced her to Harris at 45 Charles Street – a meeting that ended in blackmail.

There is no doubt she made people happier and better. In the portrait of Dorothy that he wrote after her death, Gosse describes in detail her visits to the London Hospital, going round the wards, entertaining the nurses and patients, 'the poor dear things' as she called them, comforting the latter and making everyone laugh, capping their troubles, obliterating them with her own horrifying tales so that momentarily pain was forgotten – 'Oh, that's nothing to what a friend of mine had to suffer.' The sick poor in those days would endure almost any pain before going into hospital: 'I know exactly how they feel,' quipped Dorothy, 'I'm afraid of Miss Luckes.' According to Gosse, her favourite patient was the Elephant Man, John Merrick; of whom his surgeon, Sir Frederick Treves wrote:

The most disgusting specimen of humanity I have ever seen in the course of my profession . . . At no time had I met with such a degraded or perverted version of a human being as this lone figure displayed.

Merrick had a face like a heavy trunk and skin resembling hide, which smelt quite ghastly. He was not allowed a looking-glass in his room. Covered all over with cauliflower-like protuberances, his appearance was so horrible that when he walked out he had a travelling cloak with special slits in it specially designed to cover him completely. He was extremely fastidious and his favourite article was a toilet set given to him by Treves, who carefully removed the mirror. Dorothy gave him a silver watch which he loved. She offered to take him away for a holiday and lend him a cottage at Stillians but there was a proviso: Merrick was not to leave the house until after nightfall. It never happened because poor Merrick died. It seems that Dorothy was no less a strength to him than to everyone else. In his last testament he thanked her for all her kindness.

Soon, however, her entertainments resumed their political content. Chamberlain returned from Washington in 1888, having successfully negotiated the Bayard-Chamberlain Treaty, the disputed fishing boundaries between Canada and regulating the United States. Now fifty-six and twice a widower, he brought with him an American bride of eighteen. He wrote to Dorothy:

One of those Americans whose importation into this country you once deprecated so strongly in my hearing. You said 'I like Americans very well but there are two things I wish they would keep to themselves. Their girls and their tinned lobster.' I am prepared to give up the lobster so you must be prepared to give up the girl.

He need not have worried. Everyone liked Miss Endicott: 'The new Mrs Chamberlain is really very charming, very pretty and very ladylike, and no American accent or idiom,' wrote Lord Lytton to Dorothy in a tone of surprise. Dorothy welcomed them home, warning Chamberlain that Lord Randolph needed his protection: 'The Dodos have given him up.' Lord Randolph's ideas had always attracted Chamberlain and two years previously, when Lord Randolph had resigned, they had considered the idea of forming a new National Party together. It had come to nothing largely because Churchill was so difficult. Now the time was again taken up with political overtures which were in the end only unprofitable. Dorothy wrote from Bad Homburg in August 1889:

At the risk of losing your friendship forever I really must write to ask what is the result of Lord R.C. in Birmingham.

Chamberlain replied:

He seems to have irritated our 'Dodos' more than ever and yet cannot make out how it has all ended . . . The result is a fiasco – he offended everyone including some of his warmest supporters, and only succeeded in delighting the Gladstonians. If he were to stand now against Bright he would get a well-deserved licking.

Drummond Wolff and Ralph had also returned to London, bringing the Shah with them, much to the consternation of Salisbury. What is more, 'The Master' organised many of the festivities. His mother was delighted: a good state visit was just what she liked. She enjoyed it all much more than the court for whom the entertainment was provided: the Empire Theatre; the gala night at the opera; the reception at the Persian Embassy where the Shah, splendidly dressed, received the guests serenaded by the band of the Coldstream. There were visits, too, to some of the new industrial developments. The Persian court were bored at Buckingham Palace. One courtier was nearly impaled on the railings trying to escape, and the Shah was so out of temper he is supposed to have had his masseur executed and buried at dead of night in the Palace gardens. The Persians were absolutely uninterested in the commercial elements of the country and thought only about their *placement* at dinner, especially at Hatfield, the finale of the visit, where Lord Salisbury entertained the whole entourage, including the Shah's disgusting mascot, an ugly little Persian boy with the rank of a general who had once saved his life. Dorothy, sitting near the Shah, watched the little horror plunge his hands into his neighbours' plates to extract morsels more succulent than on his own; while the Shah, taking no notice of Dorothy, took off his spectacles to wipe and then peer at especially obese ladies. He was not at all impressed by the English ladies. He was astonished that they treated their husbands like butlers.

Twelve

For Dorothy the Nineties saw the same routine: the lunch parties, canvassing and racing across the country with unabated energy, resisting Irish Home Rule from the Eridge Habitation with speeches and nigger minstrels. Chamberlain found it impossible to follow her runs.

I have been unable to answer your letters [he wrote to her]. I am very glad to find that although like a certain scriptural personage you have been wandering to and fro upon the earth you are no worse for all this travelling . . . How you manage it I cannot understand for I am sure that I should be bored to death if I had to leave my own fireside so often.

Dorothy, now over seventy, was indeed not letting up. She replied to Chamberlain:

I have been in most of the counties since we met and am more settled down here to pass that most dreadful time Xmas. Guided by you this Conservative Government is indeed going on – they perform while the next government only promise. Where are we to end? I have had consolation however – in seeing the progressives ousted at the School Board. Let us pray we may do equally well with the county councils – and then save the remnants of what has been left us.

Dorothy was persecuted by horrors of change. All her worst fears were coming true. Gladstone near the end of his life wanted power again and was determined to precipitate Home Rule through, whatever the cost. Dorothy had thought it had all been merely talk before. Once, seeing three names – Gladstone, the Duke of Argyll and Bright – in the Duke of Sutherland's visitors' book, she commented while signing her own name: 'I see, just GAB.' Now all this prattle had become a terrible threat to the Empire and to herself. Her interest in politics was her own self-interest, and 1892 was election year. The Irish camp, split by the nasty revelations during the Parnell[1] divorce case of 1890 had now divided into two, the Parnellites supporting the Conservative leadership, the anti-Parnellites adhering to Gladstone. Gone were the days when Chamberlain debating the choice between suffragettes or Home Rulers in the House had remarked: 'Of the two I prefer Parnellites to petticoats.' Now the Parnellites were on his side. He wrote to Dorothy:

The Anti-Parnellites have had a nasty blow at Waterford. What is of real importance is not the election but its effect on the spirit of the Parnellites who will be encouraged to keep up the fight. I wish them more power to their elbows.

Meanwhile Meresia, shaking as much now with St Vitus's Dance as political excitement, was frantically canvassing for the Unionists, in particular for Mr Graham in St Pancras, gliding swiftly round in a very smart blue and white dog cart fitted with new rubber wheels, her groom up behind, approaching so unexpectedly silently that she scattered the astonished pedestrians. Like Boadicea she led an army, but hers was even more extraordinary than the Warrior Queen's. Rubber tyres spinning, the Primrose Dames balanced on safety bicycles – Royal Sunbeams and Sea Skirmishers; dressed in blue and yellow facings, ribbons flying from their hair, with straw hats and woollen underwear, their long skirts falling clear of the pedals, they weaved between the horse-drawn traffic in pursuit of recalcitrant voters. There was even a book of rules for this regiment – the Primrose League Cycling Corps.

But then there was a sinister intervention. First, Meresia's little dog was killed in Berkeley Square, picked up, shaken and deposited on the ground by a large hound. Then the pony that pulled the silent chariot was struck down paralysed in its stable. Everything else began to go wrong: Horace Nevill's most important clients died; his stockbroking partnership broke down; the family income dropped. Suspicion fell on a beautiful small Buddha which lay on a red velvet cushion. It had been a gift to Dorothy. Could it be that it was the source of ill-fortune? Dorothy, not generally superstitious, was uneasy. She tried to

[1] Parnell had been cited by Captain O'Shea, M.P. for Clare, in a petition for divorce from his wife Kitty in December 1889. Parnell did not repudiate the charges and married Mrs O'Shea.

placate the god, offering it lotus leaves. The disasters continued. An enormous chimney collapsed onto Dorothy's house, destroying her water tanks and ripping away the whole bathroom. What was she to do? The last thing she wanted was to hand the inauspicious object to a friend, so she donated it to a museum, where she was appalled to hear it continued to wreak havoc. The employees went on strike, workmen fell off the roof. To crown it all the Conservatives were defeated by a combination of Liberals and Nationalists and a majority for Home Rule given to Gladstone. The Liberal Unionists suffered worst of all. In London the only successful candidate was Mr Graham; and he put it all down to Meresia's indefatigable work. They were exhausted from the campaign and horrified. Not only was a mandate given for Home Rule, but Keir Hardie, the Socialist, was elected Independent Member for South West Ham. He soon formed an Independent Working Class Party with himself as chairman and scandalised Parliament by indecorously making his entry dressed in cloth cap and tweeds.

Dorothy and Meresia decided on temporary escape. They hurried abroad, going to stay with the singular Mr Graham in Heidelberg surrounded by fruit trees. The spot seems to have been haunted (just what Dorothy needed after the little statue); they heard heavy footsteps and breathing, saw blazing lights where nobody was. Otherwise Dorothy had a marvellous time, with ample opportunity for airing her views, and plenty of beer-drinking, mingling with the students and getting *au courant* with them. This rakish student life was not for Meresia, who as usual more staid than her mother, and teetotal, steered her away to Bad Homburg where Oscar Wilde was to be heard as well as seen. There were other excitements: a vulgar group of Americans 'with a great deal of nasal twang about them, very different from my American pets', as she wrote to the Chamberlains; and the Duke of Cambridge with ghastly rumours about the new government – Home Rulers and Antis arguing more than ever. The whole Empire was at stake now, with the Arch Villain, nearly eighty- four, Prime Minister for the fourth time. He had procured young, new 'convicts' of promise for his ministry: Asquith, Acland and Edward Grey. 'Oh,' Dorothy wailed at Chamberlain,

Would we could dismember you and divide your body more equally over those dreadful counties who in their ignorance and blindness have chosen such horrors to govern them! . . . What will be the end of it all? I already see Keir Hardie ordering Citoyenne Nevill for execution . . . drawn to execution to the tune of the Marseillaise. The Duke of Cambridge is here in a terrible state over forthcoming events in all probability thinking he will accompany me to the scaffold.

To this Chamberlain replied that at least when she did go to the scaffold – 'Or would it be the Dynamo?' – she would be a credit to the British aristocracy.

On their return to England things began to look up. Dorothy sat next to Mr Gladstone at dinner. Dreadful as it seemed, he rather reassured her:

His versatility quite wonderful: I begin to think we might have worse than this government, for they are not at all what the ultra Rads want and if these people go – there will be an immense effort to get in still greater horrors.

Now even Home Rule was defeated and Gladstone retired from public life, 'his hands fixed in the cleft of the tree he had tried to split' like Milon of Creton.

But there was darkness yet again. Horace was ailing at Mannington. Red-letter days were his sister's visits. Dorothy had read Dr Jessup's book on her family, *One Generation of a Norfolk House*, and now, as usual self-interested, she used the time for researching what was to be her first book, *Mannington and the Walpoles*. In fact she had aspired to literature once before with her cousin, Henry Drummònd Wolff, proposing a book about their ancestress, Nance Oldfield, helped by Henry Irving and Ellen Terry. They sent her all the material they had as well as a slim volume on Nance Oldfield that Miss Terry possessed, but the project was finally abandoned owing to the sparsity of material and the hostility of some descendants. Prejudice against the theatre showed itself still: one granddaughter tracked down by Dorothy replied to her questionnaire that she knew nothing and cared even less about 'that despicable woman'. Dorothy, however, was undaunted and she now tracked down all the curiosities relating to Mannington, commissioning photographic plates, failing only to unearth the ghost, which in her view was the butler rifling the drink cupboard and not, as Dr Jessup had

claimed, the recusant Hugh Walpole who had resided at Mannington in the sixteenth century and ended up hung in chains for
his beliefs. But although she researched it all most capably she
complained that she lacked the ready flow of the writer's pen:
'Alas old Horace Walpole's talent has not descended to me,' she
wrote to Edmund Gosse. Now, just before the publication of
Mannington and the Walpoles, the costs of which she paid
herself, the dreadful White Lady of Wolterton was seen flitting
around the deserted grounds. 'It is either you or I this time, Dolly,
for we are the only ones left,' wrote Horace Orford to his sister. It
was for Horace that the White Lady had come. He died on 7
December 1894.

Dorothy, heartbroken to lose the last link with her childhood,
at least had the excitement over her book to distract her. She
posted off endless copies, even dispatching one to the very old
Gladstone, remembering his interest in her family. Some of her
friends were delighted, urging her to further forays into print.
'What about a book on Old Iron?' suggested Lord Wolseley.
Dorothy apparently took his advice, producing a slim volume
about her leg irons, spuds, fireguards and falconets – and other
rubbishy instruments. All the obsolete material she eventually
gave as a collection to the Victoria and Albert Museum.

Meanwhile her financial affairs were worrying, probably not
helped by the expense of her publications. 'All I am alive to is that
my money resources are more than gradually dwindling away for
the good of others,' she complained selfishly to Chamberlain.
Income tax was now 1s. 6d. in the pound, but even such a small
tariff terrified the aristocracy. Dorothy would never have
dreamed of stopping her lunch parties, or of abdicating her
position. So she gave up Stillians, the donkeys, the ponies, the
axolotls. There were no more experiments with consignments of
bizarre fish species to astonish the Sussex fishermen. Yet she still
felt the need for a country retreat, 'a green spot' in her life. For
once she tried to be practical; it must be something easy to
maintain. She found Tudor Cottage at Haslemere, conveniently
near Teddy and Edith who lived in the beautiful rectory at
Trotton, which the Nevills had not sold along with Dangstein.
But yet again Dorothy could leave nothing alone. She had to
infiltrate the fashionable Gothic into the interior, part of which

consisted of a tannery. She did manage, however, to keep the garden simple. There were tulips, hyacinths, daffodils and roses in their season for Dorothy 'to adore'. She would stay a few days relaxing in the hopelessly cluttered rooms preparing her scrapbooks and sorting out old letters: 'Dear kind ones from you,' she wrote to Blanche Airlie, 'otherwise too many heart breaking records of affectionate old friends.' Sometimes she would drive over to Sutton Place to visit her new friends, the Harmsworths, press magnates: 'I like Mr and Mrs Harmsworth very much,' she wrote. 'They have no wish to get on and never seek society – immensely rich and I am told so good and kind to poorer friends.' Then she would go to Trotton where there was great excitement as they were having the frescoes restored. Dorothy had always believed there remained wonderful paintings under the whitewash that had plastered the nave since Cromwell's day. Bit by bit they were uncovered, *The Tree of Jesse* and others. She reported:

Dear St Hubert of the time by his shoes of Richard II, his poor head has never been put on, the supposition is that the artist died of the plague before finishing it. It is all most curious, and I often think of the dear old P. Church, and my old friends the Crusaders.

The neighbours loved her and her Rabelaisian humour.

The pattern of her life was as always. After Christmas, the season she hated as it broke up her parties and which she always spent in the country, she would cover the dusty old clutter with sheets and visit the Glenesks' villa, the Château St Michel high above Cannes. Once, the Empress Eugénie came over to tea accompanied by her devoted secretary, M. Pietri, who had never left her side since the flight from the Tuileries. Afterwards they walked together in the hills, Dorothy admiring the Empress, so strong, alert and dignified; interested in everything although a little deaf; with remains of great beauty.

This is not an intellectual place [Dorothy wrote], but then the body rejoices in the cooking . . . Spring advancing every hour bursting with the colours to come, the lizards stalking through the grasses, insects darting, birds swooping and concerts of humming bees and barking frogs.

On her way back Dorothy would revisit favourite places: Bruges, staying at the little Hospital of St Jean with its Memlings and a cultured polished priesthood; then Versailles and the Trianons, where she meandered, recovering the spirit of the eighteenth century and her heroine, Marie Antoinette. But Paris itself was another matter. Dorothy could never quite forgive the French their cruelty, ever remembering David's last sketch of Marie Antoinette, drawn from the crowd as she passed by on the way to the guillotine. The wantonness of the French always distressed her. She wrote to Blanche Airlie:

I spent a charming day at St Cloud and St Germain, but I don't care for Paris for long – and all the shop windows were too immoral, nothing but ladies in their birthday suits, Danaes, Ledas etc. They [the French] are so engrained and inbornly immoral they think nothing of anything in the natural history line – and their papers are full of the most irreligious sayings – it is quite awful.

Thirteen

During the next fifteen years all Dorothy's traditional tenets were to be destroyed. First to go was the Primrose League, useful from then on only as a fund-raising body. The Boer War which broke out in 1899 was instrumental in its suppression. The League's motto, 'To support an Empire built on Liberty', seemed to be contradicted, together with the very concept of Dominion that the Habitations had avowed. Now it seemed to Dorothy that the Empire was like a house of cards that might topple at any time. What would happen to England if the European nations decided to attack? With troops far away in South Africa, there seemed not to be a man left to defend her. To a generation who knew nothing of war the campaign seemed at first thrilling, but the excitement soon wore off as it dragged on shamefully and expensively. Poor Lord Wolseley, who had supplanted the Duke of Cambridge as Commander-in-Chief in 1895, took the brunt of it all. He wrote to Dorothy, who was his chief support:

It is not physical labour that wears me out. I delight in being bodily tired but I am worn out by the opposition of a lot of d——d fools who meddle in matters without the least knowledge of war because they have the power to do so.

Needless to say, the kitchens at Charles Street began to work at full steam. Over the Sunday lunches upstairs Dorothy was airing her views to Chamberlain, now Secretary of State for the Colonies. He had in fact precipitated the war. 'Ah, if only Lord Salisbury had taken up the matter instead of J.C.,' wrote Frederic Harrison to Dorothy. 'We are all sorry for him. It will kill the Queen.' Dorothy warned Chamberlain that the country, disillusioned, would expect changes.

The very foundation of her belief was shaken when the power of the House of Lords was curtailed. Dorothy referred to it as 'the

Lord's House' as if it were some sort of sacred conventicle. For centuries its constitution had hardly changed and since George III's time it had been an exclusively Tory stronghold, a bastion against progress and reform. The Conservative Party was now in a terrible mess. Lord Salisbury had died in 1902, leaving the premiership to his nephew, Balfour. Frederic Harrison wrote to Dorothy:

They are a set of incapable lah-di-dah swells who being very well done in their own homes and having everything man can want – are playing at Government in a lazy insolent way, doing jobs, and airing their contempt for the common people.

By December 1905 they were out. In the election that ensued there was a landslide victory for the Liberals. Following the strenuous campaign, Chamberlain, the only Conservative to inspire confidence, suffered a stroke which effectively cut him off from public life. Asquith became Prime Minister in 1908, inviting inauspicious young 'convicts' for ministers. Whenever they brought in an important bill the House of Lords either rejected it or amended it out of all recognition. It seemed to Dorothy that the relationship between landowning peers and their tenants had ceased to exist. In many cases the absentee landlord had replaced the aristocrat who knew his estates and cared for his tenants. No longer was the House of Lords representative of the people: 'The country no longer cares for peers except to open bazaars and act as M.F.H.s,' moaned old Lord Ribblesdale.

In 1909 the House of Lords threw out Lloyd George's Budget. There was uproar: 'The Budget will pass whatever the Lords say or do,' wrote Dorothy. She had heard through Palace sources that the King might be forced to swamp the Lords with new peers if the Lords refused to come to their senses, and was prepared to do so. 'Down with old Peers,' she wrote, 'up with new ones, we accept our fate with patience and serenity.' She went to all the parliamentary debates, horrified by the coming indignity. At dinner with Haldane, the Secretary for War, Dorothy attacked her host over the Budget, foretelling the disappearance of the great country houses. 'As to that I feel she is probably right,' commented Marie Belloc Lowndes. Then she began denouncing Winston Churchill, adding that all the dogs in South Africa were now called Winston. But she regarded Lloyd George as the arch-criminal with his predatory policies. Early in 1910 Edward Cazalet lunched with Dorothy in Brighton. The company agreed with Dorothy that revolution was coming. She attributed it entirely to 'that beastly Lloyd George who ought to be shot a hundred times. He says he hopes there won't be a rich man left in England. What a terror he is.' The Duchess of St Albans[1] remarked that if this came to pass it would be Dorothy's head which would be the first stuck to a lamp-post.

What the Lords had reckoned without was the publication of Lady Cardigan's memoirs, calling in question Victorian behaviour and morality. Dorothy wrote to Blanche Airlie:

No one but the Lords in London and the Budget are quite overlooked in this horrid book of Lady Cardigan's. She only attacks the poor dead who have no one to protect them. At present she leaves us alone. What people are afraid of is that when the election comes these radical demons will cut pieces out just to show what the Upper Classes are!

Lady Cardigan made the most outrageous claims: for instance, that same dreadful Lord Ward, whom Dorothy had known in Florence, had forced his wife to pose naked on a black leather sofa bedecked with the family jewels. When Lady Ward died he had invited a friend to observe the body and had forced open the mouth to show the decaying teeth of the lovely corpse. The memoirs reported, too, that the very thin Maria Marchioness of Ailesbury had been fought over by her husband and Lord Wilton 'like dogs over a bone'; also that she had had an illegitimate family. 'Possibly the authoress got confused over similar incidents nearer home,' Dorothy suggested. The memoirs were actually banned in the Eton bookshop, Edward Cazalet tells us. She remembered Lady Cardigan in her youth dancing the cachuca with great verve —'Indeed from the vivacity displayed she very likely dances it still.'

Lady Cardigan was not the only one to rock the boat. Many of Dorothy's friends were doing extraordinary things. A group of Society ladies had acted in a ballet; Daisy Warwick, famous for her extravagance, had become a Socialist. Dorothy thought she had gone mad. Here was a countess, a member of her own class,

[1] Second wife of the tenth Duke. Daughter of Dorothy's friend Bernal Osborne.

preaching to her the benefits of a Socialist state. She had written to Dorothy from Amsterdam in 1903:

I wonder what you are doing and what is interesting you just now? I am having a wonderful time here at the International Congress of Socialists and have learnt very, very much . . . Right or wrong it is the one religion that unites the human race all over the world in the common cause of humanity, and it is very, very wonderful, and it is *growing* as mushrooms grow, and nothing can stem the tide!

For Dorothy at any rate the circumstances were considerably brightened by the death of Queen Victoria. After fifty-five years' ostracism she was once again accepted at court. Her first invitation from King Edward was to spend the week at Windsor: oysters, bands playing on the lawns, the arrival of the French President. Old age certainly did not stop Dorothy enjoying herself. Her worst plight seemed to be that she could not entertain at home and eat lunch at three other houses on the same day: 'People are tugging me to go and see things,' she complained to Gosse, not because she was reluctant to leave her house, but because she wanted to be everywhere: 'Such a nuisance one can't be in two places at once . . . I am hampered by perpetual outbursts of hospitality in every shape.' When Gosse congratulated her on her presence at a state funeral she replied: 'Yes, but I lost another most interesting ceremony by it being at the same hour.' Life was a treadmill of friendship, 'perpetually on the go'.

Her thoughts turned now to more serious pastimes: her memoirs. The task seemed almost beyond her, but as always in her life someone was ready to come to the rescue. 'The Master' was her literary saviour. He helped Dorothy arrange chronologically her memories and the contents of her cupboards. Without his help she never could have accomplished her *Reminiscences*, which took two years to prepare and which in 1905 were received ecstatically. 'The Press has been wonderfully good to my little efforts and to Ralph the better part is due,' she told Blanche Airlie. She made a book of congratulations received from famous people. Three other works followed over the next seven years. Only one newspaper criticised her severely, recommending her to go and eat blue beans.

A friendship of a singular nature was to enliven her last years. The meeting was not on an auspicious occasion. Against the advice of the head of the family Dorothy had attended Winston Churchill's wedding to Clementine Hozier, Blanche Airlie's granddaughter. Like Chamberlain twenty years before, he was considered the scourge of his generation. It was considered that he had let down his class. Lord Abergavenny wrote:

I trust you did not lower yourself by attending such a foolish function. I understand that the bride is charming, but surely no one in such a high position would have allowed herself to become the laughing stock of the world. As for the bridegroom . . . Who is he? A man detested in society, a man with scarcely a friend . . . Lord knows what a man to marry, I pity her.

Of course Dorothy had had to go, as much out of curiosity as to support her friend's granddaughter, even though she loathed the idea of Winston. However, it was a fruitful venture, bringing her the last great happiness in her life, her meeting with Edward Cazalet, a precocious fourteen-year-old schoolboy. Except that Edward hated politics as much as Dorothy disliked music, they seemed made to measure for each other: 'I asked her if she had seen Electra, the opera by Richard Strauss,' wrote Edward in his diary; to which Dorothy replied: 'No, but have you seen the polar bears at the Hippodrome?'

Edward was already a collector of rare books and prints and a devoted admirer of Marie Antoinette. Dorothy idolised him, and was soon writing to Mrs Cazalet, his mother, who was a friend of hers: 'Remember me to your son – my hero.' Edward had been astonished at his first visit to Charles Street: the undusted clutter, the free-flying birds, the two oddly dressed women like cardinals. Of course Dorothy had talked of politics but at last she showed him a few objects from her collections: 'A lot of odd things as well as some very nice ones,' recorded Edward. Very soon he was invited to lunch:

I am I was very nervous . . . Eight of us sat down to lunch, the male sex predominating by two, eight is the number Lady Dorothy always has to lunch: General Haldane, Mr de la Fontaine, Mr Sebright. I sat next to Miss Meresia Nevill and Mrs Sebright – so that was the party. Oh! how delightful the conversation was.

But he was by no means uncritical. The next time he thought her table rather boring:

Miss Nevill, Sir Graham Greene, Mr Ponsonby, Sir George Lambert, Mrs Evans and Mr Graham of Heidelberg . . . Found them all rather old. I sat next to Sir George who spoke so softly I could hardly hear what he said and had to make random yeses. Mr Ponsonby who is Lord Bessborough's younger brother I thought very nice except that when he spoke he came so close to me that it was quite unpleasant. Made one feel so confused.

There followed letters (so many that after Edward's death in the trenches in the First World War a large box was found full of them), and afternoon visits with his mother. Together they would choose which one of Dorothy's befruited straw bonnets she was to wear and trundle her out on the streets to visit museums, galleries and waxworks. Occasionally he called alone, and brought her flowers. 'Tell him I kept the lilies till they vanished,' wrote Dorothy to Mrs Cazalet. Dorothy's vanity blossomed with all these attentions, and he in his turn was so pleased with her that she was added to the Fairlawne[1] repertory of heroines acted in the nursery play during the holidays. On 6 January 1910, for instance, everybody dressed up their heads:

Mummie	Madame de Pompadour by Graves
Thelma [Edward's sister]	Mrs Bush by Romney
Teenie [Edward's brother]	La Tosca
Fraulein	Duchess of Devonshire!!
Myself	Lady Dorothy Nevill by Graves

'Everyone said I was exactly like Lady Dorothy with great curls round my head,' wrote Edward proudly in his diary.

There is no doubt that Dorothy was interested in young men. At Ascot there was a Master Hankey who took Dorothy baskets of eggs and vegetables from his mother. Dorothy, vain as ever, confided she liked being taken out by young men in sports cars. Edward was somewhat embarrassed to find a photograph of himself in cricketing clothes in the sanctified midst of the Cobdens and the Ellenboroughs. Dorothy admitted to Lady Bancroft:

One of the greatest treats I can now be given is to be taken by a strong young man to Piccadilly and there to be hoisted on the top of a bus and drive through the city to Whitechapel with time to look in at the London Hospital on the way.

[1] The Cazalets' house in Kent.

Dorothy loved to go to Fairlawne, where she was Edward's favourite guest. There she would be on the Sevenoaks platform, holding out her left hand, exclaiming 'How de du, how de du,' carrying with her all sorts of wonderful things: a collection of autographed fans; new memoirs; a print of their beloved Marie Antoinette. It was Dorothy's conversation that Edward fell for most of all even if she was getting repetitive and tended to tell the same story over and over again (there was one in particular about a Mrs Ridgway at Knole being licked by a stag). In spite of this flaw, however, Dorothy was the life and soul of the party, prattling nineteen to the dozen about the '1830–1860 Set': Lady Holland, Lady Palmerston, Dizzy, the 'Miss Berrys' – 'The Miss Berrys, oh I knew them; also Society was good in their days.' Lord Knutsford remembered her:

All the party would gather round her, and she would talk of old times and of past generations without posing or listening to herself as so many good talkers do. She managed to combine the past with the present in a way no one I ever heard could.

Edward was enthralled, communicating it all to his diary:

At dinner she was so charmingly attired looking so early Victorian, she never for a moment stopped talking. Very interesting I must own, but slightly trying when one wants to ask a question.

As Dorothy got older, what really angered her was the Smart Set: 'She cusses and cusses at them,' wrote Edward. The word 'smart' had been quite unknown outside the servants' hall:

I cannot imagine [Dorothy wrote] what the great ladies of other days would have thought or said had someone been introduced to them and on making enquiries being told – She is quite smart.

To her it conjured up a kitchenmaid dressed in her Sunday suit. How vulgar Society had become. Anybody could be someone by just going into a hotel or a restaurant. Money had become as though a cult to be worshipped. Currency was spent casually; fortunes easily lost. Lord Rothschild, hearing a young man speak casually of a halfpenny, remarked to Dorothy: 'That young man does not appear to know much about large transactions.'

The desire of the old time nouveau riche was to get into Society [wrote

Dorothy in *My Own Times*]. Today many of this highly esteemed much-run-after class bitterly complain they cannot keep out of it.

She herself was one of the few disinterested Society ladies, immune from gold digging, while hostesses spent fortunes trying to eclipse each other with elaborate menus and armies of liveried servants. To one apologising for there not being four footmen to wait on them, Dorothy told her not to worry, for she had never eaten more than two.

Young people were another bone of contention. Dorothy blamed it all on the results of education. In the country little girls no longer dropped a curtsy as she passed, nor did the boys touch their caps. Dorothy complained that her friends' children only knew how to spend their parents' money: 'Those horrors [the Radicals],' she would say, 'are so clever and we are so stupid.' While some girls vied with each other in reducing the dimensions of their skirts until they could scarcely hobble about, others even took exercise.

Look at the girls – playin' golf in their thumpin' boots with never a veil or a pair of gloves till their skin's like a bit of mahogany veneer. I should think the young men would as soon think of kissin' a kipper: and to make it worse they are beginning to daub themselves with lipstick and muck. I never saw such a mess.

When Edward VII died in May 1910 Dorothy hoped to see major changes in Society, with 'the Jews and Smart Set' taking 'a lower seat'. She was optimistic. The new King, George V, was not only married to a popular English Princess but could even speak English without a trace of German. Dorothy wrote to Blanche Airlie:

What a troubled time we have all had of it and how completely politics have gone from the public mind. But I am convinced that this King will take a much more conservative view of life, and he will uphold the Upper Class more than his father did. Still we have had a loss in many ways, but all think your government helped his exit out of the world.

The King had died in the middle of the House of Lords uproar. Certain peers still refused to give in: Gosse wrote to Dorothy,

What do you think of the Die Hards? I can scarcely keep my temper with them. It is really difficult to believe that 115 men could be found so obstinately to dash their heads and our heads against a stone wall.

Fortunately they gave way before the new King was forced to create peers. Even worse was to follow. Dorothy framed a caricature depicting the aristocratic plight. The Liberal programme included Partition – the prospect of Home Rule for Ireland. Asquith is handing a peer a bottle of Veto Bill hemlock: 'Now, my lord, pull yourself together and get it down.' The peer protests it is an awful dose. 'Nonsense,' the Prime Minister replies, 'this is only a draught. You will have to swallow all that behind as well presently.' In the background are ranged other bottles, labelled 'Home Rule for Ireland', 'Welsh Disestablishment', and 'Home Rule All Round.'

Fourteen

Dorothy was the matriarch of Charles Street, its canvasser, its ringleader. The Barings, the Burghcleres, Jenny Churchill, the invalid Lady Cork, whom Dorothy visited nearly ever day, all lived in the row. From her house opposite the Running Footman, Dorothy had a view of everything. It was like Coronation Street with Dorothy in the starring role. Waited on by Meresia, she visited the sick, gossiped and attended all the children's parties. When it was proposed to rename Charles Street Lytton Street, Dorothy was furious, canvassing neighbours repeatedly until they abandoned the project: 'They might just as well have proposed to call it Brummel Street' (the dandy having lived at no. 41). When Lord Lansdowne kept a particularly vociferous cow at the back of Lansdowne House (which looked on to Charles Street) Dorothy complained on behalf of the residents. She sent an anonymous note couched in the local Wiltshire dialect, postscripted: 'Dang'un! There 'ee goes again.' The lowing stopped. Then when it was suggested in Parliament people should devour horse meat, it was Dorothy who set an example by sallying forth, preceded by her maid, to choose the most succulent joint. She returned triumphantly to Charles Street with it, ignoring a jeering populace which had gathered to watch the sight.

The West End had begun to change: gorgeous liveries had given way to ordinary dress; Rotten Row was visited only for health or exercise; bowler hats or cloth caps replaced top hats. Everywhere taxis had superseded the four-wheelers and hansom cabs. Motor cars now careered between bicycles and horses. Gone was the colour, banned by Parliamentary edict, of the street vendors and the music grinders (the only form of music Dorothy enjoyed). Now, instead of shouting their wares, the hare and rabbit skin dealers went round the back door to communicate *sotto voce* with the cook and the groundsel sellers looked furtively up at balconies hung with bird cages. Everything was of a dull uniformity except for the ghastly new façades which increasingly imitated the French casino style.

At eighty-four Dorothy still liked to be in the public eye. In 1910, under the title 'The Old Regime and the New', she was photographed for the newspapers accompanied by John Burns, the trade unionist. There they were at an opening of the Victoria and Albert Museum, Dorothy looking as if she could claim exhibition space, Burns dressed like a duke: 'Did you see Burns and me locked together – me hump-backed and dreadful looking – he delighted?' wrote Dorothy to Blanche Airlie. Certainly she looked decidedly old; indeed she appeared to some the very embodiment of old age. Lady Galway wrote in *Past Revisited*:

She seemed to give points to Methuselah, yet her mind was still as busy as ever. Above conventions she took no heed of frills and tuckers . . . her umbrella too was unique, topped by a wiry hand with two stiff fingers pointing to heaven. We felt all this must have come from the Army and Navy Stores before their regeneration.

But Lady Norah Bentinck was delighted, it seems, to be compared to Dorothy as a young girl, 'because you could see how beautiful she had once been'. She remembered Dorothy sitting in a chair, her thin white arms outstretched and clutching its sides, her small feet barely touching the ground. She wore cotton stockings with black elastic sideboots, and a small flowery toque which was yellower at the back than at the front.

Not everyone was as complimentary. Sir Arthur Conan Doyle offers us a vignette at Hall Barn, the house of Lord Burnham, owner of the *Daily Telegraph*:

I see Lady Dorothy Nevill with her mittened hands and her prim, pussycat manner, retailing gossip about Disraeli's flirtations. Sir Henry James walks under the trees with bended tread, talking to the Barrister [Rufus Isaacs] who is destined as Lord Reading to be Viceroy of India. Lady Cleveland [mother of Lord Rosebery] is listening with her old head wreathed in smiles to Lady Dorothy's scandal. Young Henry Irving looks unutterably bored as Lord Burnham explains golf to him, bending his head to get a glimpse of the ball round the curve of his goodly waistcoat. Mr Asquith stands smiling beside them.

Dorothy had no peace of mind with Lloyd George in power. She hated the sound of

I can see the Old Age Pension Act, the National Insurance Act and many other acts in their trails descending, like breezes in the hills from my native land, sweeping onto the mist laden valleys and clearing the gloom away until the rays of God's sun have passed the narrowest window.

She had witnessed the debasement of the House of Lords. Now it was her own territory that was threatened. The Government had cleverly concealed the Servants' Employment Tax within the controversial National Insurance Bill. The Three Penny Tax for servants' pensions agitated employers of domestics more than the income tax had done. Dorothy was enraged. It was an unwarrantable intrusion of officialdom into her private affairs. Furthermore Insurance Act inspectors, armed with search warrants, could break into her house. The very mechanics of the Act infuriated Society ladies. They had to lick stamps to stick on the servants' cards, which was altogether an undignified process. Dorothy organised protest meetings, signed petitions, used the newspapers. She wrote to the *Daily Mail*.

I do not know if the servants and mistresses of England realise that not only is the mistress to be punished for refusing to make reductions from her servants' wages for the purpose of the Insurance Act against her will, but that the servant who refuses to produce the stamp card is equally liable to punishment by fine or imprisonment. . . . On or after July 15th therefore some fourteen millions of honest and industrious men and women will be liable to persecution and imprisonment and to be branded as criminals, for having failed to comply with regulations which even their authors cannot understand or explain.

Some millions more of employers will be liable to exacting the same treatment for respecting the personal liberty and discretion of the people they employ, and for refusing to act as tax collectors for their employees. So far has England drifted from the principles of freedom and equality . . . For my own part I refuse to act as tax collector to myself or those I employ. I refuse to write out the receipt of my own and my servants' share of the tax by cancelling the stamp with the date, and as the whole working of the Act depends on the willingness of employers to assist the state in this matter we have only ourselves to blame if we have not the courage to decline the unhonoured and unpaid post of tax collector.

All Society ladies were extremely indignant and formed an Association, complete with offices, from which they issued leaflets illustrated with the odious Lloyd George and captioned:

'the Stamp that needs a lot of licking and THE MAN.' The *Daily Mail* allowed Dorothy's letter to be reprinted for distribution. Ironically the servants (who in any case were inclined to hold the same views as their employers) were themselves enraged. The first supporter to call at the office was an old valet who had read Dorothy's letter: 'All the manservants of my acquaintance,' he declared, 'are in terrible revolt against the compulsory deductions from their wages.' But it was all to no avail. Now Dorothy was reported as lunching in Downing Street when Lloyd George entered the room. She bristled, then spluttered to Margot Asquith: 'What do you mean by asking me to meet that man?' 'You wouldn't mind,' replied Margot (supposedly), 'if I invited you to meet the Devil.' 'Certainly not,' Dorothy retorted. 'That would be quite another matter.' But her domineering ways got her nowhere. The National Insurance Act came through.

Now Dorothy felt herself threatened by infuriated females determined to get the vote. 'I hear the suffragettes are now called the Middle Sex,' she wrote to Blanche Airlie. This time they used violence. The last thing that Dorothy wanted was her windows smashed in. Her ambivalent views on the subject had been suspect for a long time. Now the women's destructiveness tipped the scales. Horrified by the hysterical and undignified behaviour of her sex, Dorothy signed a petition against their enfranchisement – surprising her friend, Helen Fawcett, one of the leaders of the Emancipation Movement.

Strikes came in the same category as suffragettes and the National Insurance Act. The Trade Unions now backed their members to use physical violence to property if necessary to achieve their goals. First the railwaymen, then the coalminers came out on strike. They wanted nothing less than nationalisation of certain industries. Frederic Harrison had written to Dorothy with his political forecast for 1912.

It is enough to frighten you. By Easter a General Strike will take place. Railways stopped – coal inaccessible – battleships stranded in port for want of coal fuel. Desperate efforts to work – chaos in England – Wales declared a Republic – Lloyd George President – Germany armed – Belgium and Holland made subject – French Civil War – Germany to annexe Belgium – German new gun at Calais to bombard Dover. F.H. commits suicide in London.

The German menace hung over all like a storm cloud ready to burst, the danger increasing with their arrogance. Dorothy, seeing the Germans stirring up things everywhere, was indignant about unlimited admissions of aliens. In 1911 her friend Edward, leaving Eton, went off to Hanover to finish his education. In her letters she warned him about Germany:

I often think of you, I suppose you will be a real German when you return. I always think of them as being a nation of ants so busy etc. but I don't want L.G. to bring their ideas and manners here. We are very independent and these wretched Germans are ruled and regulated until they are mere machines. It is all horrible – so repugnant to our liberty ideas.

By Christmas Edward was back, laden with presents, bringing Dorothy a piece of mauve silk, 'the same as the peasants wore round the bottom of their skirts'. She seemed delighted and was going to wear it, he noted his diary. Dorothy had it embroidered onto the collar of her velvet evening coat. Her adoration for Edward had increased. Their association was assuming the fervour almost of a last romance. 'But I shall not propose to My Lady as Horace did to his,' wrote Edward. All the same friends began to think of a scandal between 'a lady in her eighties and a young man in his teens'. Edward was teased by his elders who advised him against marriage to his great-grandmother. Dorothy signed her letters 'Your affectionate Dorothy': 'Surely that sounds very *intime* and affectionate for a lady of 85 to finish her letter to a boy of 17,' confided Edward to his notebook: 'I find the friendship of Miss Berry and Horace Walpole the same as Edward Cazalet and Lady D.N.' Dorothy's *billets doux*, however, were sometimes very odd:

... the second [Edward wrote] is quite incomprehensible, it has something to do with the coronation, and something to do with a curiosity shop, but she has forgotten to finish it, leaving off in the middle of the next page; on second thoughts I think she must have written it in her sleep.

The visits to Fairlawne had become more frequent. One evening when Edward, receiving a copy of *Under Five Reigns* from Dorothy, had requested her to invent a dedication, she was for once at a loss for words. 'Write something about Patience, as we play so much together,' suggested Edward; so she inscribed:

Two Idiots at Patience
Edward and Dorothy
Fairlawne 1911

She wrote Two Idiots because one of the card games I try to teach her is called 'The Idiot'!!! and after she had written Edward and Dorothy she said: 'Doesn't that sound romantic!!'

Fairlawne was not Dorothy's only weekend destination. Weeks cooped up in self-sufficient households were now curtailed to several days in 'robbed' ones. Dorothy thought that the difference between life in London and life in the country had been summed up by the gentleman who said: 'In the country if you have a leg of mutton for dinner everyone wants to know if you have caper sauce with it! Whereas in London you may have an elephant for lunch and no-one cares a pin.' Now telegrams and the telephone, faster trains and the motor car had changed the pace of country life with the result it differed very little from what went on in town. Dorothy had always taken a great interest in the automobile. When cars were first suggested she had transcribed in her scrapbook a verse from the Bible (Nahum, ii, 4):

The chariots shall rage in the streets, they shall jostle one another in the broad ways: they shall seem like torches, they shall run like the lightnings.

But now enormous houseparties motored down from London for the weekend. Dorothy complained to Edward Cazalet:

Outside driving rain – inside nothing but bridge and foolish talking . . . I am with a shooting party but I scarcely know anyone, and those I do, except the dear hostess, don't seem worth knowing. Yes – as you say – how few people take an interest in anything.

As Gosse told her: 'It is a case of suicide while one dresses for dinner.'

Dorothy was as mobile as ever. She would go to Overstrand to stay with the Batterseas; to her nephew, Colonel Walpole, at Heckfield Place; to the Mount Stephens at Brocket; to Lady Radnor at Cookham. One Sunday E. F. Benson observed Dorothy and Lady Radnor punting slowly up and down the reach of the River Thames above Boulter's Lock, contemplating developing relationships between the couples below the trees in the backwater. Dorothy turned to her hostess, younger than her by twenty years, saying: 'When we get to our age, my dear, we mustn't be shocked at anything.' On Monday morning a carriage was ordered to take Dorothy to the station. She refused to enter it:

There'll have to be a cab as well for my maid and my luggage, and I shall have to tip the coachman and have to go searchin' for my maid. Pop into your cab with your maid and your luggage I say and have done with it!

Even the remote Norfolk of her childhood had not been immune from change:

I went over to Blickling. Fancy a Mrs Buxton living there. She is very nice but it seems a bad sacrilege for anyone but that dear aristocratic Lady Lothian to be there.

Wolterton, however, was a joy – restored to full splendour by Dorothy's nephew, the fifth Lord Orford. Dorothy made the sixty stairs to her bedroom, and missed only the pen wiper. They were 'three Dorothys together' at Wolterton: 'my niece Dorothy married to the Duc de Balzo, my great-niece Lady Dorothy Walpole, and myself, most interesting.' Then there was Dorset, where Dorothy would stay with Mr De la Fontaine who had restored Athelhampton. From there she would visit Thomas Hardy, taking the somewhat patronising view that the West Country families were far too stupid to appreciate his genius. Sometimes Edward joined her there. He protected her from the unwelcome attentions of the neighbours while she showed him the haunts of her childhood, such as Ilsington House and the old Puddletown church. Rummaging around there Dorothy found the mouldering hatchment of her ancestor, Lord Orford, and carried it away in triumph. She was not so delighted with Weymouth. The celebrated mulberry tree was being felled. Dorothy gathered up some remains and had them hacked into a footstool, inscribing with characteristic vehemence:

This tree was cut down by vandals to make way for the new sailors' home. Often and often has King George III taken tea under its branches and this stool was made from the wood.

Though Dorothy's health remained astonishingly sound, poor Meresia's St. Vitus's dance was galloping. Dorothy would take her abroad to Switzerland and France. The facilities of French watering-places were improved, which was more than could be said for the behaviour of many of her fellow travellers:

Once they have crossed the Channel, mothers who in town stand over their marriageable daughters like guardian ogres . . . will set out their daughters on chairs on the sand, like the well-dressed dummies of a milliner's window; or like so many traps to catch lobsters, and to allow them to speak to any stranger of good appearance or address.

They noticed swarms of Germans everywhere, mostly Jews – 'the longest-nosed in Europe' – indulging in all sorts of luxuries and apparently richer than ever.

Fifteen

Old age made little difference to Dorothy's pace of life. There was even a new country villa – constant visits to Ascot on account of the salubrious air. Meresia kept her dogcart there, and with reins threaded through quivering fingers, a groom up behind, she would shake round the country lanes, taking her mother for invigorating drives. In the mornings Dorothy still emerged promptly from her room at 9.15, adorned with rows of amber beads, a mob-cap covering her auburn wig. 'Her maid says she has never missed going downstairs for breakfast for five years – she never has a fire in her room,' Edward wrote in his diary. Then Dorothy would settle down to work, rolling paper, emblazoning, churning out more reminiscences. Every day in London she would put on her veils and stroll out, leading Marty, her dog, around Berkeley Square and up Bond Street and Piccadilly, insufficiently wrapped up against the elements, growing even more careless with time. 'Well, I have done as I am doing for seventy years and you must admit the result hasn't been bad,' she would say.

Indeed her health had been marvellous. Apart from a slight deficiency in her sight and some deafness there was little to complain about. The odd fall left no scars. At the Tory Bloodhound's eightieth birthday celebrations in Eridge Park, Dorothy was knocked for six by a blindfolded man racing a wheelbarrow. There was more drama at the artist Alma-Tadema's studio in December 1911. Mrs Cazalet had taken Dorothy there.

Imagine my feeling [she wrote to Edward] when as we were coming out of the door Dolly who won't be helped and it was very dark, slipped and fell flat on the marble floor! She picked herself up and laughed and said: 'You see I am so small and so light that I am like a ball and never feel a tumble!

The next day Mrs Cazalet rushed round to see how she was. 'First rate,' answered Dorothy. Yet she did not really feel so spry and even made a precautionary visit to the doctor. She wrote to Gosse:

All the component parts of my body are all right, though he does not deny there are internal strifes going on and not being 17 they are difficult to fight against. I have managed between the acts of feeling dead etc. to go to some pleasant lunches.

She was as fascinated as ever by the gossip and goings on but now Edward had to act as her interpreter, to help her join in the conversation at her table – 'She finds it rather difficult now to keep up with the conversation and when she doesn't hear turns to me and says "What was that?"' Still, the entertainments went on and the guests compassed all ages. The conversation in 1912 certainly did not want for topics: the German Peril; the uncensored diaries of Harriette Wilson, the famous courtesan, and other improper books; Princess Henry of Battenberg's presumed marriage to Sir Thomas Lipton; stamp licking; Van Gogh's singular sunflowers and the Cézannes at the Post-Impressionist Exhibition held at the New Grafton Galleries (Dorothy left the opening completely stunned, chanting 'Oh dear! Oh dear! Oh dear!'); young men calling their dates 'dear' and 'darling' in public; the *Titanic* disaster ('A judgement from God on the idle rich people who want all earthly luxuries even on the water – I am told they even had a garden!'). Perhaps Dorothy's main interest, however, that summer was the great Shakespeare Pageant at Earl's Court, with refrains of the Eglinton Tournament. She wrote to Blanche Airlie:

Mrs G.W. is inaugurating a wonderful scheme for spending money, a magnificent tournament, Lady Curzon as Queen of Beauty – to last one day, seats £1 ten shillings. They are building at Earl's Court a really wonderful London in Shakespeare's time and the real Man of War of S manned by sailors in real garments – quite magnificent, all according to the most historic details. There is the Globe Theatre with a Shakespeare play to be acted. Where the money comes from, that is of no importance.

As usual there was a scapegoat – Mrs Mosscockle, a rich widow who had crashed Society:

Dear me, we have indeed sunk low, dear Lady Haliburton came and told me she had been invited to Mrs Mosscockle's musical party – Heavens what are we coming to!

Both Dorothy and Edward Cazalet collapsed with laughter at the very mention of the widow's name.[1]

Now there was the dock strike giving the country, so Dorothy thought, its first taste of what Socialism really meant. There on Tower Hill was their leader, Ben Tillett, invoking thunderbolts, shouting 'Oh God! Strike Lord Devonport[2] dead!' To Dorothy it looked like 'the eve of the French Revolution', with Tillett 'clamouring for blood, and a herd of defeated strikers inclined to take his advice'. Yet, appalling though the outlook seemed, Dorothy did not appear to feel so threatened. Age brought a certain detachment. She was even growing tired of people, preferring to turn to her favourite books, such as Gosse's *Father and Son* or Disraeli's novels:

I am dedicating my leisure hours to 'Endymion'. What a charm after the beef and mutton of ordinary novels. Yes I've come to love the friends I don't have to talk back to now. I'm getting rather old. . . . I was very happy in my dear county Dorsetshire – the neighbours delighted to welcome me – came in shoals and (beast that I am) I did not care to see them.

Dorothy wanted to be reassured. In 1911 she had told Edward Cazalet that she was not going to the South of France that winter because she did not want to be a bore to anyone. Edward told her that it was inconceivable for anyone to think that as she was so delightful – just the words that Dorothy wanted to hear. There was comfort to be found, too, at the 30 Club, a ladies' élitist luncheon club that met regularly in the back room at Rumpelmayer's the restaurant in St James's. Here Dorothy was so popular that the members hurdled over the chairs knocking each other over in their efforts to sit beside her. At least it convinced Dorothy she was an indispensable part of the institution. It made her feel important.

Then there was the matter of Disraeli's biographer, Monypenny, a *Times* journalist. Dorothy had been uncertain if

---

[1] Had the 6th Marquess of Hertford not inopportunely expired that March, Mrs Mosscockle might really have wiped the smile off their faces by becoming the Marchioness.
[2] Chairman of Port of London Authority.

Monypenny, a bachelor, was the correct choice. After publication of the first volume she had observed

that on the whole it was well done considering that Monypenny knew little of politics, and nothing of the world in which Beaconsfield had lived . . . Monypenny also seems to know nothing of love and yet love was the ruling passion and certainly played an immense part in dear Dizzy's life.

Yet when Monypenny came to research the middle part of Disraeli's life he remained closeted for hours with Dorothy in her boudoir, listening to her reminiscences. More important, he made her feel influential. She was the biographer's dream. But in November 1912 Monypenny suddenly died, just a week after publication of the second volume, which included only the period of Disraeli's first introduction to Dolly Walpole. So all in all the information was useless, and his death was a great blow to her.

Her crony in Charles Street, the witty Lady Cork, whom Dorothy visited nearly every day, died in October 1912. Dorothy wrote to Gosse:

My faculties have been so numbed lately that I have written no letters – in fact everything seems to have been going so cross it leaves me with nothing to say. I only heard from Mr Bugle that she died at four in the morning. I never heard anything more. There has never been a sound in the papers about her. I think it all the more extraordinary as she was certainly a great light of the world.

She peered from her window at the funeral cortege as it passed her door: 'I saw six wreaths. I suppose she was taken to Marston.'[1]

Although without firm religious beliefs Dorothy was not frightened by the act of dying. What frightened her was that she might be forgotten like Charlotte Walpole or Lady Cork. It was in fact a family trait to wish to make a permanent mark. Some had succeeded; the rest were remembered more for gambling away what the others had accumulated. Would Dorothy only be remembered for serving up guinea pigs and haunches of donkey? Did she do nothing 'but put food in her mouth and slip gold through her fingers'? It was by now rather late for any fresh assault on posterity. Following Lady Cork's death the family had noticed she was slowing up, although to the public gaze she

[1] The family home in Somerset.

continued to show the same quaint aspect, appearing at various functions. But soon even in public she began to show symptoms of decay. During Diaghelev's Russian Ballet season at Covent Garden, the author Robert Hichens noticed Dorothy slumped in the stalls, wrapped up in an Indian shawl, asleep.

In January 1913 Dorothy was in the back room at Rumpelmayer's, entertaining the ladies but complaining a little. Nearly all her friends had died. 'They have almost all gone,' she said. 'Are you anxious to go?' asked Marie Belloc Lowndes. 'Not at all,' retorted Dorothy, 'I fully enjoy life.' But now with Monypenny, Lady Cork and so many others dead, there seemed to be so much less point to life. She became habitually cross and even more domineering. Meresia was the chief victim, always present; Gosse another. Yet she could still be amusing, even touching and appreciative. She could still say to Gosse: 'You have made my life happier these last years – you, Lady Airlie, and dearest Winifred.' Gosse felt that to receive this from one who was proud of being as rigid as a nutcracker was worth all the protestations in the world.

That last winter Dorothy hardly moved from London. She was not feeling very well. Yet still her old governess's influence lingered. She told Frederic Harrison:

We have been here some weeks and have spent time improving my mind by going to museums etc. etc. After all that is the best education. I have profited by it all my life.

At the beginning of March Gosse received a reminder that he had been negligent:

My mind is well as body, and the few visits I ever had have all been submerged – with the rain and the Government and other miseries. I have done nothing but bend my body in utter despair over everything and this is why I have never written to you, my kind friend. When am I going to see you? Tomorrow and Saturday and Sunday I am engaged but after that my ill body will be at liberty, but for the last ten days I have scarcely had a moment and yet the world claims me not. Who does then? – for I am torn in fragments one way or another.

Gosse went to tea with Dorothy on 13 March. She was working on more reminiscences, two new works by Verlaine beside her. She complained of a slight cold. Uncertainly the malady developed, then with alarming alacrity. On 22 March,

Good Friday, the doctors diagnosed bronchitis. For the first time in her life she was confined to bed. She became immediately furious at the enforced change in the regime, defying coddling, making a terrible fuss when her children decided to light a fire in her bedroom. They had to hide it behind a screen so that Dorothy could not see the flickering flames. She warned the doctors that once she recovered she would have a lot to write about them: 'None of your hot bottles for me,' she shouted defiantly. She was correct; she did not have to have them. On Easter Sunday, 1913, at 6 p.m., Dorothy died.

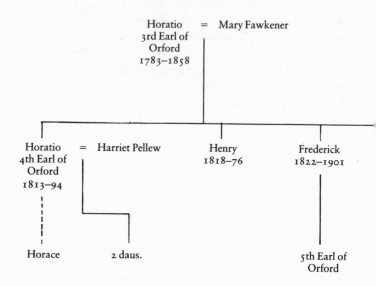

Horatio
3rd Earl of
Orford
1783–1858
= Mary Fawkener

Horatio
4th Earl of
Orford
1813–94
= Harriet Pellew

Henry
1818–76

Frederick
1822–1901

Horace

2 daus.

5th Earl of
Orford

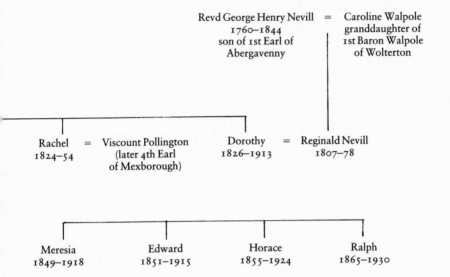

Revd George Henry Nevill = Caroline Walpole
1760–1844   granddaughter of
son of 1st Earl of   1st Baron Walpole
Abergavenny   of Wolterton

Rachel   =   Viscount Pollington   Dorothy   =   Reginald Nevill
1824–54   (later 4th Earl   1826–1913   1807–78
              of Mexborough)

Meresia   Edward   Horace   Ralph
1849–1918   1851–1915   1855–1924   1865–1930

Index

Index